How to Do Science Experiments with Children

Introduction

Experiments

Liquids

Cohesion and Adhesion

Surface Tension

Density

Effects of Temperature

Water Pressure

Refraction

Gases

Air Takes Up Space

Air Exerts Pressure

Effects of Temperature on Volume and Pressure

Properties and Changes

Chemical

Physical

Sound

Static Electricity

Forces

Balanced and Unbalanced

Action and Reaction

Inertia and Momentum

Gravity

What's in How to Do
Science Experiments with Children

73 Experiments

This book contains 73 science experiments divided into six sections. (See the Table of Contents on pages 1 and 2.) Four pages are devoted to each experiment:

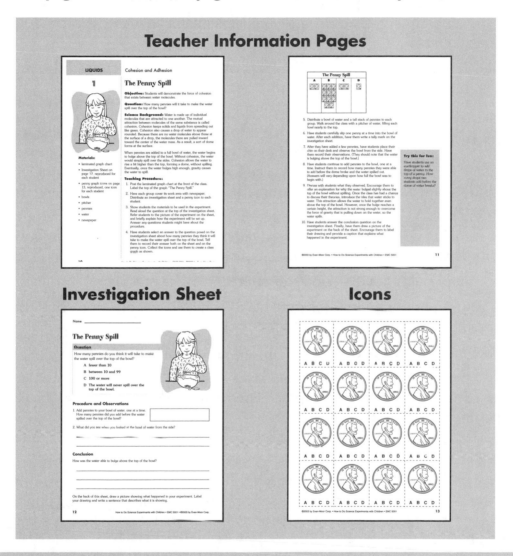

Teacher Information Pages

Investigation Sheet

Icons

Additional Resources

Parent letters are included on pages 8 and 9. The first letter explains that students will be conducting science experiments at school and encourages parents to review student investigation sheets at home once students have completed them. The other letter requests materials that might be needed in the classroom in order to perform an experiment. Send this letter home a few days before you intend to conduct an experiment so that you will be sure to have the materials on time.

Getting Ready

Before You Begin

To prepare for each experiment, follow these simple steps:

1. Read both the Teacher Information Pages and the Student Investigation Sheet.
2. Collect the materials students will need to conduct the experiment. Decide how many groups you will divide the class into, and make sure you have enough materials for each group. (See page 6 for more on group size.)
3. Try out the experiment in advance to familiarize yourself with the procedure and expected result.
4. Post the laminated graph chart at the front of the room. (See page 5 for more on the graph chart.)

Helpful Hints

Before beginning any experiment, decide which area of the classroom students will be working in, and the materials they will be using. Follow these ideas for making cleanup as easy as possible:

- For experiments using water or other liquids, have students cover their work area with newspaper to absorb spills.
- Keep plenty of paper towels handy for spills and other messes.
- Set up "Distribution Stations" for students to come collect bulk materials they might need during an experiment (such as salt, water, sugar, and so on).
- Designate a "Materials Area" to store materials that will be used in more than one experiment.
- Go over experiment and cleanup procedures with students before you begin an experiment.

Safety

Safety is always a top concern when conducting science experiments with young children. Go over the safety rules of the science lab with your students before beginning any experiment:

- If a teacher demonstration involves fire, hot water, or flying objects, clearly mark off areas where students can stand and areas that are "off-limits."
- Use plastic containers instead of glass whenever possible.
- Remind students *never* to eat or drink anything in science lab unless instructed to do so by you.

Graph Chart

Early in an experiment, students will be asked to guess what they think will happen in the experiment. While these responses are not technically "predictions," they can be useful in identifying student misconceptions before the experiment begins. These misconceptions may then be discussed once the experiment is complete. The graph charts also function to get students excited about learning the outcome of the experiment.

Prepare a single graph chart that can be reused for each experiment. Use a permanent marker to draw the outline of the chart on a large piece of tagboard. If you are able to laminate the chart, all the better. Then you can use erasable markers to write the name of the experiment at the top of the chart as shown.

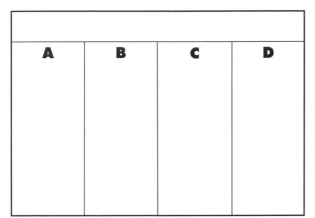

Blank Graph Chart

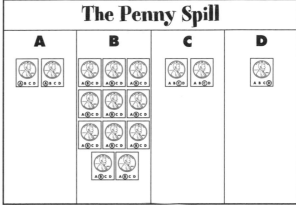

Completed Graph Chart

Post the chart on a corkboard or other place that will accommodate the pushpins used to hold the graph icons to the chart.

Portfolios

Create individual portfolios for each student to keep his or her completed investigation sheets in. Use a colorful file folder secured with ribbon.

- Reproduce the cover on page 303 for students to color and glue to the front of their portfolios.
- Reproduce the experiments log on page 304. After doing each experiment, help students add the experiment to the log.

Decide on a place where the portfolios will be kept, and instruct students to add their investigation sheet to their portfolio after each experiment is completed. The portfolios will allow you and the students to keep track of the work they have completed. Students may take their portfolio home and share their work with their family.

Conducting the Experiments

These experiments were written for use in second-, third-, and fourth-grade classrooms. Of course, they may also be used in home-school situations, as well as by parents of children who just want to know more about science!

For younger students, the experiments may be performed as class demonstrations. For older students, small groups or even individuals can perform the experiments themselves. (There are a few exceptions, such as experiments that involve the use of fire. These experiments must be performed by the teacher/parent.)

Hands-on experience is always better than simple observation, so try to have students perform the experiments whenever possible. You might want to recruit parent volunteers to help student groups as they work on their experiments.

Many experiments suggest that you divide the class into groups to perform the experiment. Use whatever group size works best for your situation, or have students perform the experiment individually if you have enough materials and feel students would benefit most from doing it themselves.

Science Content Information

Science content information is provided for the teacher on the first page of each experiment (see "Science Background"). A simplified version of that explanation is offered to students in the discussion step that follows the experiment. In some cases, the student explanation has been substantially simplified. For more advanced students, you might want to offer some of the more technical information provided in the teacher section. For younger students, you might choose to skip the science explanation entirely and focus instead on their observations alone. It is up to you to decide how much information your students can process and benefit from. Technical jargon and abstract explanations can dampen students' enthusiasm for doing science, so make sure you don't "over-explain."

Working with Younger Students

Each experiment includes an investigation sheet on which students are asked to record their observations and conclusions. If your students are emergent or beginning writers, you may choose to use the investigation sheet to simply guide the investigation along. Students may share their observations and conclusions verbally rather than in writing. Younger students may still use the back of the sheet to draw what happened in their experiment.

National Science Education Standards

The *National Science Education Standards* (National Academy Press, 1996) outlines what students need to know, understand, and be able to do to be "scientifically literate." What does it mean to be scientifically literate? It means being able to use scientific information to make choices and engage intelligently in public debate about important issues that involve science and technology.

Content Standards for Grades K–4

The *Standards* states that as a result of activities, students should develop an understanding of the following content:

Physical Science

Properties of objects and materials

Position and motion of objects

Light, heat, electricity, and magnetism

Life Science

Characteristics of organisms

Life cycles of organisms

Organisms and environments

Earth and Space Science

Properties of earth materials

Objects in the sky

Changes in earth and sky

Experiments in *How to Do Science Experiments with Children* cover the content areas set in italics above.

Scientific Inquiry

The *Standards* states that "as a result of activities in grades K–4, all students should develop

• the abilities necessary to do scientific inquiry and

• an understanding about scientific inquiry."

Younger students should be developing their abilities to do science and their understanding of science in accordance with their developmental capabilities. This means understanding the process of investigation, learning how to ask scientific questions, making careful observations, using evidence to construct reasonable explanations, and communicating results to others. Experiments in *How to Do Science Experiments with Children* promote the development of these skills.

Dear Parents,

Our class will be doing a series of science experiments over the next several months. These experiments will look at properties of liquids and gases, how matter changes, how sound and static electricity are produced, and some of the forces that exist in nature. As part of each experiment, students will record their observations and conclusions on an investigation sheet. These sheets allow the student to keep a record of the experiment and the results obtained.

Your child may be bringing home these investigation sheets after each experiment is complete. You can take part in extending your child's learning by encouraging him or her to explain to you the purpose of the experiment, the steps followed, the results obtained, and the conclusions drawn. Reviewing the experiment with you verbally will help reinforce the scientific knowledge your child gained while doing the experiment.

Your child might want to repeat an experiment at home. Please help your child to set up and carry out the experiments, as needed. Stress that your child should always ask permission before performing any science experiment at home.

Thank you for participating in your child's science experience.

Sincerely,

Dear Parents,

Our class will be doing several science experiments this month.

Can you help by sending in any of the following items?

We will need them by _____.

_____

_____

_____

_____

_____

_____

Thank you for participating in your child's science experience.

Sincerely,

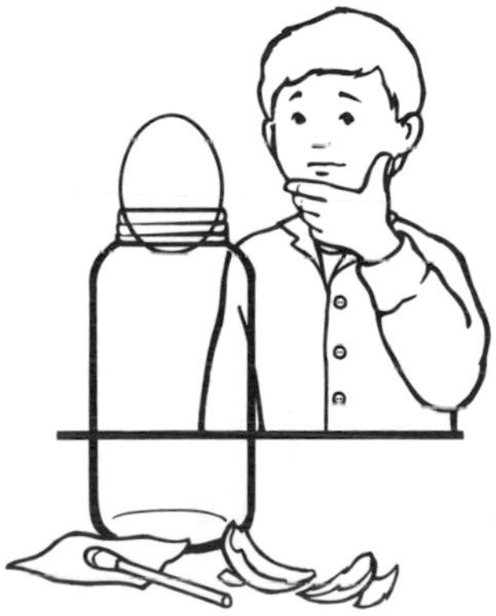

1

The Penny Spill

Objective: Students will demonstrate the force of cohesion that exists between water molecules.

Question: How many pennies will it take to make the water spill over the top of the bowl?

Science Background: Water is made up of individual molecules that are attracted to one another. The mutual attraction between molecules of the same substance is called **cohesion**. Cohesion keeps solids and liquids from spreading out like gases. Cohesion also causes a drop of water to appear rounded. Because there are no water molecules above those at the surface of a drop, the molecules there are pulled inward toward the center of the water mass. As a result, a sort of dome forms at the surface.

When pennies are added to a full bowl of water, the water begins to bulge above the top of the bowl. Without cohesion, the water would simply spill over the sides. Cohesion allows the water to rise a bit higher than the top, forming a dome, without spilling. Eventually, once the water bulges high enough, gravity causes the water to spill.

Materials:

- laminated graph chart
- page 12, reproduced for each student
- page 13, reproduced, one icon for each student
- bowls
- pitcher
- pennies
- water
- newspaper

Teaching Procedure:

1. Post the laminated graph chart at the front of the class. Label the top of the graph "The Penny Spill."

2. Have each group cover its work area with newspaper. Distribute an investigation sheet and a penny icon to each student.

3. Show students the materials to be used in the experiment. Read aloud the question at the top of the investigation sheet. Refer students to the picture of the experiment on the sheet and briefly explain how the experiment will be set up. Answer any questions students might have about the procedure.

4. Have students select an answer to the question posed on the investigation sheet about how many pennies they think it will take to make the water spill over the top of the bowl. Tell them to record their answer both on the sheet and on the penny icon. Collect the icons and use them to create a class graph as shown.

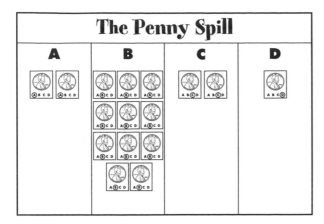

5. Distribute a bowl of water and a tall stack of pennies to each group. Walk around the class with a pitcher of water, filling each bowl nearly to the top.

6. Have students carefully slip one penny at a time into the bowl of water. After each addition, have them write a tally mark on the investigation sheet.

7. After they have added a few pennies, have students place their chin on their desk and observe the bowl from the side. Have them record their observations. (They should note that the water is bulging above the top of the bowl.)

8. Have students continue to add pennies to the bowl, one at a time. Instruct them to record how many pennies they were able to add before the dome broke and the water spilled out. (Answers will vary depending on how full the bowl was to begin with.)

9. Discuss with students what they observed. Encourage them to offer an explanation for why the water bulged slightly above the top of the bowl without spilling. Once the class has had a chance to discuss their theories, introduce the idea that water sticks to water. This attraction allows the water to hold together even above the top of the bowl. However, once the bulge reaches a certain height, the attraction is not strong enough to overcome the force of gravity that is pulling down on the water, so the water spills.

10. Have students answer the conclusion question on the investigation sheet. Finally, have them draw a picture of the experiment on the back of the sheet. Encourage them to label their drawing and provide a caption that explains what happened in the experiment.

Try this for fun:

Have students use an eyedropper to add drops of water to the top of a penny. How many drops can they add before the dome of water breaks?

The Penny Spill

Question

How many pennies do you think it will take to make the water spill over the top of the bowl?

A fewer than 10

B between 10 and 99

C 100 or more

D The water will never spill over the top of the bowl.

Procedure and Observations

1. Add pennies to your bowl of water, one at a time. How many pennies did you add before the water spilled over the top of the bowl?

2. What did you see when you looked at the bowl of water from the side?

_____

_____

Conclusion

How was the water able to bulge above the top of the bowl?

_____

_____

_____

On the back of this sheet, draw a picture showing what happened in your experiment. Label your drawing and write a sentence that describes what it is showing.

2

Water Works

Objective: Students will demonstrate the force of cohesion that exists between water molecules.

Question: What will happen to a drop of water as it is pulled along a sheet of waxed paper by a toothpick?

Science Background: Water is made up of individual molecules that are attracted to one another. This attraction is known as **cohesion**. Cohesion will keep a drop of water together even as it is being poked at and pulled with a toothpick. Because the water molecules stick together, as part of the drop is dragged forward, the rest follows. The waxed paper keeps the water molecules from sticking to the absorbent maze surface.

Teaching Procedure:

1. Post the laminated graph chart at the front of the class. Label the top of the graph "Water Works."

2. Distribute an investigation sheet, a water droplet icon, and a water maze to each student.

3. Show students the materials to be used in the experiment. Read aloud the question at the top of the investigation sheet. Refer students to the picture of the experiment on the sheet and briefly explain how the experiment will be set up. Answer any questions students might have about the procedure.

4. Have students select an answer to the question posed on the investigation sheet about what they think will happen to a drop of water if they try to pull it across a sheet of waxed paper with a toothpick. Tell them to record the answer both on the sheet and on the water droplet icon. Collect the icons and use them to create a class graph as shown.

Materials:

- laminated graph chart
- page 16, reproduced for each student
- page 17, reproduced, one icon for each student
- Water Maze on page 302, reproduced for each student
- toothpicks
- waxed paper
- plastic cups
- water

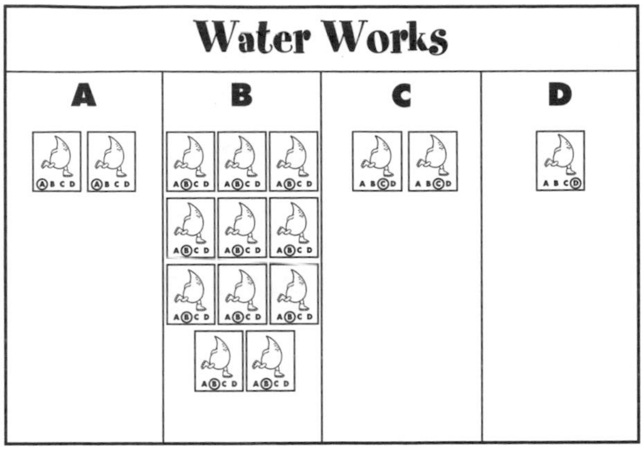

Water Works

A	B	C	D

5. Distribute a cup of water, a toothpick, and a sheet of waxed paper to each student. Have students place the waxed paper over the maze and add a drop of water at the "Start" of the maze. Then have them use the toothpick to try to drag the drop along the trail. Are they successful? (The drop should hold together as it is dragged along.) Have students record their observations on the investigation sheet.

6. Discuss with students what they observed. Encourage them to offer an explanation for why they were able to drag the drop of water through the maze without the drop breaking apart. Once the class has had a chance to discuss their theories, introduce the idea that water sticks to water. This attraction allows the drop to hold together even as it is being dragged across the waxed paper.

7. Have students answer the conclusion question on the investigation sheet. Finally, have them draw a picture of the experiment on the back of the sheet. Encourage them to label their drawing and provide a caption that explains what happened in the experiment.

Try this for fun:

Have students create their own water mazes. Suggest that they place the mazes on a gradual incline. Can students drag the drops uphill? (Yes, as long as the incline is not too steep.)

Name _____

Water Works

Question

What do you think will happen to a drop of water if you try to pull it along a sheet of waxed paper with a toothpick?

The drop of water will _____.

    A be absorbed by the waxed paper

    B hold together as it moves

    C not move

    D break apart

Procedure and Observations

1. Put a sheet of waxed paper over the maze. Place a drop of water at the "Start" of the maze.

2. Now use the toothpick to drag the drop through the maze. Are you able to do it?

_____

Conclusion

How can you explain the behavior of the water droplet in this experiment?

_____

_____

_____

On the back of this sheet, draw a picture showing what happened in your experiment. Label your drawing and write a sentence that describes what it is showing.

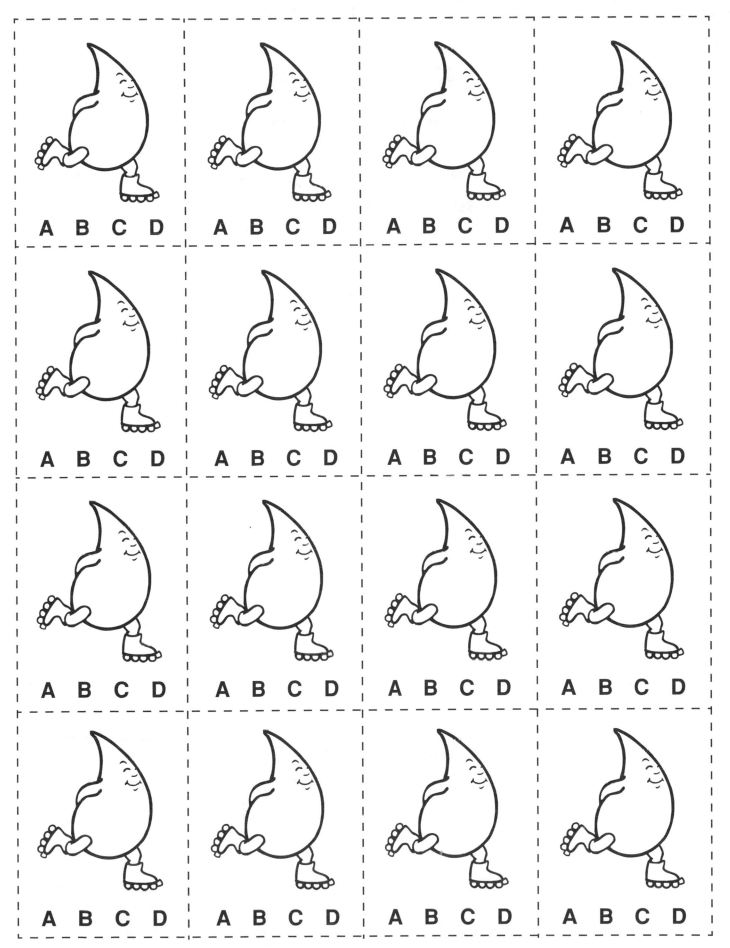

A B C D   A B C D   A B C D   A B C D

A B C D   A B C D   A B C D   A B C D

A B C D   A B C D   A B C D   A B C D

A B C D   A B C D   A B C D   A B C D

3

Paper Buddies

Objective: Students will demonstrate the forces of cohesion and adhesion that exist between two wet sheets of paper.

Question: How will water affect the stickiness of paper?

Science Background: Water molecules are **polar**, which means they each have a positive end and a negative end. The positive end of one water molecule is attracted to the negative end of another water molecule. This attractive force is called **cohesion**.

Paper molecules also have a certain polarity. When two polar substances, like water and paper, come into contact, the negative parts of water are attracted to the positive parts of paper, and the positive parts of water are attracted to the negative parts of paper. In other words, the water and paper stick together. The attractive force that exists between molecules of two different substances is known as **adhesion**.

So what forces are at work when two wet pieces of paper come into contact? Adhesion (between the paper and water) and cohesion (between the water molecules on opposite strips) work simultaneously to make the wet paper sheets stick together.

Materials:

- laminated graph chart
- page 20, reproduced for each student
- page 21, reproduced, one icon for each student
- sheets of plain paper or newspaper
- plastic cups
- water

Teaching Procedure:

1. Post the laminated graph chart at the front of the class. Label the top of the graph "Paper Buddies."

2. Distribute an investigation sheet and a paper sheets icon to each student.

3. Show students the materials to be used in the experiment. Read aloud the question on the investigation sheet. Refer students to the picture of the experiment on the sheet and briefly explain how the experiment will be set up. Answer any questions students might have about the procedure.

4. Distribute two sheets of paper to each group. Have students investigate what happens when they set one piece down on top of the other and then lift it again. Do the pieces of paper stick together? (No.)

5. Have students select an answer to the question posed on the investigation sheet about how they think wetting the pieces of paper will affect their stickiness. Tell them to record their answer both on the sheet and on the paper sheets icon. Collect the icons and use them to create a class graph as shown.

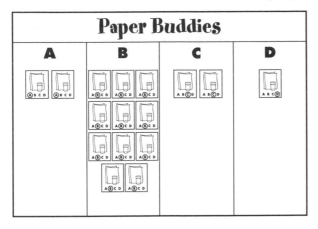

6. Distribute a cup of water to each group. Have students wet both pieces of paper and then set one on top of the other again. Have them try to lift the top piece of paper off the bottom one and record their observations. (They should note that the two pieces of paper now stick together and have to be "peeled" apart.)

7. Discuss with students what they observed. Encourage them to offer an explanation for why the pieces of paper stuck together after they were wetted. Once the class has had a chance to discuss their theories, introduce the idea that water sticks to paper (adhesion) and water sticks to water (cohesion). Together, these two forces act to hold the wet pieces of paper together.

8. Have students answer the conclusion question on the investigation sheet. Finally, have them draw a picture of the experiment on the back of the sheet. Encourage them to label their drawing and provide a caption that explains what happened in the experiment.

Try this for fun:

Have students try to slide the pieces of paper apart rather than simply peeling them. What do they notice? (It is much harder to slide than to peel the pieces of paper apart because sliding involves breaking many more water-water bonds.)

Paper Buddies

Question

How do you think water will affect the stickiness of the paper?

  A Water will make the paper less sticky.

  B Water will make the paper more sticky.

  C Water will not affect the stickiness of the paper.

  D Water will make the two sheets of paper easier to pull apart.

Procedure and Observations

1. Place one piece of paper on top of another. Now lift the top sheet off. Do the pieces of paper stick together?

   _____

2. Wet the two pieces of paper. Now set them one on top of the other again and try to lift the top piece off the bottom piece. What do you notice?

   _____

   _____

Conclusion

How can you explain the behavior of the pieces of paper once they were wetted?

   _____

   _____

   _____

On the back of this sheet, draw a picture showing what happened in your experiment. Label your drawing and write a sentence that describes what it is showing.

A B C D | A B C D | A B C D | A B C D

A B C D | A B C D | A B C D | A B C D

A B C D | A B C D | A B C D | A B C D

A B C D | A B C D | A B C D | A B C D

Cohesion and Adhesion

4

Celery Surprise

Objective: Students will demonstrate the forces of cohesion and adhesion at work in a celery stalk.

Question: What will happen to a stalk of celery when it is left in a cup of colored water?

Science Background: Capillary action describes the movement of water up narrow tubes, such as those that exist along the length of some plants, including celery. The forces of **adhesion** and **cohesion** act together to pull the water up the tubes. Adhesion exists between the water molecules and the sides of the tubes. Cohesion exists between individual water molecules. If the force of adhesion is greater than the force of cohesion, the liquid will rise in the tube. Plants use capillary action to pull water and dissolved nutrients from their roots to the upper parts of the plant.

Materials:

- laminated graph chart
- page 24, reproduced for each student
- page 25, reproduced, one icon for each student
- plastic cups
- food coloring
- plastic knife
- celery stalks
- water
- newspaper

Teaching Procedure:

1. Use the knife to cut the bottom centimeter off all the celery stalks. (This exposes the tubes inside the celery stalk, allowing water to flow up the stalk more easily.)

2. Post the laminated graph chart at the front of the class. Label the top of the graph "Celery Surprise."

3. Have each group cover its work area with newspaper. Distribute an investigation sheet and a celery stalk icon to each student.

4. Show students the materials to be used in the experiment. Read aloud the question at the top of the investigation sheet. Refer students to the picture of the experiment on the sheet and briefly explain how the experiment will be set up. Answer any questions students might have about the procedure.

5. Have students select an answer to the question posed on the investigation sheet about what they think will happen to the celery if they leave it in a cup of colored water. Tell them to record their answer both on the sheet and on the celery stalk icon. Collect the icons and use them to create a class graph as shown.

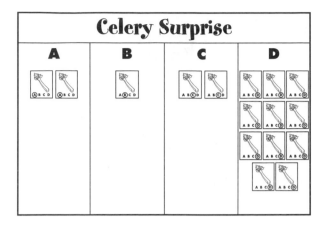

Celery Surprise

6. Distribute a plastic cup of colored water and a celery stalk to each group. Have students place the stalk in the cup of colored water, with the leaves sticking out of the cup. Tell students to set the cup aside for an hour.

7. After an hour, have students observe their celery stalk. Walk around and cut each group's stalk in half to expose the colored dots that are cross sections of the tubes. What do students notice? (The colored liquid must have moved up the tubes in the stalk.)

8. Discuss with students what they observed. Encourage them to offer an explanation for why the colored water moved up the stalk. Once the class has had a chance to discuss their theories, introduce the idea that water sticks to water (cohesion) and water also sticks to other materials, like the sides of the tubes in the celery (adhesion). When the adhesive force between the water and the tubes is stronger than the cohesive force between water molecules, the water gets pulled up the tubes to the top of the stalk. Discuss with students the value of this action in helping the plant get nutrients from the soil.

9. Have students answer the conclusion question on the investigation sheet. Finally, have them draw a picture of the experiment on the back of the sheet. Encourage them to label their drawing and provide a caption that explains what happened in the experiment.

Try this for fun:

Have students repeat the experiment using white carnations instead of celery stalks.

Celery Surprise

Question

What do you think will happen to a stalk of celery when it is left in a cup of colored water?

The celery will _____.

    A wilt

    B grow more leaves

    C grow longer

    D change color inside

Procedure and Observations

1. Place the stalk of celery in the cup of colored water. Leave it alone for one hour.

2. Look at the stalk of celery after your teacher has cut it in half. What do you notice?

_____

_____

Conclusion

How can you explain what happened in this experiment?

_____

_____

_____

On the back of this sheet, draw a picture showing what happened in your experiment. Label your drawing and write a sentence that describes what it is showing.

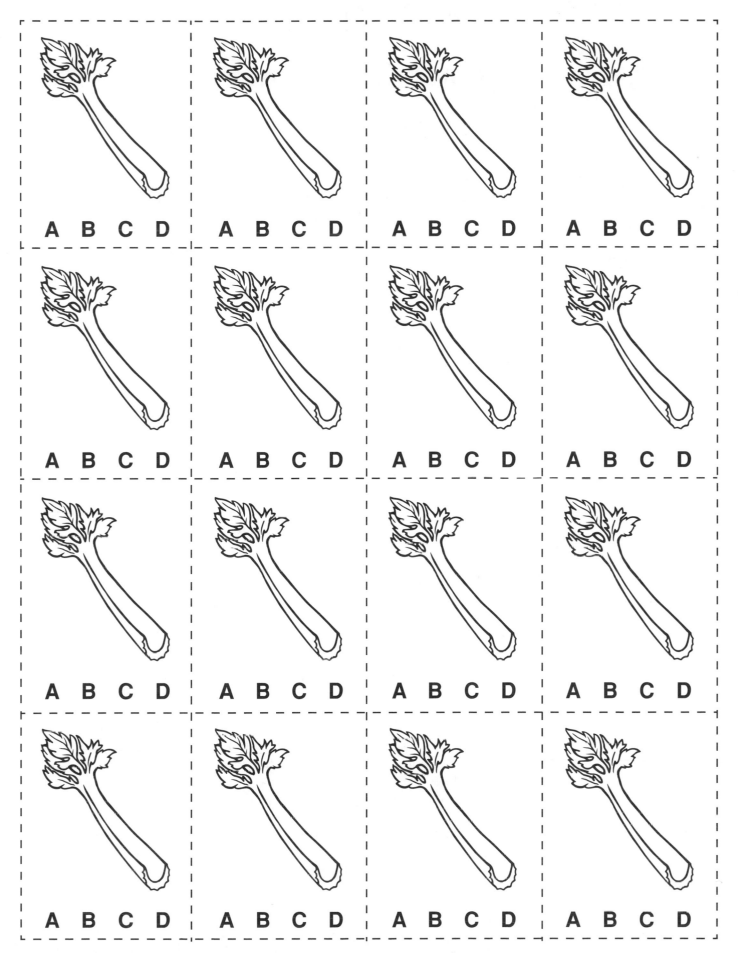

5

Materials:

- laminated graph chart
- page 28, reproduced for each student
- page 29, reproduced, one icon for each student, and one larger boat per group
- liquid detergent
- small paper or plastic cups
- flat toothpicks or plastic knives
- aluminum pie pans
- water
- newspaper
- scissors

Good Clean Fun

Objective: Students will demonstrate that detergent reduces the surface tension of water.

Question: What will happen to a paper boat floating on a pan of water when liquid detergent is dropped into a notch cut out of the rear of the boat?

Science Background: Surface tension is the tendency of water molecules on the surface of water to pull on one another and on objects floating on the water's surface. (This tension creates a sort of membrane that water striders and some other insects can use to "walk" along the water's surface without falling in.) Cohesion, the attraction between water molecules, is what creates surface tension.

An object floating on the water's surface will be pulled equally in all directions by the surface tension, and so will stay still (unless affected by wind or other forces). Soaps and detergents break down the surface tension of water. In this activity, when detergent is added to the water on one side of a boat, the surface tension of the water on that side is reduced. On the opposite side of the boat, the surface tension of the water remains intact. As a result, the boat is pulled toward the side where the surface tension is still strong.

Teaching Procedure:

1. Post the laminated graph chart at the front of the class. Label the top of the graph "Good Clean Fun."

2. Have each group cover its work area with newspaper. Distribute an investigation sheet and a boat icon to each student, and one precut larger boat to each group.

3. Show students the materials to be used in the experiment. Read aloud the question on the investigation sheet. Refer students to the picture of the experiment on the sheet and briefly explain how the experiment will be set up. Answer any questions students might have about the procedure.

4. Distribute an aluminum pie pan of water, a toothpick, and a small cup to each group. Place about a thimbleful of detergent in each group's cup.

5. Have students "launch" their boats on the water and observe what they do. (The boats may drift a bit, but then come to a stop and stay there.) Instruct students to record their observations on the investigation sheet.

6. Have students select an answer to the question posed on the investigation sheet about what they think will happen when they add liquid detergent to the notch at the rear of the boat. Tell them to record their answer both on the sheet and on the paper boat icon. Collect the icons and use them to create a class graph as shown.

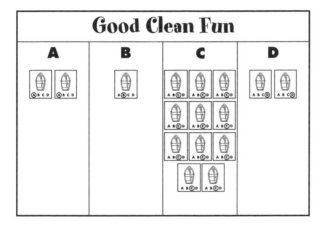

7. Now have students use the toothpick to place a small amount of detergent in the notch at the back of the boat. Again, have them record their observations. (The boat should move forward, away from the detergent.)

8. Discuss with students what they observed. Encourage them to offer an explanation for what made the boat move forward. Once the class has had a chance to discuss their theories, introduce the idea that water sticks to water and to objects floating on it, and that detergent makes it stick less. By putting detergent in the water on one end of the boat, they made the water on that side less "sticky," and so the boat was pulled in the opposite direction—forward!

9. Have students answer the conclusion question on the investigation sheet. Finally, have them draw a picture of the experiment on the back of the sheet. Encourage them to label their drawing and provide a caption that explains what happened in the experiment.

Try this for fun:

Have students cut another notch in the boat, this time on the side. Then have them add a few drops of detergent to that notch. This should make the boat travel in a circle.

Name _____

Good Clean Fun

Question

What do you think will happen to the paper boat when drops of liquid detergent are placed in the notch at the rear of the boat? The boat will _____.

    A sink

    B flip over

    C travel forward

    D travel backward

Procedure and Observations

1. Set your boat down gently on top of the water in your pan. What does the boat do?

_____

_____

2. Now place a few drops of detergent on your toothpick and dip the toothpick in the notch at the rear of the boat. What happens?

_____

_____

Conclusion

What caused the boat to do what it did in the experiment?

_____

_____

_____

On the back of this sheet, draw a picture showing what happened in your experiment. Label your drawing and write a sentence that describes what it is showing.

    How to Do Science Experiments with Children • EMC 5001 • ©2003 by Evan-Moor Corp.

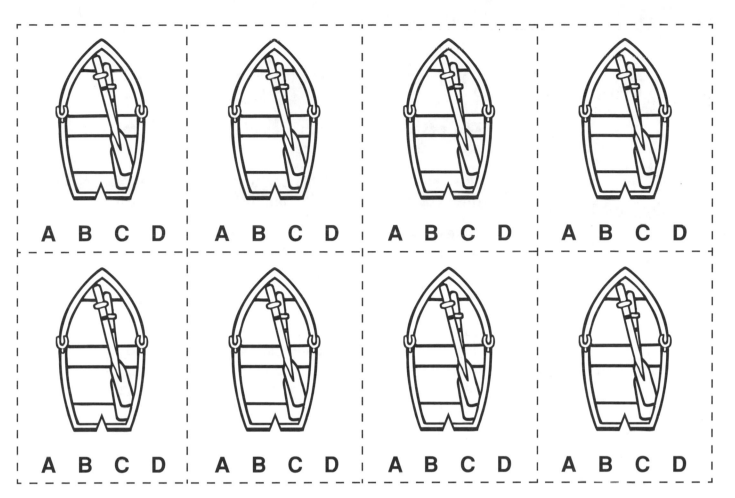

A B C D | A B C D | A B C D | A B C D

A B C D | A B C D | A B C D | A B C D

6

Materials:

- laminated graph chart

- page 32, reproduced for each student

- page 33, reproduced, one icon for each student, and one larger newspaper man for each group

- aluminum pie pans

- liquid detergent

- water

- newspaper

- scissors

All Washed Up

Objective: Students will demonstrate that detergent reduces the surface tension of water.

Question: What will happen to two newspaper men when one is placed in plain water and the other in soapy water?

Science Background: Detergent acts to reduce the **surface tension** of water, the tendency of water molecules at the surface to stick together. As the water molecules become less attracted to one another, they attach themselves more readily to other materials that happen to be in the water. Thus, an absorbent material like newspaper will take a few seconds to become wet when placed in plain water, but will do so almost immediately when placed in soapy water. As a result, the newspaper man placed in soapy water will become wet and sink before the newspaper man that was placed in plain water.

Teaching Procedure:

1. Post the laminated graph chart at the front of the class. Label the top of the graph "All Washed Up."

2. Use the larger icon shape to cut out two newspaper men for each group from a sheet of real newspaper.

3. Have each group cover its work area with newspaper. Distribute an investigation sheet and a newspaper man icon to each student, and two newspaper men cutouts to each group.

4. Show students the materials to be used in the experiment. Read aloud the question at the top of the investigation sheet. Refer students to the picture of the experiment on the sheet and briefly explain how the experiment will be set up. Answer any questions students might have about the procedure.

5. Have students select an answer to the question posed on the investigation sheet about what they think will happen to the two newspaper men. Tell them to record their answer both on the sheet and on the newspaper man icon. Collect the icons and use them to create a class graph as shown.

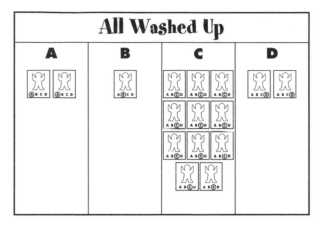

6. Distribute two pie pans of water to each group. Place several drops of detergent in one of each group's pans. Each group should have one pan of plain water and one pan of soapy water.

7. Have students place a newspaper man flat on the surface of each pan of water. Remind them to lay the men down gently, being careful not to "dunk" them underwater. Instruct students to record their observations of what happens to the men. (The newspaper man in the soapy water should get wet faster and sink sooner than the newspaper man in the plain water.)

8. Discuss with students what they observed. Encourage them to offer an explanation for what made the newspaper man in the soapy water sink first. Once the class has had a chance to discuss their theories, introduce the idea that water molecules at the surface of water tend to stick to one another. When detergent is added to the water, the water molecules separate from one another and are then free to stick to the newspaper more readily. So the newspaper man in the soapy water got wet quicker and therefore sank before the newspaper man placed in plain water.

9. Have students answer the conclusion question on the investigation sheet. Finally, have them draw a picture of the experiment on the back of the sheet. Encourage them to label their drawing and provide a caption that explains what happened in the experiment.

Try this for fun:

Have students repeat the experiment using different types of soap (such as bar soap, powdered detergent, shampoo, and bubble bath).

Name _____

All Washed Up

Procedure and Observations

At the same time, gently place one newspaper man facedown in the pan of plain water and the other man facedown in the pan of soapy water. What does each man do?

_____

_____

_____

_____

Conclusion

What caused the men to act as they did in the experiment?

_____

_____

_____

On the back of this sheet, draw a picture showing what happened in your experiment. Label your drawing and write a sentence that describes what it is showing.

A B C D   A B C D   A B C D   A B C D

A B C D   A B C D   A B C D   A B C D

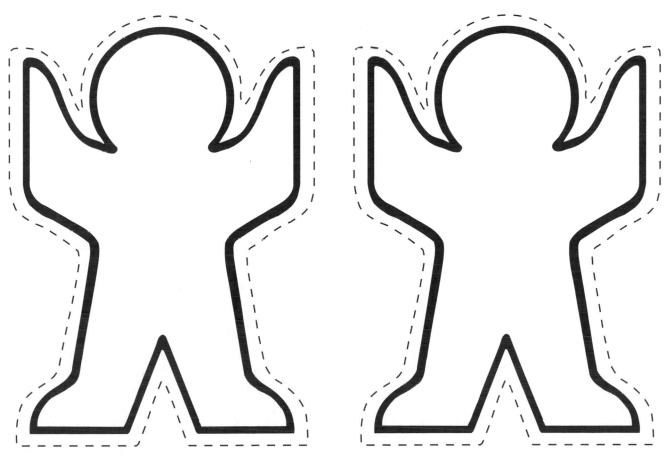

7

Materials:

- laminated graph chart
- page 36, reproduced for each student
- page 37, reproduced, one icon for each student
- aluminum pie pans
- baby powder
- bar of soap
- paper clips
- water
- newspaper

Surface Tension

Take a Powder

Objective: Students will demonstrate that detergent reduces the surface tension of water.

Question: What will happen when a soapy paper clip is dipped into water that has baby powder floating in it?

Science Background: Surface tension is the tendency of water molecules on the surface of water to pull on one another and on objects floating on the water's surface. Objects floating on the water's surface will be pulled equally in all directions by the surface tension, and so will stay still (unless affected by wind or other forces).

Soaps and detergents break down the surface tension of water. When a soapy paper clip is lowered into a dish of water with powder floating in it, the surface tension of the water around the soapy clip is reduced. Surface tension near the sides of the dish, however, remains intact. As a result, the powder is pulled toward the sides of the dish.

Teaching Procedure:

1. Post the laminated graph chart at the front of the class. Label the top of the graph "Take a Powder."

2. Have each group cover its work area with newspaper. Distribute an investigation sheet and a powder jar icon to each student.

3. Show students the materials to be used in the experiment. Read aloud the question on the investigation sheet. Refer students to the picture of the experiment on the sheet and briefly explain how the experiment will be set up. Answer any questions students might have about the procedure.

4. Distribute a pie pan of water to each group. Sprinkle a small amount of powder on each pan of water. Have students record their observations. (The powder should float freely all over the surface of the water.)

5. Have students select an answer to the question posed on the investigation sheet about what they think will happen when they dip the soapy paper clip into the center of the pan of water. Tell them to record their answer both on the sheet and on the powder jar icon. Collect the icons and use them to create a class graph as shown.

Take a Powder

A	B	C	D

6. Distribute a paper clip to each group. Instruct students to straighten out one end of the clip. Offer help as needed.

7. Walk around the class with a bar of soap. Tell students to stick the straight end of the paper clip into the soap. Then instruct them to dip the soapy end of the clip into the pan of water. Have them record their observations. (The powder should move quickly away from the soapy clip, toward the sides of the pan.)

8. Discuss with students what they observed. Encourage them to offer an explanation for what made the powder move to the sides of the pan. Once the class has had a chance to discuss their theories, introduce the idea that water sticks to water and to objects floating on it, and that soap makes it stick less. By putting soap in the center of the pan of water, they made the water there less "sticky," reducing its pull on the powder. However, water at the sides of the pan continued to pull on the powder as before. As a result, the powder in the center moved toward the sides of the pan.

9. Have students answer the conclusion question on the investigation sheet. Finally, have them draw a picture of the experiment on the back of the sheet. Encourage them to label their drawing and provide a caption that explains what happened in the experiment.

Try this for fun:

Have students repeat the experiment, this time using liquid detergent instead of soap, and black pepper grains instead of powder.

Name _____

Take a Powder

Question

What do you think will happen to the baby powder when a soapy paper clip is dipped into the water in the center of the pan? The baby powder will _____.

    A spread out away from the paper clip

    B dissolve

    C stick to the paper clip

    D blow away

Procedure and Observations

1. Watch as your teacher sprinkles powder on your pan of water. What does the powder do?

_____

_____

2. Now dip the soapy end of your paper clip into the center of the pan of water. What do you observe?

_____

_____

Conclusion

What caused the powder to act as it did when you dipped the soapy paper clip into the water?

_____

_____

_____

On the back of this sheet, draw a picture showing what happened in your experiment. Label your drawing and write a sentence that describes what it is showing.

 How to Do Science Experiments with Children • EMC 5001 • ©2003 by Evan-Moor Corp.

8

Materials:

- laminated graph sheet
- page 40, reproduced for each student
- page 41, reproduced, one icon for each student
- uncooked eggs
- plastic cups
- plastic spoons
- pitcher
- water
- food coloring
- salt
- cornstarch
- vinegar
- newspaper

Density

The Incredible Egg

Objective: Students will observe that different liquids have different densities.

Question: In which liquid mixture will an egg float?

Science Background: Density is a measure of mass (we'll use the term *weight* here) per unit volume. Some substances are denser than others; that is, they have more mass (they weigh more) per unit volume. For example, salt water is denser than plain water. This is because it contains dissolved particles of salt that increase its weight per unit volume.

The other liquid mixtures tested in this experiment are not noticeably denser than plain water. A few drops of food coloring do not add much to water's overall weight per unit volume. The same is true of vinegar. Cornstarch does not dissolve in water as salt does. Instead, it forms a "suspension," where small particles of cornstarch are suspended within the water, but eventually settle out. Because its particles don't form a solution with water, cornstarch does not increase water's overall density.

The density of an uncooked egg is slightly greater than the density of fresh water, but slightly less than that of salt water. Thus, an uncooked egg will float in salt water, but sink in the other liquid mixtures tested.

Teaching Procedure:

1. Post the laminated graph chart at the front of the class. Label the top of the graph "The Incredible Egg."

2. Distribute an investigation sheet and a swimming egg icon to each student. Read aloud the question at the top of the investigation sheet. Refer students to the picture of the experiment on the sheet and briefly explain how the experiment will be set up. Answer any questions students might have about the procedure.

3. Have students select an answer to the question posed on the investigation sheet about which liquid mixture they think the egg will float in. Tell them to record their answer both on the sheet and on the swimming egg icon. Collect the icons and use them to create a class graph as shown.

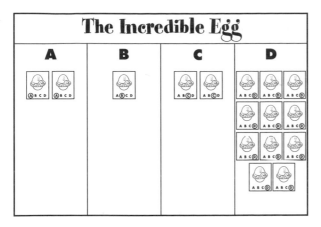

4. Have each group cover its work area with newspaper. Then give each group four plastic cups filled with water, an egg, and a plastic spoon. Place the containers of food coloring, salt, cornstarch, and vinegar at the front of the room. Invite the groups to prepare their liquid mixtures, as follows: Add a few drops of food coloring to one cup, two spoonfuls of cornstarch to a second cup, four spoonfuls of salt to a third cup, and two spoonfuls of vinegar to a fourth cup. Stir each liquid mixture.

5. Once students have prepared the four liquid mixtures, have them carefully set the uncooked egg into each and observe what the egg does. (The egg will float in the salt water and sink in all the others. If the egg sinks in the salt water, have students continue adding salt and stirring until the egg begins to float.) Instruct students to record their observations on the investigation sheet.

6. Discuss with students what they observed. Encourage them to offer an explanation for why the egg floated in the salt water and sank in all the other liquid mixtures. Once the class has had a chance to discuss their theories, introduce the idea that the egg is less dense than the salt water. Therefore, the egg floats in the salt water as less dense materials float in more dense materials. The egg was denser than the other three liquid mixtures, and therefore sank in them.

7. Have students answer the conclusion question on the investigation sheet. Finally, have them draw a picture of the experiment on the back of the sheet. Encourage them to label their drawing and provide a caption that explains what happened in the experiment.

Try this for fun:

Have students try the experiment again using a hard-boiled egg. Are the results the same? (The hard-boiled egg will sink in all the liquid mixtures, including salt water.)

The Incredible Egg

Question

In which liquid mixture do you think an egg will float?

The egg will float in _____.

A food coloring and water

B cornstarch and water

C salt and water

D vinegar and water

Procedure and Observations

Follow your teacher's instructions to make the four different liquid mixtures. Place your egg in each one. What does the egg do? Circle the correct choice.

In food coloring and water:	sink	float
In cornstarch and water:	sink	float
In salt and water:	sink	float
In vinegar and water:	sink	float

Conclusion

How can you explain what the egg did in the different liquid mixtures?

_____

_____

_____

On the back of this sheet, draw a picture showing what happened in your experiment. Label your drawing and write a sentence that describes what it is showing.

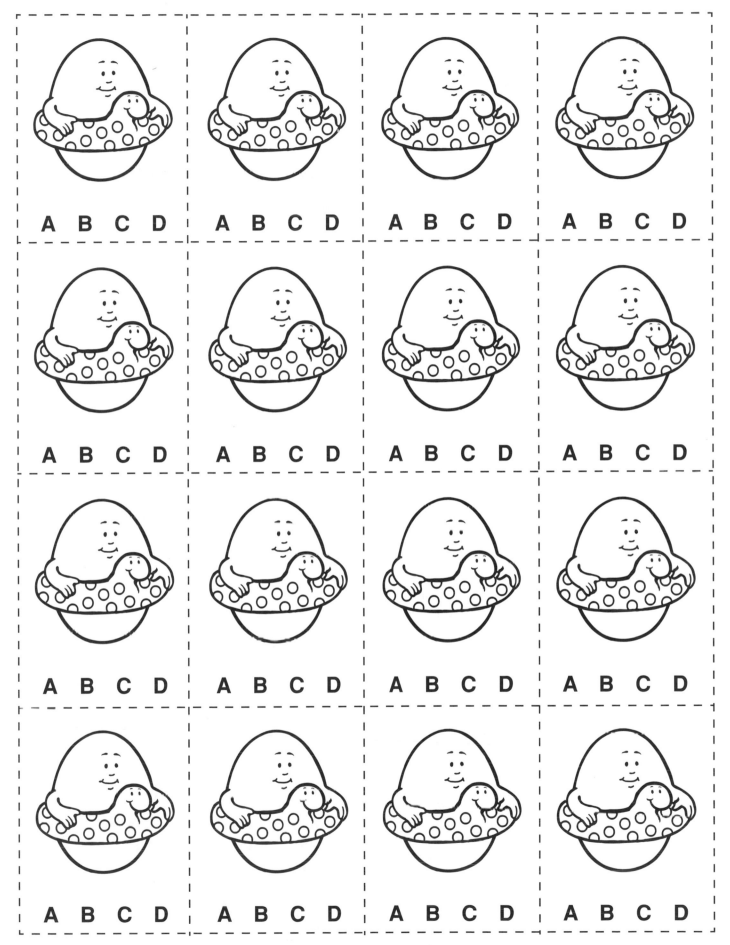

Materials:

- laminated graph sheet
- page 44, reproduced for each student
- page 45, reproduced, one icon for each student
- jars with tight-fitting lids (baby food jars work well)
- vegetable oil
- pitcher
- water
- food coloring
- paper towels

Density

Surf's Up

Objective: Students will demonstrate that liquids of different densities don't mix.

Question: What happens when water is mixed with oil?

Science Background: Density is a measure of a substance's mass (weight) per unit volume. Oil is less dense than water. Less dense liquids float on top of denser liquids because they weigh less. So, oil floats on water. Oil and water placed together in a jar and shaken will separate, with the oil on top. When gently rocked back and forth, the liquids will form a sort of "wave" in the jar.

Another reason that oil and water don't mix is because, unlike water, oil molecules are nonpolar—they do not have a positively charged end and a negatively charged end. This is why oil will briefly form individual droplets when shaken up with water rather than mixing into it. (These droplets eventually join together again to form one layer floating on top of the water.) The polarity of water and oil molecules will not be discussed with students.

Teaching Procedure:

1. Post the laminated graph chart at the front of the class. Label the top of the graph "Surf's Up."

2. Distribute an investigation sheet and a surfboard icon to each student.

3. Show students the materials to be used in the experiment. Read aloud the question at the top of the investigation sheet. Refer students to the picture of the experiment on the sheet and briefly explain how the experiment will be set up. Answer any questions students might have about the procedure.

4. Have students select an answer to the question posed on the investigation sheet about what they think will happen when water is mixed with oil. Tell them to record their answer both on the sheet and on the surfboard icon. Collect the icons and use them to create a class graph as shown.

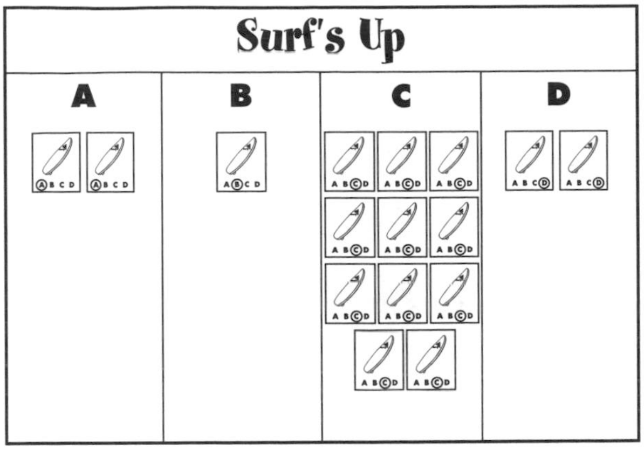

Surf's Up

A	B	C	D

5. Add several drops of food coloring to a pitcher of water and stir.

6. Distribute a jar to each group. Add (or have students add) equal amounts of colored water and vegetable oil to the jars, filling them about three-quarters full. Screw the lids on tightly. Use paper towels to wipe off the outside of the jars.

7. Instruct students to rock the jar gently back and forth. What happens to the oil and water? Have them record their observations on the investigation sheet. (The oil will float above the water, making a sort of wave as the jar is rocked back and forth.)

8. Discuss with students what they observed. Encourage them to offer an explanation for why the water and oil did not mix. Once the class has had a chance to discuss their theories, introduce the idea that different liquids have different densities. Density is a measure of mass per unit of volume. Because liquids of higher density have more mass, they are heavier and therefore sink below those of lower density. (For younger students, define density simply as weight. "The water is heavier than the oil, and so it sinks below the oil in the jar.") Liquids of different densities don't mix.

9. Have students answer the conclusion question on the investigation sheet. Finally, have them draw a picture of the experiment on the back of the sheet. Encourage them to label their drawing and provide a caption that explains what happened in the experiment.

Try this for fun:

Have students add a few drops of detergent into the jars and watch what happens to the water and oil. (The oil will form tiny droplets that distribute themselves throughout the water and stay there.)

Name _____

Surf's Up

Question

What do you think will happen when water is mixed with oil?

The water and oil will _____.

    A mix and change color

    B become cloudy

    C separate

    D form a solid

Procedure and Observations

Gently rock your jar of water and oil back and forth. What do you observe in the jar?

_____

_____

_____

_____

Conclusion

Why did the oil and water act as they did in the jar?

_____

_____

_____

_____

On the back of this sheet, draw a picture showing what happened in your experiment. Label your drawing and write a sentence that describes what it is showing.

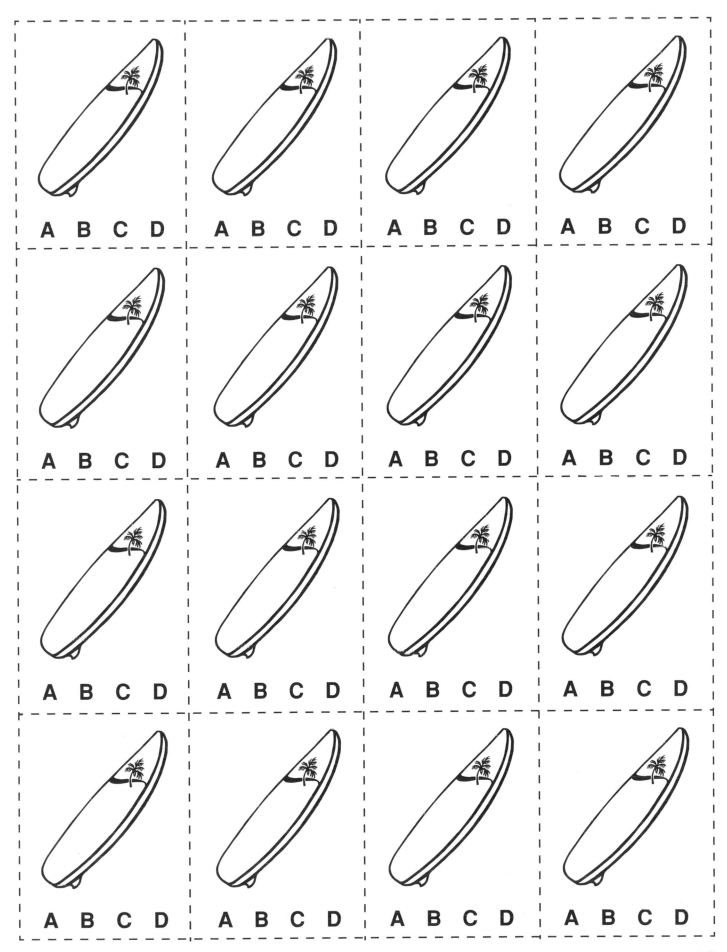

A B C D   A B C D   A B C D   A B C D

A B C D   A B C D   A B C D   A B C D

A B C D   A B C D   A B C D   A B C D

A B C D   A B C D   A B C D   A B C D

Density

10

Let It Drop

Objective: Students will demonstrate that liquids of different densities don't mix.

Question: What will happen to drops of colored water when they are added to vegetable oil?

Science Background: Density is a measure of a substance's mass (weight) per unit volume. Water is denser than oil. Denser liquids sink in less dense liquids, so drops of water added to a cup of oil will sink through the oil and settle at the bottom of the cup. Because liquids of different densities don't mix together, the water droplets will retain their shape as they fall, rather than mixing into the oil.

Materials:

- laminated graph sheet
- page 48, reproduced for each student
- page 49, reproduced, one icon for each student
- vegetable oil
- plastic cups
- plastic spoons
- pitcher
- water
- food coloring
- newspaper

Teaching Procedure:

1. Post the laminated graph chart at the front of the class. Label the top of the graph "Let It Drop."

2. Mix several drops of food coloring into a pitcher of water. The water should be visibly colored.

3. Have each group cover its work area with newspaper. Then give each group a plastic cup half-filled with oil, a plastic cup half-filled with colored water, and a plastic spoon.

4. Distribute an investigation sheet and a water droplet icon to each student. Read aloud the question at the top of the investigation sheet. Refer students to the picture of the experiment on the sheet and briefly explain how the experiment will be set up. Answer any questions students might have about the procedure.

5. Have students select an answer to the question posed on the investigation sheet about what they think will happen to the drops of colored water when they are added to the oil. Tell them to record their answer both on the sheet and on the water droplet icon. Collect the icons and use them to create a class graph as shown.

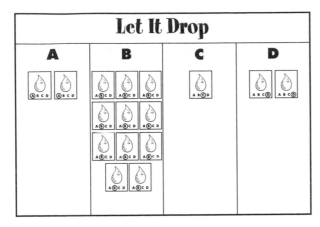

6. Have students add drops of colored water to their cup of oil and observe what the drops do. (They will sink to the bottom of the cup, retaining their droplet shape as they fall.) Encourage students to try different-sized drops. (No matter their size, the water droplets will sink to the bottom and keep their shape.) Instruct students to record their observations on the investigation sheet.

7. Discuss with students what they observed. Encourage them to offer an explanation for why the drops sank in the oil, and why they retained their droplet shape rather than mixing into the oil. Once the class has had a chance to discuss their theories, introduce the idea that water is denser than oil and will therefore sink when placed in a cup of oil. Because liquids of different densities don't mix together, the drops retain their original shape as they fall.

8. Have students answer the conclusion question on the investigation sheet. Finally, have them draw a picture of the experiment on the back of the sheet. Encourage them to label their drawing and provide a caption that explains what happened in the experiment.

Try this for fun:

Have students add drops of other kinds of liquids to their cup of oil. Do the drops sink or float? If they sink, do they retain their droplet shape? (Answers will vary, depending on the liquids used.)

Name _____

Let It Drop

Question

What do you think will happen to drops of colored water when they are added to oil?

The colored droplets will _____.

    A mix with the oil and lose their color

    B remain as colored droplets

    C change to clear droplets

    D move up and down in the oil

Procedure and Observations

1. Carefully spoon several drops of colored water into the cup of oil. What happens to the drops?

_____

_____

2. Try drops of different sizes. Do bigger drops act differently than smaller drops?

_____

_____

Conclusion

What caused the drops to do what they did in the experiment?

_____

_____

_____

On the back of this sheet, draw a picture showing what happened in your experiment. Label your drawing and write a sentence that describes what it is showing.

 How to Do Science Experiments with Children • EMC 5001 • ©2003 by Evan-Moor Corp.

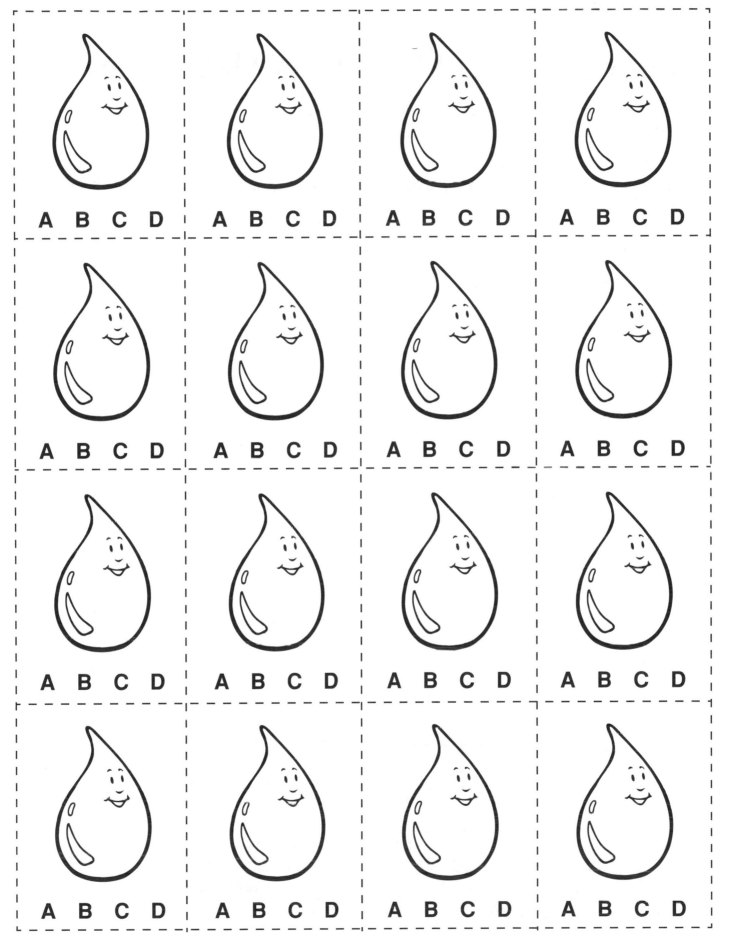

A B C D   A B C D   A B C D   A B C D

A B C D   A B C D   A B C D   A B C D

A B C D   A B C D   A B C D   A B C D

A B C D   A B C D   A B C D   A B C D

11

A Chip Off the Old Potato

Objective: Students will demonstrate that a sugar-water solution is denser than plain water.

Question: What will happen when plain water is added to a cup containing a sugar-water solution and a potato slice?

Science Background: Sugar dissolves in water to form a sugar-water solution. This solution is denser than plain water because the dissolved sugar particles increase the water's weight per unit volume. A potato has a **density** slightly higher than that of plain water, but slightly lower than that of sugar water. Thus, a piece of potato will float in sugar water but will sink in plain water. When plain water is slowly poured into a cup of sugar water with a potato piece floating in it, the plain water will sit above the sugar water, and the potato will remain at the intersection of the two liquid layers.

Materials:

- laminated graph sheet
- page 52, reproduced for each student
- page 53, reproduced, one icon for each student
- uncooked potatoes
- knife
- plastic cups
- plastic spoons
- granulated sugar
- pitcher
- water
- food coloring
- newspaper

Teaching Procedure:

1. Post the laminated graph chart at the front of the class. Label the top of the graph "A Chip Off the Old Potato."

2. Distribute an investigation sheet and a potato icon to each student.

3. Show students the materials to be used in the experiment. Read aloud the question on the investigation sheet. Refer students to the picture of the experiment on the sheet and briefly explain how the experiment will be set up. Answer any questions students might have about the procedure.

4. Fill two pitchers with plain water. Add several drops of food coloring to one pitcher and stir. Place the sugar and pitchers of water at the front of the room.

5. Have each group cover its work area with newspaper. Distribute two plastic cups, a plastic spoon, and a piece of potato to each group. Have each group stir a spoonful of sugar into half a cup of plain (clear) water. Tell them to fill the other cup with colored water.

6. Have students gently set the piece of potato into the cup containing the sugar water. Where does the potato come to rest? (at the top of the solution) Instruct students to record their observations on the investigation sheet.

7. Have students select an answer to the question posed on the investigation sheet about what they think will happen when plain water is added to the cup containing the sugar water and piece of potato. Tell them to record their answer both on the sheet and on the potato icon. Collect the icons and use them to create a class graph as shown.

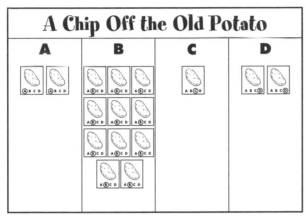

8. Now have students tip the cup of sugar water gently to one side and carefully pour the colored water into it until almost full. (The colored water will come to rest above the layer of sugar water. The piece of potato will rest at the junction of the two liquid layers.) Have students record their observations on the investigation sheet.

9. Discuss with students what they observed. Encourage them to offer an explanation for why the potato floated between the layers. Once the class has had a chance to discuss their theories, introduce the idea that different liquids have different densities. The sugar water had a higher density than the plain (colored) water, so it sat below the plain water in the cup. The potato had a slightly lower density than the sugar water, but a slightly higher density than the plain water. As a result, it came to rest at the junction of the two layers.

10. Have students answer the conclusion question on the investigation sheet. Finally, have them draw a picture of the experiment on the back of the sheet. Encourage them to label their drawing and provide a caption that explains what happened in the experiment.

Try this for fun:

Have students try the experiment again, using a saltwater solution instead of a sugar-water solution.

Name _____

A Chip Off the Old Potato

Question

What do you think will happen when plain water is added to the cup containing the sugar-water solution and piece of potato?

The piece of potato will _____.

    A sink

    B float on top of the plain water

    C float between the liquid layers

    D get bigger

Procedure and Observations

1. Place your piece of potato in the cup of sugar-water solution. Where does it go?

_____

_____

2. Slowly pour the plain water into the cup with the potato in it. Where does the potato go now?

_____

_____

Conclusion

How can you explain where the potato ended up?

_____

_____

_____

On the back of this sheet, draw a picture showing what happened in your experiment. Label your drawing and write a sentence that describes what it is showing.

     How to Do Science Experiments with Children • EMC 5001 • ©2003 by Evan-Moor Corp.

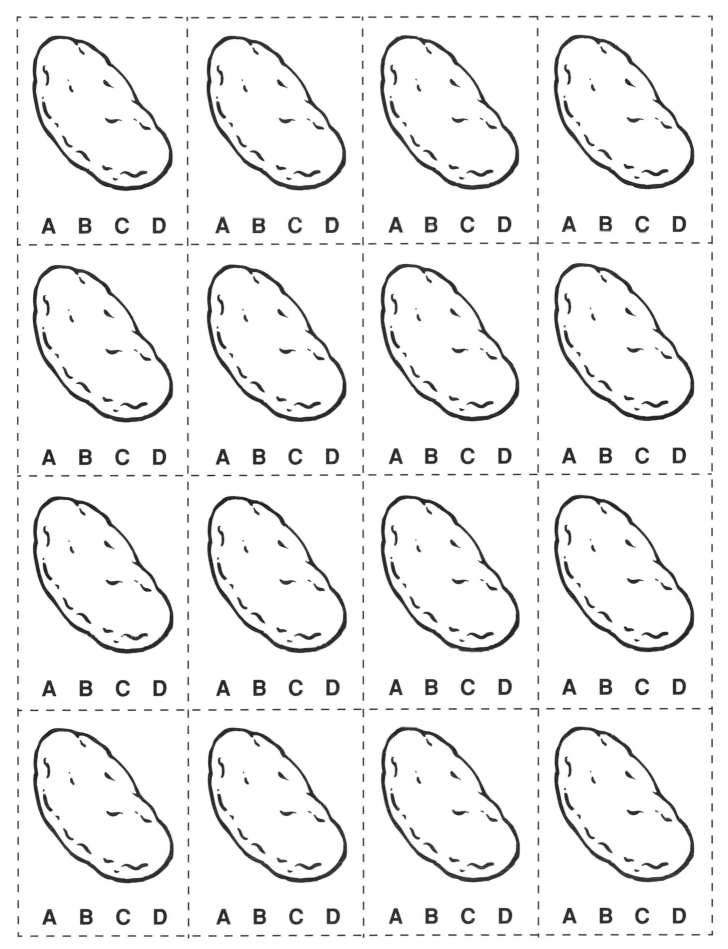

Density

12

Great Eggs-pectations

Objective: Students will demonstrate that objects float more readily in liquids of high density than in liquids of low density.

Question: What will happen to an egg in a cup of water when salt is added to the water?

Science Background: Salt dissolves in water to form a saltwater solution. Salt water is denser than plain water. This is because it contains dissolved particles of salt that increase its weight per unit volume.

The density of an uncooked egg is slightly greater than the density of fresh water, but slightly less than that of salt water. Thus, an uncooked egg will sink in plain water but will float when salt is added to the water to form a saltwater solution.

Teaching Procedure:

1. Post the laminated graph chart at the front of the class. Label the top of the graph "Great Eggs-pectations."

2. Distribute an investigation sheet and a swimming egg icon to each student. Read aloud the question on the investigation sheet. Refer students to the picture of the experiment on the sheet and briefly explain how the experiment will be set up. Answer any questions students might have about the procedure.

3. Have each group cover its work area with newspaper. Then give each group a plastic cup of water, an egg, and a plastic spoon. Place the container of salt at the front of the room.

4. Tell students to place their egg in the cup of water and observe what it does. (It sinks to the bottom of the cup.) Instruct students to record their observations on the investigation sheet.

5. Have students select an answer to the question posed on the investigation sheet about what they think will happen to the egg when they add salt to the cup of water. Tell them to record their answer both on the sheet and on the swimming egg icon. Collect the icons and use them to create a class graph as shown.

Materials:

- laminated graph sheet
- page 56, reproduced for each student
- page 57, reproduced, one icon for each student
- uncooked eggs
- plastic cups
- plastic spoons
- water
- salt
- newspaper

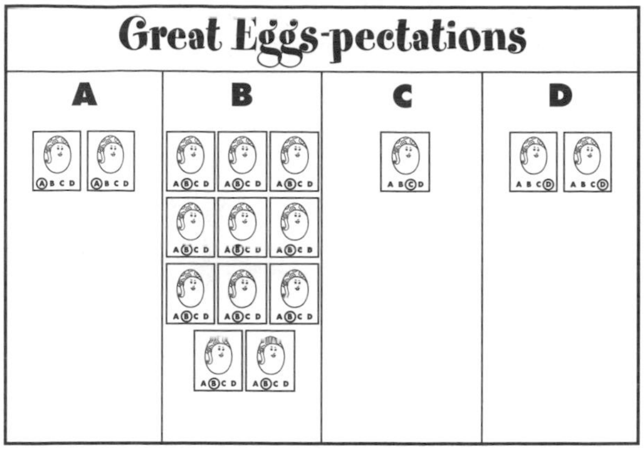

Great Eggs-pectations

A	B	C	D

6. Now have each group come up to the front of the room and add four large spoonfuls of salt to their cup and stir. Tell students to be careful not to damage the egg as they stir. Have them record their observations. (As the salt dissolves into the solution, the egg will begin to float.)

7. Discuss with students what they observed. Encourage them to offer an explanation for why the egg sank in the plain water but floated in the salt water. Once the class has had a chance to discuss their theories, introduce the idea that plain water is less dense than the uncooked egg. Therefore, the egg sank in the plain water. Salt water, on the other hand, is denser than the uncooked egg. Therefore, the egg floated in the salt water because less dense materials float in more dense materials.

8. Have students answer the conclusion question on the investigation sheet. Finally, have them draw a picture of the experiment on the back of the sheet. Encourage them to label their drawing and provide a caption that explains what happened in the experiment.

Try this for fun:

Have students try the experiment again, substituting different objects for the egg. Which float in salt water? Which do not float in either plain or salt water? What can students infer about objects that don't float in salt water? (They are denser than salt water.)

Name _____

Great Eggs-pectations

Question

What do you think will happen to the egg when salt is added to the water?

The egg will _____.

    A crack open

    B begin to float

    C stay on the bottom

    D change color

Procedure and Observations

1. Place your egg in a cup of plain water. What does the egg do?

_____

_____

2. Add four large spoonfuls of salt to the cup and stir. What does the egg do now?

_____

_____

_____

Conclusion

How can you explain what the egg did after the salt was added to the water?

_____

_____

_____

On the back of this sheet, draw a picture showing what happened in your experiment. Label your drawing and write a sentence that describes what it is showing.

 How to Do Science Experiments with Children • EMC 5001 • ©2003 by Evan-Moor Corp.

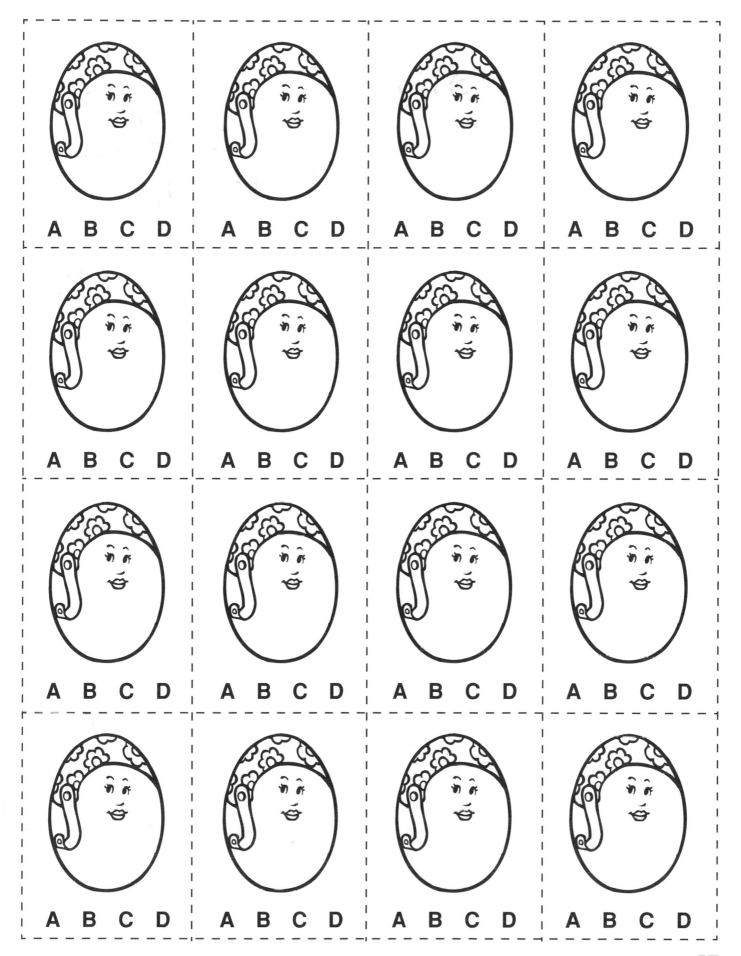

13

Materials:

- laminated graph sheet

- page 60, reproduced for each student

- page 61, reproduced, one icon for each student

- raisins

- plastic cups

- water

- clear soda pop (like 7-UP®)

- newspaper

Dancing Raisins

Objective: Students will demonstrate that substances less dense than water will float.

Question: What will happen to raisins dropped into a cup of soda pop?

Science Background: Raisins by themselves are denser than water. Thus, a raisin placed in a glass of water will sink to the bottom. Soda pop is carbonated; that is, it contains carbon dioxide that exits the solution to form bubbles of carbon dioxide gas. These bubbles are less dense than water, and so float to the surface of the liquid.

When raisins are placed in a cup of soda pop, some of the carbon dioxide bubbles attach themselves to the raisins, reducing each raisin's overall density temporarily and causing it to rise to the surface of the liquid. At the surface, the bubbles pop, and the raisin once again falls to the bottom of the cup. As more bubbles form and attach themselves to the raisins, the cycle of rising and sinking continues, producing a sort of "raisin dance."

Teaching Procedure:

1. Post the laminated graph chart at the front of the class. Label the top of the graph "Dancing Raisins."

2. Explain that students will use raisins and soda pop in this experiment, but that they are not to consume either. ***Remind them that they should never eat or drink in science class unless instructed to do so by their teacher.***

3. Have each group cover its work area with newspaper. Then give each group two plastic cups, a can of clear soda, and a handful of raisins. Fill one of the cups three-quarters full with water, or show students where they can fill them.

4. Distribute an investigation sheet and a raisin icon to each student. Read aloud the question on the investigation sheet. Refer students to the picture of the experiment on the sheet and briefly explain how the experiment will be set up. Answer any questions students might have about the procedure.

5. Have students drop a few raisins into the cup of water. What happens to the raisins? (They sink to the bottom of the cup.) Instruct students to record their observations on the investigation sheet. Then review with students the fact that raisins are denser than water and so sink when dropped in water.

6. Have students select an answer to the question posed on the investigation sheet about what they think will happen when raisins are added to a cup of soda pop. Tell them to record their answer both on the sheet and on the raisin icon. Collect the icons and use them to create a class graph as shown.

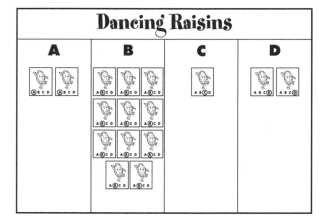

7. Now have students fill the other cup about three-quarters full with clear pop. Have them drop a few raisins into the cup. Instruct them to record their observations of the raisins over the next few minutes. (The raisins will sink at first, then be carried to the surface as carbon dioxide gas bubbles attach themselves to the raisins. Once they reach the surface of the soda, the bubbles will burst and the raisins will sink again. As they rise and fall over and over, the raisins will appear to be "dancing.")

8. Discuss with students what they observed. Encourage them to offer an explanation for why the raisins rose and sank again and again in the soda pop. Once the class has had a chance to discuss their theories, introduce the idea that bubbles of gas in the soda pop attached themselves to the raisins, temporarily reducing each raisin's overall density. Since less dense materials float in more dense materials, the raisins floated to the surface of the liquid. Once the bubbles burst at the surface, each raisin's overall density was increased again, and the raisins sank.

9. Have students answer the conclusion question on the investigation sheet. Finally, have them draw a picture of the experiment on the back of the sheet. Encourage them to label their drawing and provide a caption that explains what happened in the experiment.

Try this for fun:

Have students try the experiment again, using different carbonated beverages or different types of small fruits.

Dancing Raisins

Question

What do you think will happen to raisins dropped into a glass of clear soda pop?

The raisins will _____.

    A dissolve

    B sink to the bottom and stay there

    C move up and down in the cup

    D float to the top and stay there

Procedure and Observations

1. Place a few raisins in a glass of water. What happens to the raisins?

_____

_____

2. Place a few raisins in a glass of clear soda pop. What happens to the raisins?

_____

_____

Conclusion

How can you explain what the raisins did in the soda pop?

_____

_____

_____

On the back of this sheet, draw a picture showing what happened in your experiment. Label your drawing and write a sentence that describes what it is showing.

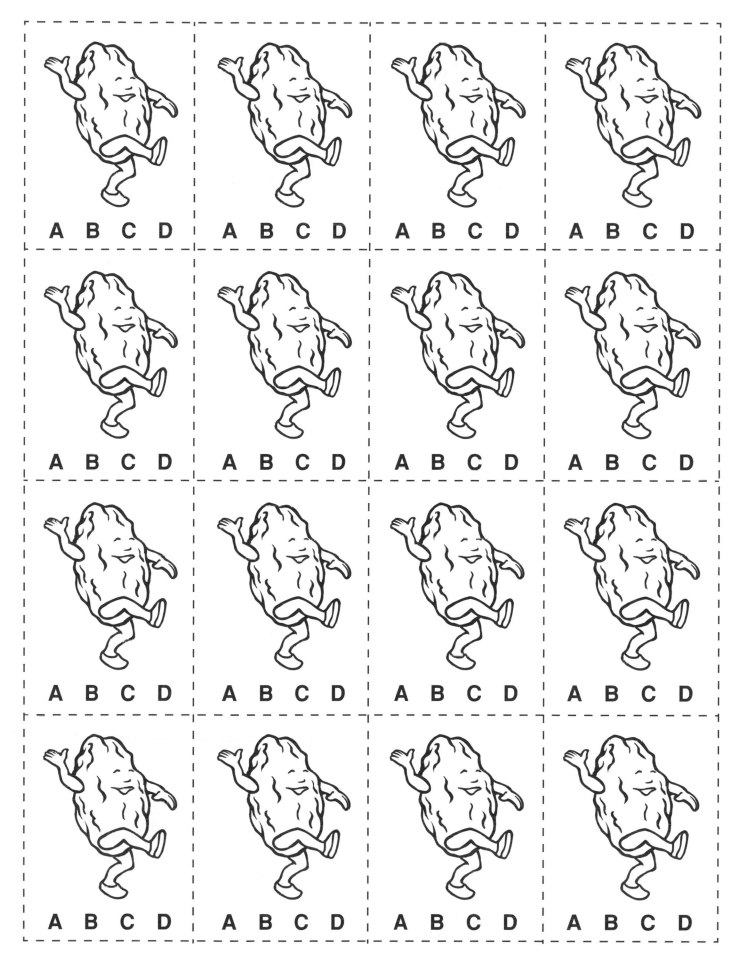

14

Materials:

- laminated graph sheet
- page 64, reproduced for each student
- page 65, reproduced, one icon for each student
- warm water
- cold water
- food coloring
- small bottles
- bowls
- newspaper

Plip, Plop, Drip, Drop

Objective: Students will demonstrate that cold water sinks and warm water rises.

Question: What will happen to cold water when it is poured into a bowl of warm water?

Science Background: Water is made up of many tiny molecules. These molecules, like the molecules that make up all matter, vibrate. Molecules of warmer water vibrate more than those of colder water because they have more energy. Because warmer water molecules vibrate more, they become more spread out and take up more space than the same quantity of cold water. As a result, warm water is less dense than cold water.

As the previous experiments have shown, liquids of different densities do not mix. When cold water is poured carefully into a container of warm water, the cold water will sink and form a distinct layer beneath the warm water. The cold water sinks because it is denser and therefore heavier than the warm water.

Teaching Procedure:

1. Post the laminated graph chart at the front of the class. Label the top of the graph "Plip, Plop, Drip, Drop."

2. Fill each of the small bottles halfway with cold water and add a few drops of food coloring. Each group will need one bottle of cold colored water.

3. Distribute an investigation sheet and a water droplet icon to each student.

4. Show students the materials to be used in the experiment. Read aloud the question at the top of the investigation sheet. Refer students to the picture of the experiment on the sheet and briefly explain how the experiment will be set up. Answer any questions students might have about the procedure.

5. Have students select an answer to the question posed on the investigation sheet about what they think will happen to the cold water when it is poured into the warm water. Tell them to record their answer both on the sheet and on the water droplet icon. Collect the icons and use them to create a class graph as shown.

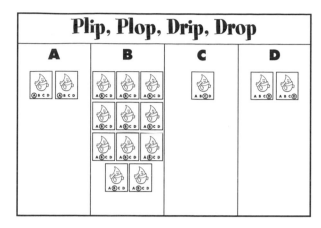

Plip, Plop, Drip, Drop

6. Have each group cover its work area with newspaper. Distribute a bowl of warm water and a bottle of cold colored water to each group.

7. Have students hold their thumb over the bottle opening, tip the bottle sideways, and slowly lower it into the bowl of warm water. Then have them release their thumb and observe what happens. **Warn students not to shake their bottle or otherwise create waves in the bowl. The cold water should be allowed to pour out of the bottle on its own.** Instruct students to record their observations on the investigation sheet. (The colored cold water will sink below the clear warm water and form a layer beneath it.)

8. Discuss with students what they observed. Encourage them to offer an explanation for why the cold water sank below the warm water and formed its own layer. Once the class has had a chance to discuss their theories, introduce the idea that cold water and warm water have different densities. Draw on students' experience with previous density experiments in this book, if you have performed them. Challenge students to identify which liquid is denser and why. (The cold water must be denser because it sank beneath the warm water.)

9. Have students answer the conclusion question on the investigation sheet. Finally, have them draw a picture of the experiment on the back of the sheet. Encourage them to label their drawing and provide a caption that explains what happened in the experiment.

Try this for fun:

Have students try the experiment in reverse, pouring warm water into cold.

Name _____

Plip, Plop, Drip, Drop

Question

What do you think will happen to cold water when it is poured into a bowl of warm water?

The cold water will _____.

    A float on top of the warm water

    B mix into the warm water

    C sink under the warm water

    D form an ice cube

Procedure and Observations

1. Hold your thumb over the opening of the bottle of cold colored water, turn the bottle on its side, and lower it into the bowl of warm water. Release your thumb. What do you observe?

_____

_____

2. Where did the cold water end up?

_____

Conclusion

How can you explain what happened to the cold water in the bowl?

_____

_____

On the back of this sheet, draw a picture showing what happened in your experiment. Label your drawing and write a sentence that describes what it is showing.

15

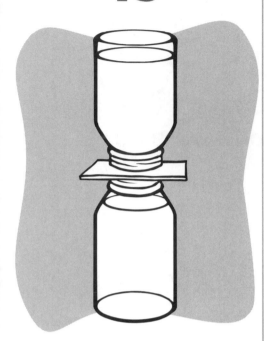

Water Wonder

Objective: Students will demonstrate that warm water rises and cold water sinks.

Question: What will happen to a bottle of warm water when it is placed upside down over a bottle of cold water?

Science Background: Molecules of warmer water vibrate more than those of colder water because they have more energy. Because warmer water molecules vibrate more, they take up a greater volume of space than the same quantity of cold water. As a result, warm water is less dense than cold water.

Liquids of different densities do not mix. When a bottle of warm water is inverted over a bottle of cold water, the warm water will stay above the cold water and will not mix into it. The less dense warm water floats on top of the denser cold water.

Materials:

- laminated graph chart
- page 68, reproduced for each student
- page 69, reproduced, one icon for each student
- wide-mouth jars, such as large baby food jars
- warm water
- cold water
- food coloring
- lightweight cardboard squares
- newspaper

Teaching Procedure:

1. Post the laminated graph chart at the front of the class. Label the top of the graph "Water Wonder."

2. You might want to perform this experiment as a class demonstration, as it requires fairly advanced motor skills and can get quite messy if mistakes are made.

3. Distribute an investigation sheet and a water droplet icon to each student.

4. Show students the materials to be used in the experiment. Read aloud the question at the top of the investigation sheet. Refer students to the picture of the experiment on the sheet and briefly explain how the experiment will be set up. Answer any questions students might have about the procedure.

5. Have students select an answer to the question posed on the investigation sheet about what they think will happen when a bottle of warm water is placed upside down over a bottle of cold water. Tell them to record their answer both on the sheet and on the water droplet icon. Collect the icons and use them to create a class graph as shown.

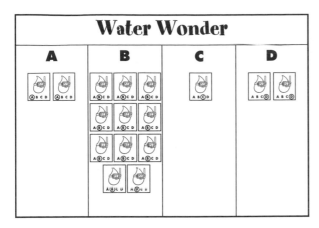

Water Wonder

6. Cover your demonstration area with newspaper and have students gather around. (If you decide to have students perform the experiment themselves, distribute the materials to each group.) Fill one jar to the top with warm water and a second jar to the top with cold water. Place several drops of red food coloring into the warm water jar, and several drops of blue food coloring into the cold water jar.

7. Place the cardboard square over the top of the warm water jar. Hold the cardboard in place as you carefully invert the jar. Now place the warm water jar on top of the cold water jar so that the piece of cardboard is between them.

8. Hold the two jars steady with one hand. Then, with your other hand, quickly pull out the piece of cardboard between the jars. What do students observe? (The red water stays in the jar above, and the blue water stays in the jar below. They do not mix.) Instruct students to record their observations on the investigation sheet.

9. Discuss with students what they observed. Encourage them to offer an explanation for why the warm and cold water did not mix together. Once the class has had a chance to discuss their theories, introduce the idea that warm water and cold water have different densities. Liquids of different densities don't mix. That's why the warm water stayed separate from the cold water, even after the cardboard was removed. Challenge students to identify which liquid was denser. How do they know? (The cold water was denser because it stayed at the bottom of the jar and did not rise.)

10. Have students answer the conclusion questions on the investigation sheet. Finally, have them draw a picture of the experiment on the back of the sheet. Encourage them to label their drawing and provide a caption that explains what happened in the experiment.

Try this for fun:

Repeat the experiment, but this time reverse the positions of the warm and cold water jars so that the cold water is on top. (The cold water will sink, mixing the liquids together and turning them purple.)

Name _____

Water Wonder

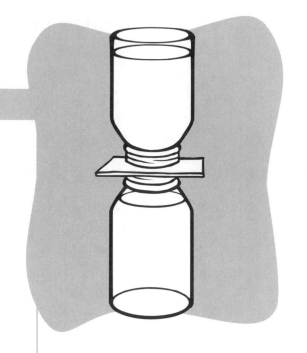

Question

What do you think will happen to a bottle of warm water when it is placed upside down over a bottle of cold water?

The warm water will _____.

    A mix with the cold water and turn purple

    B evaporate

    C not mix with the cold water

    D mix with the cold water and form steam

Procedure and Observations

Look at the jar of warm water on top of the jar of cold water. Watch as your teacher removes the cardboard between the jars. What happens?

_____

_____

Conclusions

1. How can you explain what happened in the experiment?

_____

_____

_____

2. Which is denser, warm water or cold water? How do you know?

_____

_____

On the back of this sheet, draw a picture showing what happened in your experiment. Label your drawing and write a sentence that describes what it is showing.

        How to Do Science Experiments with Children • EMC 5001 • ©2003 by Evan-Moor Corp.

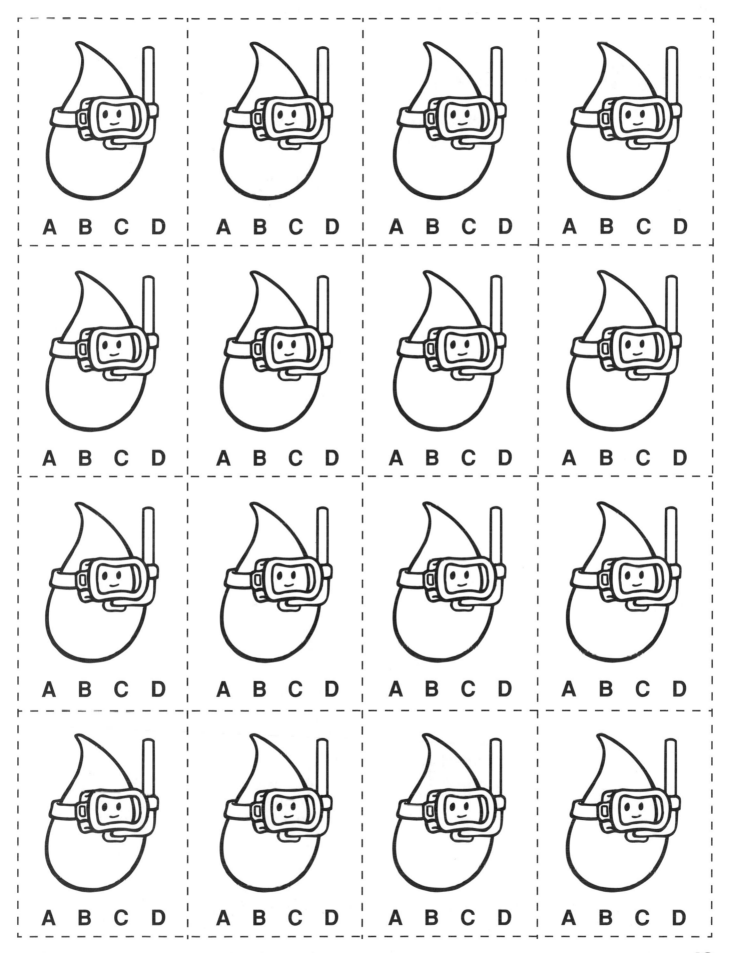

16

Materials:

- laminated graph chart
- page 72, reproduced for each student
- page 73, reproduced, one icon for each student
- hot water
- cold water
- plastic cups
- flavored gelatin
- newspaper

Mix It Up

Objective: Students will demonstrate that some substances dissolve more quickly in hot water than in cold water.

Question: What will happen to gelatin when it is added to hot water?

Science Background: Water is made up of many tiny molecules. These molecules, like the molecules that make up all matter, vibrate. Molecules of hot water vibrate faster than those of cold water because they contain more energy.

Consider a package of drink mix that is added to two glasses of water: one hot and one cold. The particles of water in each glass mix with the particles of drink mix, separating them and causing them to **dissolve**. However, the vibration of the molecules in the hot water makes the particles of powder separate and spread out more quickly. Thus, generally speaking, powders dissolve more quickly in hot water than in cold water.

Teaching Procedure:

1. Post the laminated graph chart at the front of the class. Label the top of the graph "Mix It Up."

2. Distribute an investigation sheet and a gelatin box icon to each student.

3. Show students the materials to be used in the experiment. Read aloud the question on the investigation sheet. Refer students to the picture of the experiment on the sheet and briefly explain how the experiment will be set up. Answer any questions students might have about the procedure.

4. Have each group cover its work area with newspaper. Distribute a cup of hot water, a cup of cold water, and a small amount of gelatin in another plastic cup to each group.

5. Have students add a pinch of gelatin to the cup of cold water and observe what happens to the gelatin. (It will sink and slowly begin to dissolve in the water.) Instruct students to record their observations on the investigation sheet.

6. Have students select an answer to the question posed on the investigation sheet about what they think will happen when they add the gelatin to the hot water. Tell them to record their answer both on the sheet and on the gelatin box icon. Collect the icons and use them to create a class graph as shown.

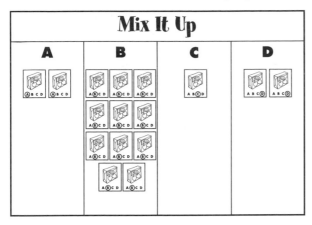

7. Now have students add a pinch of gelatin to the cup of hot water and observe what happens to the gelatin. (It will dissolve almost immediately.) Have students again record their observations on the investigation sheet.

8. Discuss with students what they observed. Encourage them to offer an explanation for why the gelatin dissolved so much faster in the hot water. Once the class has had a chance to discuss their theories, introduce the idea that water is made up of tiny particles that have energy. Hot water particles have more energy than cold water particles. This energy helps to break up the gelatin particles and dissolve them into the water.

9. Have students answer the conclusion question on the investigation sheet. Finally, have them draw a picture of the experiment on the back of the sheet. Encourage them to label their drawing and provide a caption that explains what happened in the experiment.

Try this for fun:

Have students repeat the experiment using warm water (the gelatin will dissolve faster than it did in cold water but not as fast as it did in hot water) or hot and cold milk (results will be similar to those seen for the hot and cold water).

Mix It Up

Question

What do you think will happen to the gelatin when it is added to hot water?

The gelatin will _____.

    A swirl and quickly mix with the water

    B float on top of the water

    C instantly harden

    D react just as it did in cold water

Procedure and Observations

1. Add a pinch of gelatin to the cup of cold water. What happens to the gelatin?

_____

_____

2. Now add a pinch of gelatin to the cup of hot water. What happens to the gelatin?

_____

_____

Conclusion

How can you explain the difference in how the gelatin behaved in each cup?

_____

_____

_____

On the back of this sheet, draw a picture showing what happened in your experiment. Label your drawing and write a sentence that describes what it is showing.

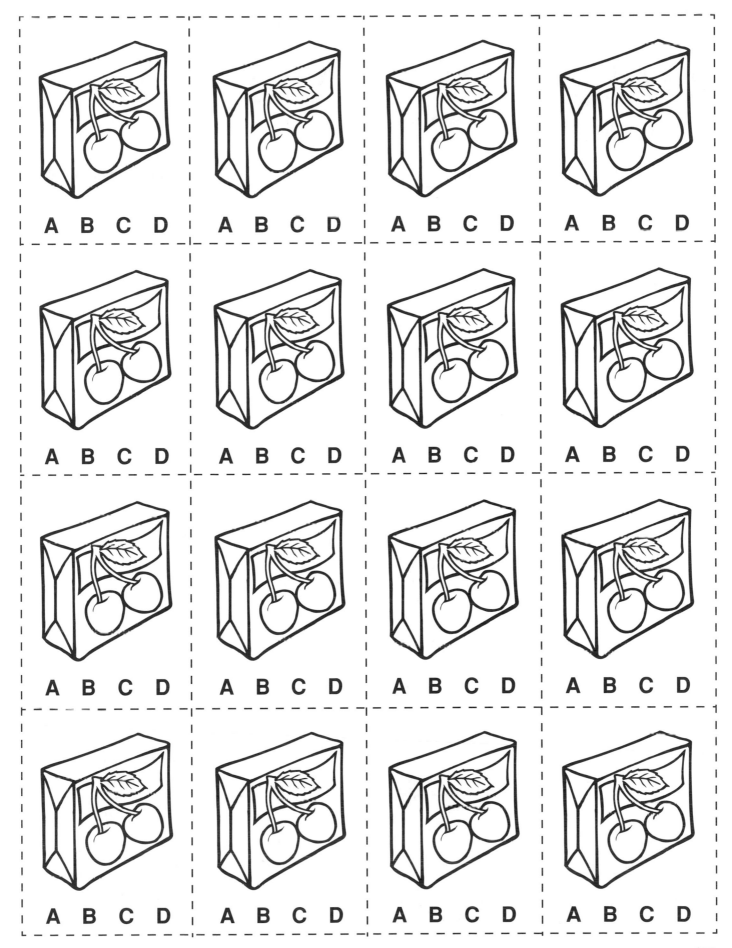

A B C D | A B C D | A B C D | A B C D

A B C D | A B C D | A B C D | A B C D

A B C D | A B C D | A B C D | A B C D

A B C D | A B C D | A B C D | A B C D

17

Materials:

- laminated graph chart
- page 76, reproduced for each student
- page 77, reproduced, one icon for each student
- empty milk cartons, quart or half-gallon
- water
- plastic tubs
- pushpins
- masking tape

A Moo-ving Experiment

Objective: Students will demonstrate that water pressure increases with depth.

Question: Which of three holes punched in the side of a milk carton will produce the longest stream of water: the top, middle, or bottom hole?

Science Background: Consider a glass of water. Water has weight and therefore exerts **pressure** on objects beneath its surface, including the water located at the bottom of the glass! How much pressure the water exerts at any point depends on the height of the column of water above that point. The higher the column, the greater the pressure. Thus, water at the bottom of the glass will be under greater pressure than water near the middle or top of the glass.

Now consider a milk carton full of water. Water near the bottom of the carton has a higher column of water sitting on top of it than water near the center of the carton does. If three holes are punched in the side of the carton—one near the bottom, one near the middle, and one near the top—water will exit each of the holes at different rates. The greater the pressure on the water, the greater the speed at which it will exit the hole, and the farther it will squirt. Thus, water squirts farther out of the bottom hole than it does out of the middle hole, and farther out of the middle hole than it does from the top hole.

Teaching Procedure:

1. Post the laminated graph chart at the front of the class. Label the top of the graph "A Moo-ving Experiment."

2. Distribute an investigation sheet and a milk carton icon to each student.

3. Show students the materials to be used in the experiment. Read aloud the question at the top of the investigation sheet. Refer students to the picture of the experiment on the sheet and briefly explain how the experiment will be set up. Answer any questions students might have about the procedure.

4. Have students select an answer to the question posed on the investigation sheet about which of the three holes they think will produce the longest stream of water. Tell them to record their answer both on the sheet and on the milk carton icon. Collect the icons and use them to create a class graph as shown.

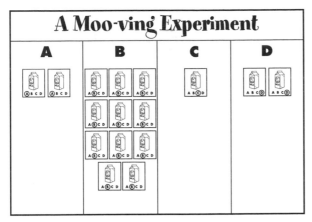

5. Distribute an empty milk carton, a pushpin, a 20-cm length of masking tape, and a plastic tub to each group. Have students poke three holes in the side of the carton: one near the bottom, one near the middle, and one near the top. The holes should all be the same size, aligned one above the other, and evenly spaced.

6. Next, have students place the length of tape over the holes so that all three are blocked. Have students fill the carton with water and place it in the tub. Instruct them to remove the tape quickly and observe the stream of water that exits each hole. (The water will shoot farthest out of the bottom hole, followed by the middle hole and then the top hole.) Instruct students to record their observations on the investigation sheet.

7. Discuss with students what they observed. Encourage them to offer an explanation for why the water squirted a different distance from each hole. Once the class has had a chance to discuss their theories, introduce the idea that water exerts pressure—it presses down on things. Point out that water near the bottom of the carton had more water pushing on it from above, and so was pushed out of the bottom hole with greater force and squirted farther than the water from the holes above it.

8. Have students answer the conclusion question on the investigation sheet. Finally, have them draw a picture of the experiment on the back of the sheet. Encourage them to label their drawing and provide a caption that explains what happened in the experiment.

Try this for fun:

Have students place a ruler in the plastic tub and measure the distance that the water squirts out of each hole.

A Moo-ving Experiment

Question

Which of three holes punched in the side of a milk carton do you think will produce the longest stream of water: the bottom, middle, or top hole?

A the bottom hole

B the middle hole

C the top hole

D all will be the same

Procedure and Observations

1. Follow your teacher's instructions on how to poke three holes in the side of your carton. Cover the holes with tape. Fill the carton with water and place it in the plastic tub. Remove the tape quickly. What do you observe?

_____

_____

2. From which hole did the water shoot farthest?

_____

Conclusion

How can you explain what happened in your experiment?

_____

_____

_____

On the back of this sheet, draw a picture showing what happened in your experiment. Label your drawing and write a sentence that describes what it is showing.

18

Materials:

- laminated graph chart
- page 80, reproduced for each student
- page 81, reproduced, one icon for each student
- water
- plastic cups
- pencils

What Do I See?

Objective: Students will observe that light rays refract (bend) as they pass from one medium to another.

Question: What will a pencil placed in a glass half full of water look like?

Science Background: Light travels in straight lines called rays. Light rays move in all directions away from their source. The rays bounce off objects and enter our eyes. Our brains use this information to create an image of the objects.

Light rays travel at different speeds in different mediums (materials). As light rays pass from one medium to another—for example, from water to air—they change direction slightly, or bend, as their speed changes. This phenomenon is known as **refraction**.

Half of the pencil in the glass of water is submerged and half is not. Light rays bouncing off the submerged parts of the pencil pass from the water to the air as they travel to our eyes, and are bent at the water's surface. Light rays bouncing off the parts of the pencil that are not submerged do not move from one medium to another, and so are not bent. As a result, we see the two halves of the pencil from slightly different perspectives, making the pencil appear to be broken.

Teaching Procedure:

1. Post the laminated graph chart at the front of the class. Label the top of the graph "What Do I See?"

2. Distribute an investigation sheet and a pencil icon to each student.

3. Show students the materials to be used in the experiment. Read aloud the question at the top of the investigation sheet. Refer students to the picture of the experiment on the sheet and briefly explain how the experiment will be set up. Answer any questions students might have about the procedure.

4. Have students select an answer to the question posed on the investigation sheet about what they think a pencil placed in a glass of water will look like. Tell them to record their answer both on the sheet and on the pencil icon. Collect the icons and use them to create a class graph as shown.

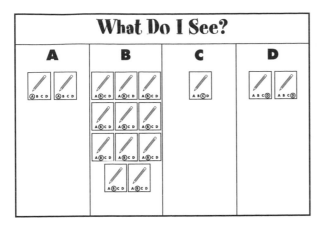

5. Distribute a cup of water (filled halfway) to each group. Have students place the pencil in the glass of water and observe it from the side. (The pencil will appear to be "broken" at the surface of the water.) Instruct students to record their observations on the investigation sheet.

6. Have students take their pencils out of the water and observe them again. Are they broken? (No.) Have students again record their observations on the investigation sheet.

7. Discuss with students what they observed. Encourage them to offer an explanation for why the pencil appeared to be broken, even though it wasn't. Once the class has had a chance to discuss their theories, introduce the idea that we see objects when light rays bounce off them and then enter our eyes. When these rays pass from one kind of material to another—such as from water to air—they are bent. So light rays bouncing off the submerged half of the pencil don't line up with those bouncing off the dry part of the pencil. Therefore, the pencil looks like it is broken, even though it isn't.

8. Have students answer the conclusion question on the investigation sheet. Finally, have them draw a picture of the experiment on the back of the sheet. Encourage them to label their drawing and provide a caption that explains what happened in the experiment.

Try this for fun:

Have students try the experiment again with a different liquid or a different object.

Name _____

What Do I See?

What do you think a pencil placed in a glass half full of water will look like?

The pencil will look _____.

    A like it's moving up and down

    B smaller

    C broken

    D upside down

Procedure and Observations

1. Place a pencil in half a cup of water. Observe the pencil from the side. How does the pencil look?

_____

_____

2. Take the pencil out of the water and look at it. Does it look like it did when it was in the glass of water?

_____

_____

Conclusion

How can you explain the difference between how the pencil looked in and out of the cup of water?

_____

_____

On the back of this sheet, draw a picture showing what happened in your experiment. Label your drawing and write a sentence that describes what it is showing.

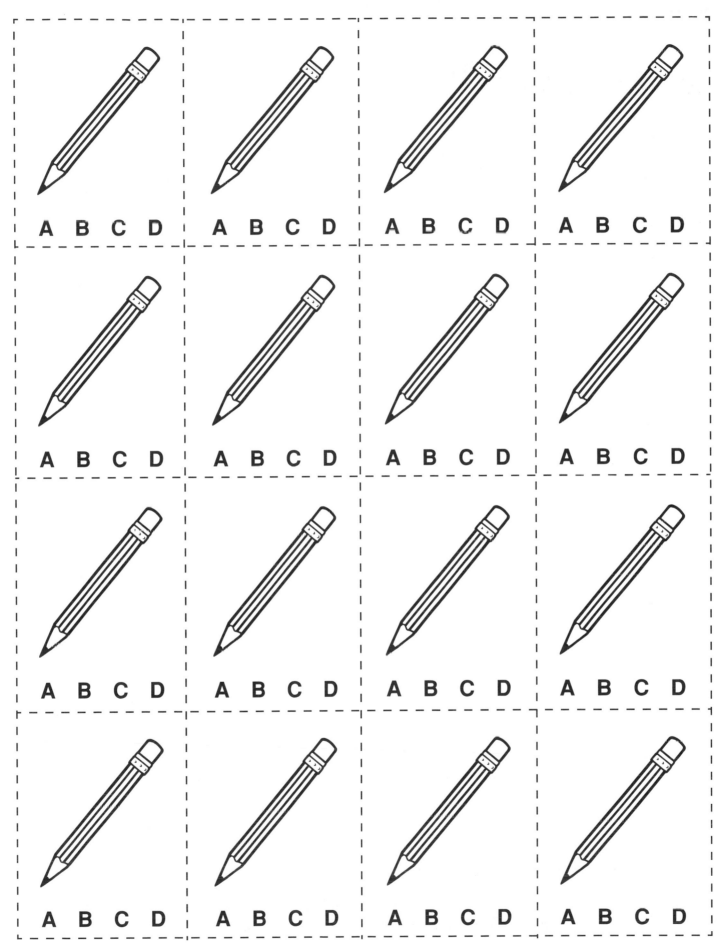

19

Materials:

- laminated graph chart
- page 84, reproduced for each student
- page 85, reproduced, one icon for each student
- plastic cups
- paper napkins
- bowls
- water
- newspaper

No Vacancy

Objective: Students will demonstrate that air takes up space.

Question: What will happen to a crumpled napkin in a plastic cup when the cup is placed upside down in a bowl of water?

Science Background: Because air is invisible, students have a hard time understanding that it is "something" and takes up space. In this experiment, the crumpled napkin placed at the bottom of the cup does not get wet when the cup is inverted and pushed down into a bowl of water. That's because a pocket of air between the water and the napkin keeps the water from reaching the napkin. If the air had a way to escape the cup—for instance, if there were a hole in the bottom of the cup—the water would displace the air and wet the napkin. But because the cup is intact, the napkin stays dry.

Teaching Procedure:

1. Post the laminated graph chart at the front of the class. Label the top of the graph "No Vacancy."

2. Have each group cover its work area with newspaper. Distribute an investigation sheet and a napkin icon to each student.

3. Show students the materials to be used in the experiment. Read aloud the question at the top of the investigation sheet. Refer students to the picture of the experiment on the sheet and briefly explain how the experiment will be set up. Answer any questions students might have about the procedure.

4. Have students select an answer to the question posed on the investigation sheet about what they think will happen when the cup with the napkin in it is placed upside down in a bowl of water. Tell them to record their answer both on the sheet and on the napkin icon. Collect the icons and use them to create a class graph as shown.

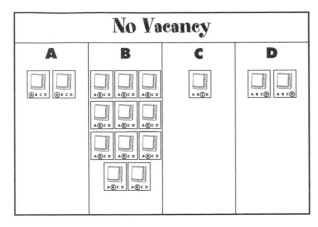

5. Distribute a plastic cup, a bowl of water, and a paper napkin to each group. Have students crumple up the napkin and stuff it into the bottom of the plastic cup.

6. Instruct students to invert the cup and push it straight down into the bowl of water. ***Emphasize that the cup must be kept perpendicular to the water's surface or the experiment will not work. Offer help as needed.*** Then have students record their observations of what happens when they push the cup underwater. (The napkin will stay dry.)

7. Discuss with students what they observed. Encourage them to offer an explanation for why the napkin did not get wet. Once the class has had a chance to discuss their theories, introduce the idea that air is a real thing that takes up space. Between the crumpled napkin and the top of the cup was a pocket of air. When the cup was inverted and pushed down into the water, the pocket of air prevented the water from reaching the napkin and wetting it.

8. Have students answer the conclusion question on the investigation sheet. Finally, have them draw a picture of the experiment on the back of the sheet. Encourage them to label their drawing and provide a caption that explains what happened in the experiment.

Try this for fun:

Have students push the cup into the water again, this time at an angle, and see what happens. (The water will rush into the cup and wet the napkin. Tilting the cup creates a way for the air inside it to escape. The water then displaces the air, wetting the napkin.)

No Vacancy

Question

What do you think will happen to a crumpled napkin in a plastic cup when the cup is placed upside down in a bowl of water?

The napkin will _____.

    A stay dry

    B get wet

    C fall apart

    D absorb all the water in the bowl

Procedure and Observations

Crumple up your napkin and stuff it into the bottom of your plastic cup. Turn the cup over and push it straight down into the bowl of water. What happens to the napkin?

_____

_____

_____

Conclusion

How can you explain what happened to the napkin?

_____

_____

_____

On the back of this sheet, draw a picture showing what happened in your experiment. Label your drawing and write a sentence that describes what it is showing.

A B C D   A B C D   A B C D   A B C D

A B C D   A B C D   A B C D   A B C D

A B C D   A B C D   A B C D   A B C D

A B C D   A B C D   A B C D   A B C D

20

Materials:

- laminated graph chart
- page 88, reproduced for each student
- page 89, reproduced, one icon for each student
- plastic soda bottles
- plastic cups
- funnels
- clay
- water
- newspaper

Funnel Fun

Objective: Students will demonstrate that air takes up space.

Question: What will happen when water is poured into a funnel resting on a bottle that has been sealed with clay?

Science Background: Because air is invisible, students have a hard time understanding that it is a real thing and takes up space. In this experiment, a funnel is placed in the mouth of a bottle, and the joint between the funnel and bottle is sealed with clay. Water is then poured into the funnel, but the water cannot enter the bottle because the bottle is already full of air. If the bottle/funnel joint were not sealed with clay, the air would be forced out of the bottle through the joint as the water pushed down on the air from above. But because the joint is sealed, the air cannot leave the bottle and so the water cannot enter the bottle.

Teaching Procedure:

1. Post the laminated graph chart at the front of the class. Label the top of the graph "Funnel Fun."

2. Have each group cover its work area with newspaper. Distribute an investigation sheet and a funnel icon to each student.

3. Show students the materials to be used in the experiment. Read aloud the question at the top of the investigation sheet. Refer students to the picture of the experiment on the sheet and briefly explain how the experiment will be set up. Answer any questions students might have about the procedure.

4. Have students select an answer to the question posed on the investigation sheet about what they think will happen when water is poured into the funnel. Tell them to record their answer both on the sheet and on the funnel icon. Collect the icons and use them to create a class graph as shown.

How to Do Science Experiments with Children • EMC 5001 • ©2003 by Evan-Moor Corp.

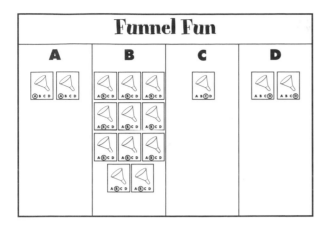

5. Distribute a plastic soda bottle, a funnel, a small lump of clay, and a plastic cup filled with water to each group. Have students place the funnel in the opening of the bottle and use the clay to seal the joint. Refer them to the picture on the investigation sheet as needed.

6. Ask students what is in the bottle. (Many students will suggest that the bottle is empty. Some may recognize that the bottle is filled with air.) Instruct students to record their ideas on the investigation sheet.

7. Instruct students to pour water from the cup into the funnel. Have them observe what happens to the water. (It stays in the funnel.) Tell them to record their observations on the investigation sheet.

8. Discuss with students what they observed. Encourage them to offer an explanation for why the water did not enter the bottle. Once the class has had a chance to discuss their theories, introduce the idea that air takes up space. The bottle was full of air when they poured the water into the funnel. The air prevented the water from entering the bottle!

9. Have students answer the conclusion question on the investigation sheet. Finally, have them draw a picture of the experiment on the back of the sheet. Encourage them to label their drawing and provide a caption that explains what happened in the experiment.

Try this for fun:

Have students pour water into the funnel again, but first tell them to remove the clay from the bottle opening. What happens? (The water will enter the bottle because it can displace the air, forcing it out of the joint between the funnel and the bottle opening.)

Funnel Fun

Question

What do you think will happen when water is poured into a funnel resting on a bottle that has been sealed with clay?

The water will _____.

    A stay in the funnel

    B flow into the bottle smoothly

    C enter the bottle in gulps

    D dissolve the clay

Procedure and Observations

1. Set the funnel in the bottle opening and seal the joint with clay. What is in the bottle?

_____

2. Pour water into the funnel. What does the water do?

_____

_____

Conclusion

How can you explain what the water did?

_____

_____

_____

On the back of this sheet, draw a picture showing what happened in your experiment. Label your drawing and write a sentence that describes what it is showing.

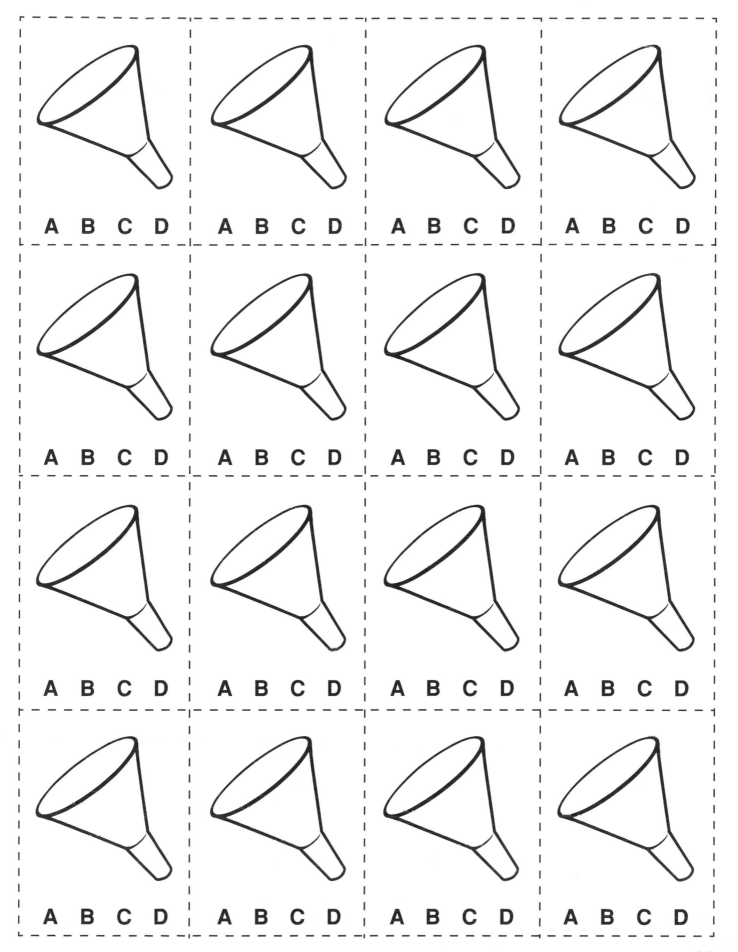

21

Materials:

- laminated graph chart
- page 92, reproduced for each student
- page 93, reproduced, one icon for each student
- plastic bottles
- small balloons

Air Takes Up Space

Blow Out

Objective: Students will demonstrate that air takes up space.

Question: What will happen to a balloon in a bottle when you blow into it?

Science Background: Because air is invisible, students have a hard time understanding that it is real and takes up space. In this experiment, the balloon body is inserted in a bottle, and the neck is stretched around the mouth of the bottle. The bottle, of course, is full of air, and the balloon, in effect, seals the bottle.

When students attempt to blow into the balloon, the balloon inflates slightly as the walls of the balloon compress the air in the bottle. Inflation can only go so far, however, because the compressed air pushes back against the balloon, preventing it from expanding further. If there were a hole in the bottle, the air in the bottle could be forced out as students blew into the balloon. But because the bottle is sealed, the air cannot escape and the balloon cannot be inflated.

Teaching Procedure:

1. Post the laminated graph chart at the front of the class. Label the top of the graph "Blow Out."

2. Distribute an investigation sheet and a balloon icon to each student.

3. Show students the materials to be used in the experiment. Read aloud the question at the top of the investigation sheet. Refer students to the picture of the experiment on the sheet and briefly explain how the experiment will be set up. Answer any questions students might have about the procedure.

4. Have students select an answer to the question posed on the investigation sheet about what they think will happen when they blow into the balloon in the bottle. Tell them to record their answer both on the sheet and on the balloon icon. Collect the icons and use them to create a class graph as shown.

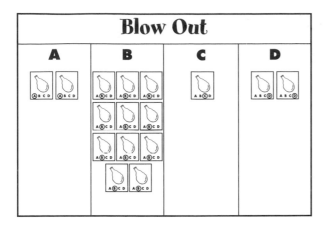

Blow Out

A	B	C	D

5. Distribute a plastic bottle and a small balloon to each student. Show students how to insert the balloon into the bottle, and how to stretch the neck of the balloon over the bottle's mouth.

6. Ask students what is in their bottle. (The bottle contains a balloon and is full of air.)

7. Now have students try to inflate the balloon inside the bottle by blowing air into it. Tell them to record their observations on the investigation sheet. (It will not inflate, no matter how hard students blow.)

8. Discuss with students what they observed. Encourage them to offer an explanation for why they could not inflate the balloon. Once the class has had a chance to discuss their theories, introduce the idea that air takes up space. When they tried to inflate the balloon by blowing into it, the balloon could not expand because the space it would have expanded into was already occupied by air. Because the bottle was sealed, air could not escape the bottle, and so the balloon could not inflate.

9. Have students answer the conclusion question on the investigation sheet. Finally, have them draw a picture of the experiment on the back of the sheet. Encourage them to label their drawing and provide a caption that explains what happened in the experiment.

Try this for fun:

Poke a hole in one of the students' bottles and have that student try to inflate the balloon inside again. What happens? (The balloon inflates this time.) Ask students to explain why. (The hole allowed the air inside the bottle to escape when the expanding balloon pressed on it. The balloon could therefore expand as it normally would outside the bottle.)

Name _____

Blow Out

Question

What do you think will happen to a balloon in a bottle when you blow into it?

The balloon will _____.

    A inflate

    B pop

    C do nothing

    D get flatter

Procedure and Observations

1. Put the balloon inside the bottle and stretch the neck over the bottle mouth as shown in the picture above. What is in the bottle?

_____

_____

2. Blow into the balloon inside your bottle. Blow as hard as you can! What happens to the balloon?

_____

_____

Conclusion

How can you explain what happened to the balloon?

_____

_____

_____

On the back of this sheet, draw a picture showing what happened in your experiment. Label your drawing and write a sentence that describes what it is showing.

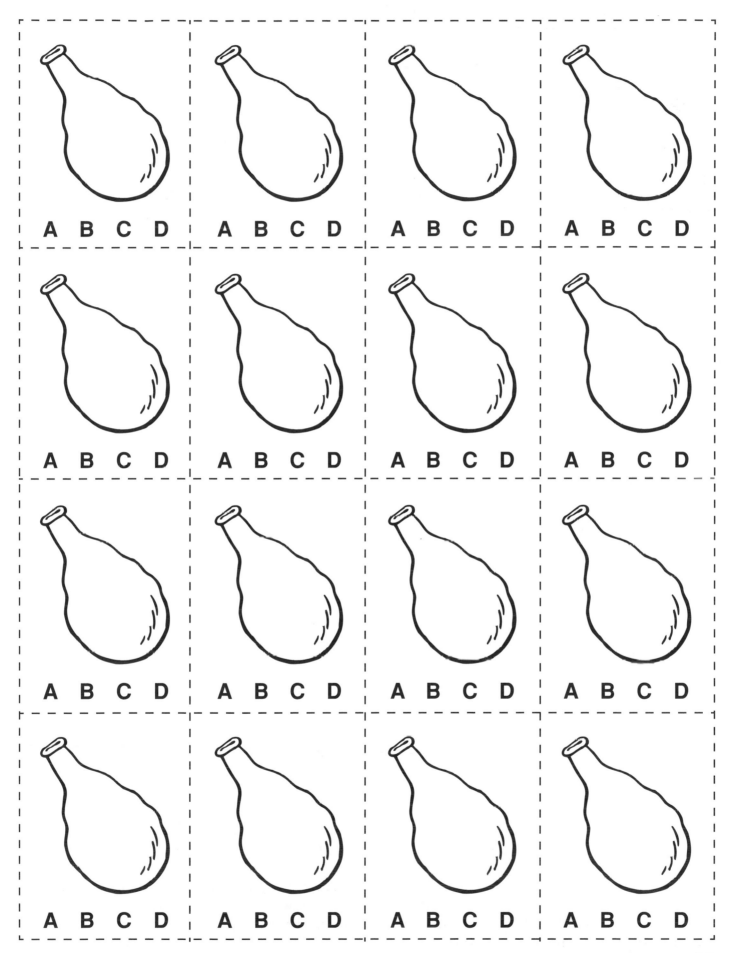

Air Exerts Pressure

22

Materials:

- laminated graph chart
- page 96, reproduced for each student
- page 97, reproduced, one icon for each student
- stiff rulers
- sheets of plain paper

Paper Magic

Objective: Students will demonstrate that air has weight and exerts pressure.

Question: What will happen to a piece of paper on top of a ruler when you hit the end of the ruler really hard?

Science Background: Air exerts pressure. The tiny particles that make up air are constantly moving. These particles have weight and therefore exert a force on objects they strike. **Pressure** is a measure of the force applied per unit of area $(P = F/A)$.

Consider a sheet of paper lying on top of a ruler on a desk. The sheet of paper, while not heavy, has a relatively large surface area. Thus, the force of all the air particles bumping into it from above is considerable. The force is great enough to resist the sudden thrust of the ruler as one end is struck. If the ruler is struck hard, the air particles at the surface of the paper do not have a chance to be pushed out of the way and their force is felt. This force holds the ruler down to the table. If one end of the ruler is pressed slowly instead of struck, the air particles are simply pushed away from the paper's surface as the ruler rises with ease.

Teaching Procedure:

1. Post the laminated graph chart at the front of the class. Label the top of the graph "Paper Magic."

2. Distribute an investigation sheet and a paper magic icon to each student.

3. Show students the materials to be used in the experiment. Read aloud the question at the top of the investigation sheet. Refer students to the picture of the experiment on the sheet, and briefly explain how the experiment will be set up. Answer any questions students might have about the procedure.

4. Have students select an answer to the question posed on the investigation sheet about what they think will happen to the sheet of paper when they strike the end of the ruler really hard. Tell them to record their answer both on the sheet and on the paper magic icon. Collect the icons and use them to create a class graph as shown.

5. Distribute a stiff ruler and a sheet of plain paper to each group. Have students set the ruler on the edge of a table as shown in the picture on the investigation sheet. Have them place the sheet of paper over the portion of the ruler that is on the table.

6. Now have students take turns striking the end of the ruler that hangs over the side of the desk. Instruct them to record their observations of what happens to the paper and the ruler. (The sheet of paper will not move much; it will hold the ruler down on the table.)

7. Discuss with students what they observed. Encourage them to offer an explanation for why the ruler and paper did not fly up when they struck the end of the ruler. Once the class has had a chance to discuss their theories, introduce the idea that air exerts pressure on objects it touches. The pressure exerted by all the air particles above the sheet of paper held the paper and ruler to the table as the end of the ruler was struck, making the paper seem heavy.

8. Have students answer the conclusion question on the investigation sheet. Finally, have them draw a picture of the experiment on the back of the sheet. Encourage them to label their drawing and provide a caption that explains what happened in the experiment.

Try this for fun:

Have students try the experiment again with larger and smaller pieces of paper. What do they notice? (The larger the surface area of the paper, the greater the pressure exerted on it by the air and the less it moves when the ruler is struck. This makes the paper feel heavier than it really is.)

Have students try pushing the ruler down slowly instead of striking it and see how their results differ. (The slow-moving ruler will simply push the air molecules above the paper out of the way as it rises. As a result, the paper will feel lighter.)

Paper Magic

Question

What do you think will happen to the piece of paper on top of the ruler when you hit the end of the ruler really hard?

The paper will _____.

A fly up in the air

B tear apart

C fall to the ground

D not move much

Procedure and Observations

1. Place your ruler on a table, so that part of the ruler hangs over the edge, as shown above. Set the sheet of paper over the part of the ruler that is on the table.

2. Strike the overhanging end of the ruler really hard. What happens to the paper? What happens to the ruler?

_____

_____

Conclusion

How can you explain the behavior of the paper and the ruler in this experiment?

_____

_____

_____

On the back of this sheet, draw a picture showing what happened in your experiment. Label your drawing and write a sentence that describes what it is showing.

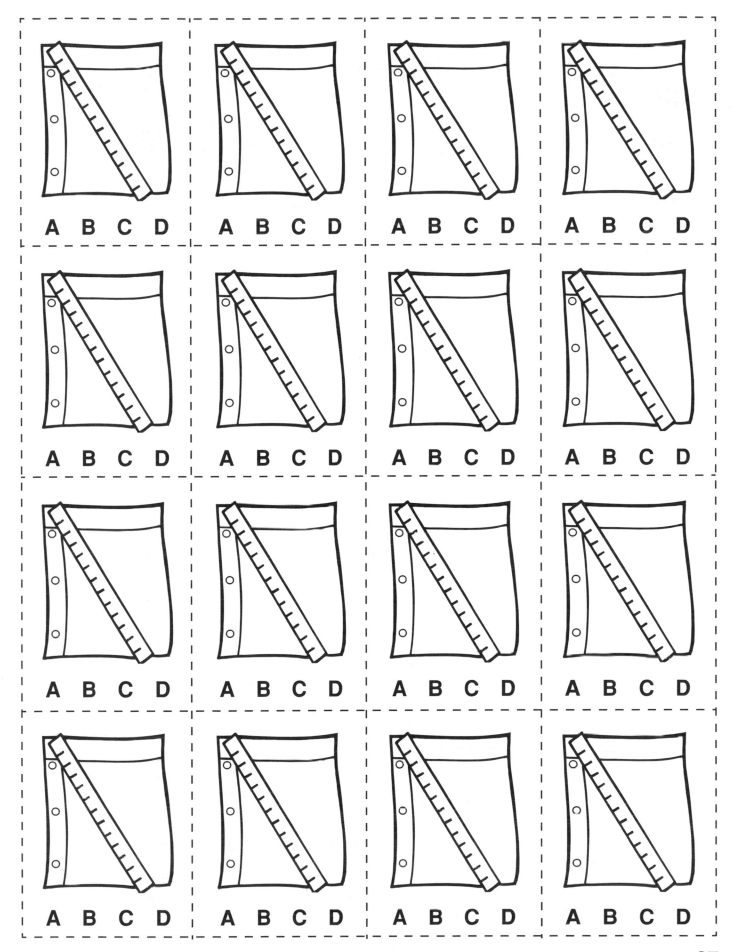

A B C D   A B C D   A B C D   A B C D

A B C D   A B C D   A B C D   A B C D

A B C D   A B C D   A B C D   A B C D

A B C D   A B C D   A B C D   A B C D

23

Bottled Up

Objective: Students will demonstrate that air exerts pressure.

Question: What will happen to the water in a sealed plastic bottle when the bottle is punctured with a pushpin?

Science Background: Air exerts pressure. The tiny particles that make up air are constantly moving. These particles have weight and therefore exert a force on objects they strike. **Pressure** is a measure of the force applied per unit of area (P = F/A).

Consider a sealed bottle of water with a small hole punctured in its side. At the hole, two opposing forces are at work: Water pressure inside the bottle is working to force the water out of the bottle, and air pressure outside the bottle is working to keep the water inside the bottle. As long as the bottle is sealed at the top, the forces will remain equal and the water will not leak out the pinhole. If the bottle cap is removed, however, air pressure above the water will force the water out of the pinhole.

Materials:

- laminated graph chart
- page 100, reproduced for each student
- page 101, reproduced, one icon for each student
- plastic bottles with caps
- pushpins
- water
- newspaper

Teaching Procedure:

1. Post the laminated graph chart at the front of the class. Label the top of the graph "Bottled Up."

2. Have each group cover its work area with newspaper. Distribute an investigation sheet and a pushpin icon to each student.

3. Show students the materials to be used in the experiment. Read aloud the question at the top of the investigation sheet. Refer students to the picture of the experiment on the sheet and briefly explain how the experiment will be set up. Answer any questions students might have about the procedure.

4. Have students select an answer to the question posed on the investigation sheet about what they think will happen to the water in the bottle when the bottle is punctured with a pushpin. Tell them to record their answer both on the sheet and on the pushpin icon. Collect the icons and use them to create a class graph as shown.

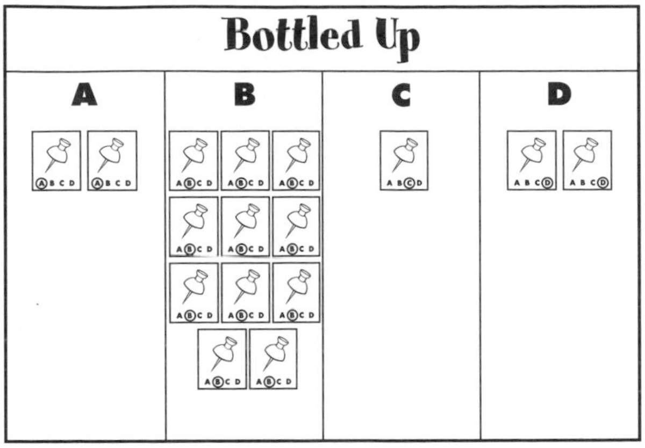

Bottled Up			
A	**B**	**C**	**D**

5. Distribute a capped plastic bottle filled with water and a pushpin to each group. Have students poke the pushpin into the side of the bottle near the bottom, as shown on the investigation sheet.

6. Now tell students to remove the pin from the bottle and watch what happens. Have students record their observations on the investigation sheet. (The water will stay in the bottle.)

7. Discuss with students what they observed. Encourage them to offer an explanation for why the water did not leak out of the hole left by the pushpin. Once the class has had a chance to discuss their theories, introduce the idea that air outside the bottle exerted pressure on the water at the hole. This pressure held the water inside the bottle, even as water pressure inside the bottle was trying to force the water out of the hole.

8. Have students answer the conclusion question on the investigation sheet. Finally, have them draw a picture of the experiment on the back of the sheet. Encourage them to label their drawing and provide a caption that explains what happened in the experiment.

Try this for fun:

Have students try the experiment again. After they have removed the pushpin from the side of the bottle, have them remove the bottle cap. What happens? Why? (The water will start squirting out of the pinhole. The air pressure above the water forces the water out of the bottle.)

Name _____

Bottled Up

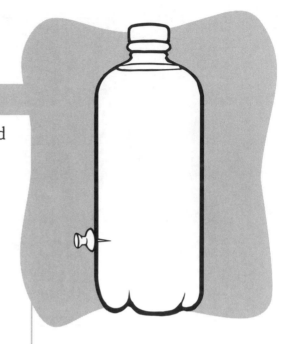

What do you think will happen to the water in a sealed plastic bottle when the bottle is punctured with a pushpin?

The water will _____.

    A   stay inside

    B   squirt out

    C   pop off the cap

    D   make a hissing sound

Procedure and Observations

1. Poke a pushpin into the side of your capped bottle of water, near the bottom.

2. Remove the pushpin from the bottle. What happens to the water in the bottle?

_____

_____

Conclusion

How can you explain what happened to the water in this experiment?

_____

_____

_____

On the back of this sheet, draw a picture showing what happened in your experiment. Label your drawing and write a sentence that describes what it is showing.

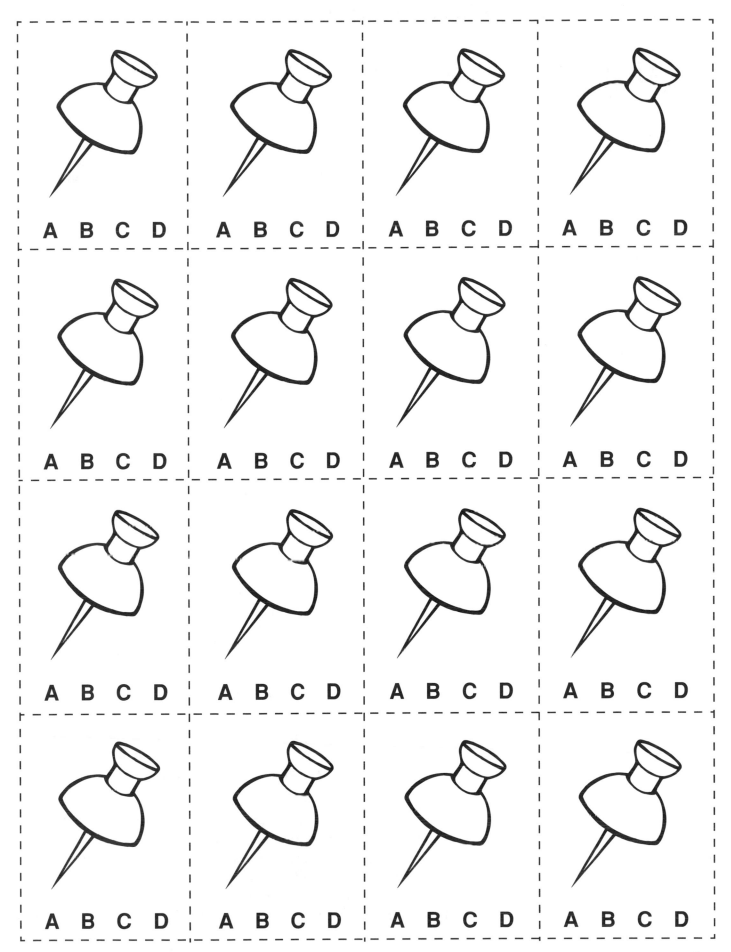

GASES

24

Materials:

- laminated graph chart
- page 104, reproduced for each student
- page 105, reproduced, one icon for each student
- plastic cups
- water
- plastic tubs
- newspaper
- cardboard squares

Flip Flop

Objective: Students will demonstrate that air exerts pressure.

Question: What will happen when you turn over a glass of water topped with cardboard and then let go of the cardboard?

Science Background: Air exerts pressure. The tiny particles that make up air are constantly moving. These particles have weight and therefore exert a force on objects they strike. **Pressure** is a measure of the force applied per unit of area ($P = F/A$).

Air exerts pressure in all directions—up, down, and sideways. Consider what happens when a cup of water topped with cardboard is turned over, and the cardboard is released. Because the air pressure pushing up on the cardboard is greater than the weight of the water pushing down on the cardboard, the cardboard stays in place and the water stays in the cup!

Teaching Procedure:

1. Post the laminated graph chart at the front of the class. Label the top of the graph "Flip Flop."

2. Have each group cover its work area with newspaper. Distribute an investigation sheet and a cup icon to each student.

3. You might choose to perform this experiment as a class demonstration instead of having individual groups do it. If not, plastic tubs at each work area will help to contain spills. In any case, try the experiment yourself over a sink a few times before instructing students how to set it up.

4. Show students the materials to be used in the experiment. Read aloud the question at the top of the investigation sheet. Refer students to the picture of the experiment on the sheet and briefly explain how the experiment will be set up. Answer any questions students might have about the procedure.

5. Have students select an answer to the question posed on the investigation sheet about what they think will happen when they turn the cup of water over and let go of the cardboard. Tell them to record their answer both on the sheet and on the cup icon. Collect the icons and use them to create a class graph as shown.

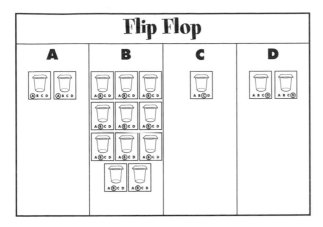

Flip Flop

| A | B | C | D |

6. Distribute to each group a plastic tub, a plastic cup filled to the brim with water, and a square of cardboard slightly larger than the diameter of the cup. Working over the tub, have students slide the piece of cardboard over the top of the cup.

7. Now instruct students to hold the cardboard square to the cup, turn the cup upside down, and then take their hand off the cardboard. Tell students to record their observations on the investigation sheet. (The cardboard will stick to the cup and the water will stay inside.)

8. Discuss with students what they observed. Encourage them to offer an explanation for why the water did not spill out of the cup. Once the class has had a chance to discuss their theories, introduce the idea that air exerts pressure in all directions, including up! The pressure exerted upward on the cardboard by air particles beneath it was greater than the weight of the water pressing down on the cardboard, so the cardboard and water stayed in place.

9. Have students answer the conclusion question on the investigation sheet. Finally, have them draw a picture of the experiment on the back of the sheet. Encourage them to label their drawing and provide a caption that explains what happened in the experiment.

Try this for fun:

Have students try the experiment again, this time with light tagboard. Does the water stay in the cup? (Yes, the experiment will work as long as the material is stiff enough to hold its shape. Once it gets wet, however, it will no longer be able to support the weight of the water.)

Name _____

Flip Flop

Question

What do you think will happen when you turn over
a glass of water topped with cardboard and then
let go of the cardboard?

A The water will spill all over.

B The water will sprinkle out slowly.

C The cardboard will stick to the cup and
hold the water in.

D The water will change color.

Procedure and Observations

1. Make sure your cup of water is filled to the brim. Now slide a piece of cardboard over the top
of the cup.

2. Hold the cup over your plastic tub. Pressing tightly on the cardboard, turn the cup upside
down. Now let go of the cardboard. What happens?

_____

_____

_____

Conclusion

How can you explain what happened in the experiment?

_____

_____

_____

On the back of this sheet, draw a picture showing what happened in your experiment. Label
your drawing and write a sentence that describes what it is showing.

How to Do Science Experiments with Children • EMC 5001 • ©2003 by Evan-Moor Corp.

A B C D A B C D A B C D A B C D

A B C D A B C D A B C D A B C D

A B C D A B C D A B C D A B C D

A B C D A B C D A B C D A B C D

25

Materials:

- laminated graph chart
- page 108, reproduced for each student
- page 109, reproduced, one icon for each student
- plastic soda bottles, 16-oz., empty
- cans of clear soda pop or sparkling water, 12-oz.
- corks
- paper towels
- newspaper

Rock-a-Bye Bottle

Objective: Students will demonstrate that gases (like air) exert pressure.

Question: What will happen when a soda bottle filled with pop and sealed with a cork is gently rocked back and forth?

Science Background: Like all fluids, air exerts pressure. Air is made up of tiny particles that are constantly moving. These particles push on objects they strike, and all these tiny pushes add up to create a force that is exerted on the objects. **Pressure** is simply a measure of the force applied per unit of area ($P = F/A$).

The soda pop in this experiment is full of dissolved gas (carbon dioxide). Some of the gas comes out of the solution when the can is opened. When the soda is poured into a plastic bottle and sealed with a cork, the gas that remains exerts pressure on the closed bottle. When the bottle is shaken, more gas is released and more pressure is exerted on the bottle. Eventually, the force created by the gas particles is great enough to rupture the bottle. In the case of this experiment, the cork is pushed off the bottle by the force of the moving carbon dioxide gas particles.

Teaching Procedure:

1. Post the laminated graph chart at the front of the class. Label the top of the graph "Rock-a-Bye Bottle."

2. Have each group cover its work area with newspaper. Distribute an investigation sheet and a soda bottle icon to each student.

3. Show students the materials to be used in the experiment. Read aloud the question on the investigation sheet. Refer students to the picture of the experiment on the sheet and briefly explain how the experiment will be set up. Answer any questions students might have about the procedure.

4. Distribute an empty plastic soda bottle, a cork, a can of clear soda pop or sparkling water, and several paper towels to each group. Have students pour the can of soda into the plastic bottle. Invite students to observe the soda in the bottle and record their observations on the investigation sheet. When they are finished, have them insert the cork firmly into the mouth of the bottle.

5. Have students select an answer to the question posed on the investigation sheet about what they think will happen when they begin to rock the bottle back and forth. Tell them to record their answer both on the sheet and on the soda bottle icon. Collect the icons and use them to create a class graph as shown.

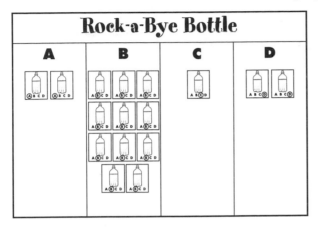

6. Instruct students to begin rocking the bottle of pop back and forth. **Warn them to point the mouth of the bottle away from their face and away from other students.** Tell them to record their observations on the investigation sheet. (The cork will eventually pop out of the bottle as the pressure in the bottle builds up.)

7. Discuss with students what they observed. Encourage them to offer an explanation for why the cork popped out of the bottle. Once the class has had a chance to discuss their theories, introduce the idea that gas particles in the soda pop were released into the bottle when the bottle was rocked. These particles moved around the bottle and pushed on the surfaces they hit, including the cork. Eventually, the gas particles exerted so much pressure that they forced the cork out of the bottle.

8. Have students answer the conclusion question on the investigation sheet. Finally, have them draw a picture of the experiment on the back of the sheet. Encourage them to label their drawing and provide a caption that explains what happened in the experiment.

Try this for fun:

Have students try the experiment again, this time with "homemade" pop made from baking soda, vinegar, and water. (Warn them not to drink the foul-tasting mixture.)

Name _____

Rock-a-Bye Bottle

Question

What do you think will happen to a soda bottle filled with pop and sealed with a cork when it is gently rocked back and forth?

The cork will _____.

 A shoot off the top of the bottle

 B be sucked into the bottle

 C expand and break the bottle

 D do nothing

Procedure and Observations

1. Pour your can of soda pop into the plastic bottle. What do you notice about the soda?

_____

_____

2. Place a cork in the mouth of the bottle. The cork should fit snugly. Point the cork end of the bottle away from your face and away from other students. Then rock the bottle gently back and forth. What happens?

_____

_____

Conclusion

How can you explain what happened in the experiment?

_____

_____

_____

On the back of this sheet, draw a picture showing what happened in your experiment. Label your drawing and write a sentence that describes what it is showing.

How to Do Science Experiments with Children • EMC 5001 • ©2003 by Evan-Moor Corp.

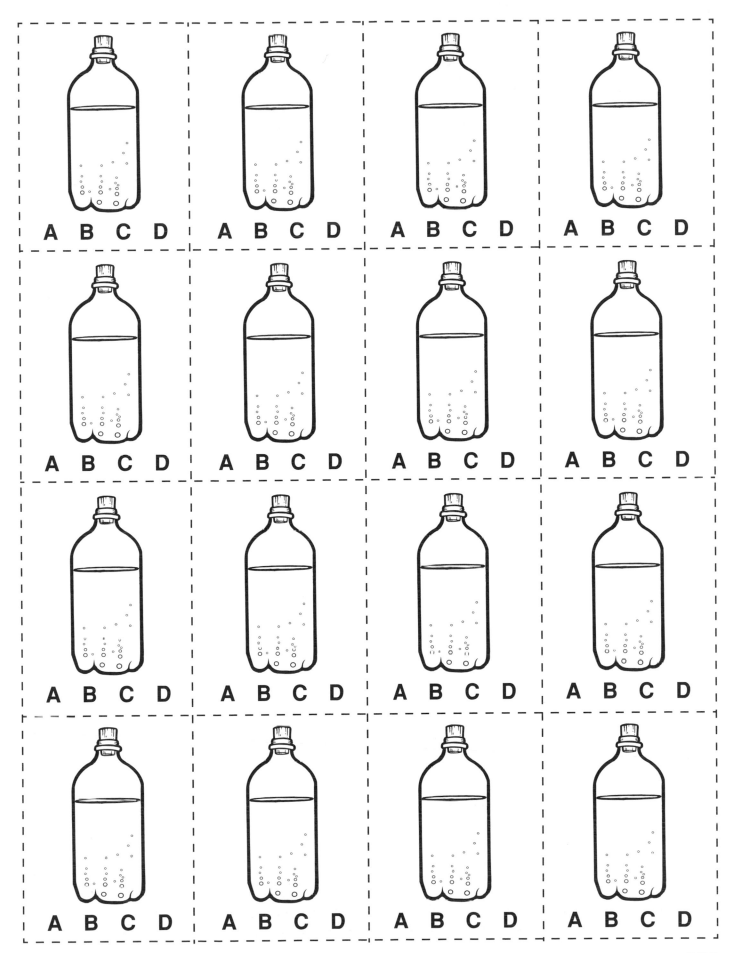

A B C D A B C D A B C D A B C D

A B C D A B C D A B C D A B C D

A B C D A B C D A B C D A B C D

A B C D A B C D A B C D A B C D

26

Materials:

- laminated graph chart
- page 112, reproduced for each student
- page 113, reproduced, one icon for each student
- glass bottles
- hard-boiled eggs, peeled
- matches
- paper
- cooking oil

Air Exerts Pressure

Egg Rescue

Objective: Students will demonstrate that adding air to a sealed container increases the air pressure inside the container.

Question: How can you get a hard-boiled egg out of a bottle without breaking either the bottle or the egg?

Science Background: Air pressure is directly related to the number of air particles there are in a given area. The more air particles there are in an area, the greater the pressure will be. So, for example, when the amount of air in a container is increased, the pressure in that container is also increased.

In this experiment, a slippery hard-boiled egg is trapped inside a bottle whose opening is slightly smaller than the diameter of the egg. By blowing hard around the egg and into the bottle, students add air particles to the bottle and therefore increase the air pressure behind the egg. This higher pressure forces the egg out of the bottle.

Teaching Procedure:

1. Post the laminated graph chart at the front of the class. Label the top of the graph "Egg Rescue."

2. Insert an egg inside each bottle, following the directions in Experiment 27 (pp. 114–117). Wash out all the charred bits of paper from the bottles. The bottle openings must be slightly smaller than the diameter of the eggs for the experiment to work.

3. Distribute an investigation sheet and an egg icon to each student.

4. Show students the materials to be used in the experiment. Read aloud the question at the top of the investigation sheet. Refer students to the picture of the experiment on the sheet and briefly explain how the experiment will be set up. Answer any questions students might have about the procedure.

5. Have students select an answer to the question posed on the investigation sheet about how they think they can get the egg out of the bottle. Tell them to record their answer both on the sheet and on the egg icon. Collect the icons and use them to create a class graph as shown.

Egg Rescue

6. Divide the class into groups based on their responses to the question posed on the investigation sheet. (For example, all students who think they can get the egg out by shaking the bottle should be in one group, and so on.) Distribute a bottle with an egg inside to each group. Have students take turns testing their group's method for getting the egg out. Have students record their results.

7. If one group figures out how to blow into the bottle to make the egg come out, have them demonstrate for the rest of the class. Otherwise, demonstrate yourself: Turn the bottle upside down, so that the egg is plugging the bottle opening. Then blow as hard as you can on the end of the egg sticking out of the bottle. (As the stream of air lifts the egg slightly, air particles will flow past it and into the bottle. When you stop blowing, the egg will fall again and close the opening. Then the egg should pop out.) Now have the rest of the class try it.

8. Discuss with students what they observed. Encourage them to offer an explanation for why the egg popped out when they blew on it. Once the class has had a chance to discuss their theories, introduce the idea that the more air there is inside a container, the higher the pressure will be. By blowing around the egg and into the bottle, students increased the quantity of air and therefore the air pressure behind the egg. The increased pressure forced the egg out of the bottle.

9. Have students answer the conclusion question on the investigation sheet. Finally, have them draw a picture of the method of egg removal that worked. Encourage them to label their drawing and provide a sentence that explains what happened in the experiment.

Try this for fun:

Have students poke a hole in the bottom of their bottle, and then repeat the experiment. What happens? (The hole allows air blown into the bottle to escape, so the air pressure in the bottle never increases sufficiently to force the egg out.)

Egg Rescue

Question

How can you get the hard-boiled egg out of the bottle
without breaking either the bottle or the egg?

A by pulling the egg out with my fingers

B by shaking the bottle

C by tapping on the end of the bottle

D by blowing around the egg and into
the bottle

Procedure and Observations

Try to get the egg out of the bottle using the method you chose above. What happens?

_____

_____

Conclusion

Draw a picture showing which method of egg removal finally worked. Label your drawing and
write a sentence that describes what it is showing.

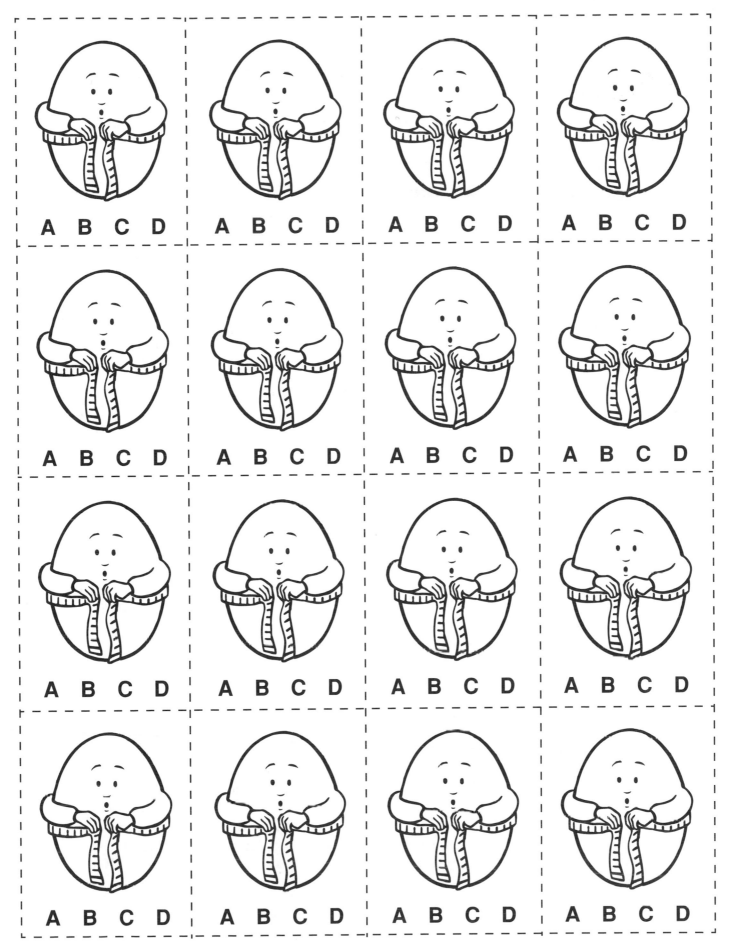

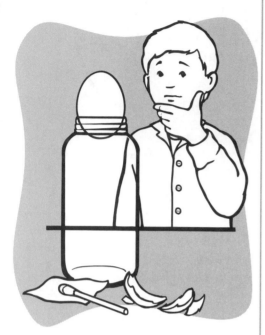

Materials:

- laminated graph chart
- page 116, reproduced for each student
- page 117, reproduced, one icon for each student
- glass bottles
- hard-boiled eggs, peeled
- paper
- matches
- cooking oil

Air Exerts Pressure

Eggstra-ordinary Experiment

Objective: Students will demonstrate that removing air from a sealed container decreases the air pressure inside the container.

Question: What will happen to a hard-boiled egg when it is placed on top of a bottle that has a burning piece of paper inside it?

Science Background: Air pressure is directly related to the number of air particles there are in a given area. For example, the more air particles there are in a given container, the greater the air pressure inside the container. Likewise, the fewer air particles there are, the lower the pressure inside the container.

In this experiment, paper is burned inside a bottle whose mouth is sealed with a hard-boiled egg. The burning paper raises the temperature of the air inside the bottle and causes it to expand. Some of the air is forced out around the egg. By the time the fire burns out and the air inside has cooled, there are fewer air particles in the bottle than there were before. Fewer air particles means lower pressure. When the air pressure inside the bottle is lower than the air pressure outside the bottle, the higher pressure air outside the bottle forces the egg into the bottle.

Teaching Procedure:

1. Locate glass bottles whose openings are slightly smaller than the diameter of the hard-boiled eggs you've prepared. Wipe the openings of the bottles with a little cooking oil so that the eggs can slide in more easily.

2. Post the laminated graph chart at the front of the class. Label the top of the graph "Eggstra-ordinary Experiment."

3. Distribute an investigation sheet and an egg icon to each student.

4. Show students the materials to be used in the experiment. Read aloud the question at the top of the investigation sheet. Refer students to the picture of the experiment on the sheet and briefly explain how the experiment will be set up. Answer any questions students might have about the procedure.

5. Have students select an answer to the question posed on the investigation sheet about what they think will happen to the egg when it is placed on top of a bottle that contains a burning piece of paper. Tell them to record their answer both on the sheet and on the egg icon. Collect the icons and use them to create a class graph as shown.

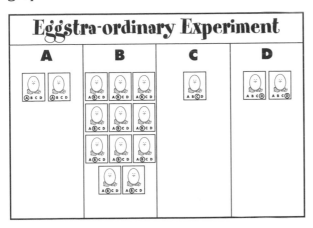

6. Distribute a glass bottle and a peeled hard-boiled egg to each group. Walk around to each group and drop a lit piece of paper into their bottle. Have students quickly place the egg upright in the mouth of the bottle. (The egg should seal the hole.) Instruct students to watch the egg carefully for several minutes. (The flame will go out. Shortly after that, the egg will be sucked into the bottle.) Have them record their observations on the investigation sheet.

7. Discuss with students what they observed. Encourage them to offer an explanation for why the egg was sucked into the bottle. Once the class has had a chance to discuss their theories, introduce the idea that the amount of air in a container affects the air pressure inside the container. Heating the air inside the bottle caused the air to expand, and some of the air escaped around the egg at the top of the bottle. That left fewer air particles in the bottle, and the fewer air particles there are in the bottle, the lower the pressure. When the air pressure inside the bottle becomes lower than the air pressure outside the bottle, the higher pressure air outside forces the egg into the bottle.

8. Have students answer the conclusion question on the investigation sheet. Finally, have them draw a picture of the experiment on the back of the sheet. Encourage them to label their drawing and provide a caption that explains what happened in the experiment.

Try this for fun:

Have students try the experiment again, this time placing a scrap of paper on top of the bottle instead of an egg. Does the piece of paper get sucked into the bottle? (No, the paper does not form a seal with the bottle the way the egg did. Instead, it allows outside air to enter the bottle to replace the air particles that escaped during heating. So the pressure inside the bottle stays the same as the pressure outside the bottle.)

Name _____

Eggstra-ordinary Experiment

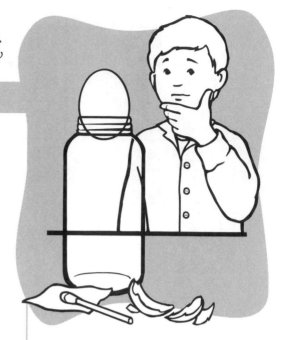

Question

What do you think will happen to the hard-boiled egg when it is placed on top of a bottle that has a burning piece of paper inside it?

The egg will _____.

    A begin to burn

    B pop off

    C be sucked into the bottle

    D just sit on top of the bottle

Procedure and Observations

1. Watch as your teacher drops a burning piece of paper into your bottle. Now set your hard-boiled egg in the mouth of the bottle so that it plugs the hole.

2. Observe the egg for several minutes. What does it do?

_____

_____

Conclusion

How can you explain what happened to the egg in this experiment?

_____

_____

_____

On the back of this sheet, draw a picture showing what happened in your experiment. Label your drawing and write a sentence that describes what it is showing.

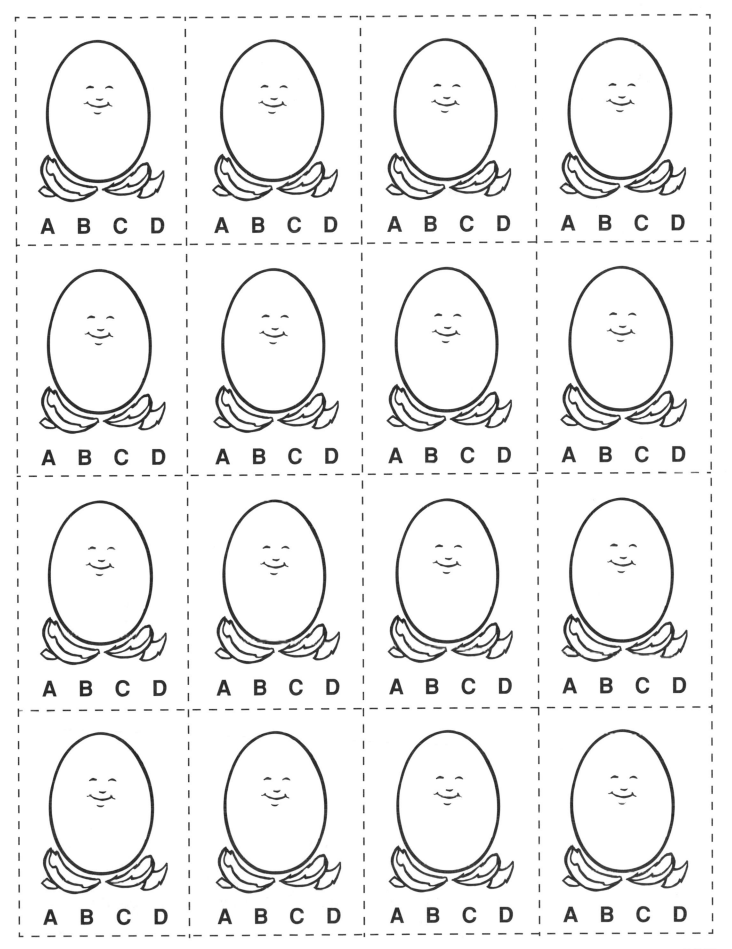

A B C D   A B C D   A B C D   A B C D

A B C D   A B C D   A B C D   A B C D

A B C D   A B C D   A B C D   A B C D

A B C D   A B C D   A B C D   A B C D

28

Materials:

- laminated graph chart
- page 120, reproduced for each student
- page 121, reproduced, one icon for each student
- plastic jug with cap
- hot water

Jug of Fun

Objective: Students will demonstrate that removing air from a sealed container decreases the air pressure inside the container.

Question: What will happen to a plastic jug when it is heated with hot water, emptied, then sealed and allowed to cool?

Science Background: Air pressure is directly related to the number of air particles there are in a given area. For example, the more air particles there are in a given container, the greater the air pressure inside the container. Likewise, the fewer air particles there are, the lower the pressure inside the container.

In this experiment, a jug is heated by pouring some hot water into it and letting it sit a minute. The hot water is then poured out, but the walls of the jug remain warm. As the air particles inside the jug warm up, they start to move around more quickly, and some escape through the jug opening. When the jug is capped, no more air particles can enter or leave the jug. The capped jug now contains fewer air particles than it did before it was heated, but each particle exerts more pressure, so the pressure inside and outside the jug is equal. But as the air inside the jug cools, the particles exert less pressure. Eventually, the pressure exerted by each air particle inside and outside the jug is equal, but there are fewer particles inside the jug than outside. Fewer particles mean lower pressure. When the pressure inside the jug becomes lower than the pressure outside the jug, the outside air presses in on the jug, collapsing it slightly.

Teaching Procedure:

1. Post the laminated graph chart at the front of the class. Label the top of the graph "Jug of Fun."

2. Perform this experiment as a demonstration, as it involves hot water that could burn students.

3. Distribute an investigation sheet and a jug icon to each student.

4. Show students the materials to be used in the experiment. Read aloud the question at the top of the investigation sheet. Refer students to the picture of the experiment on the sheet and briefly explain how the experiment will be set up. Answer any questions students might have about the procedure.

5. Have students select an answer to the question posed on the investigation sheet about what they think will happen to the jug after is heated, sealed, and allowed to cool. Tell them to record their answer both on the sheet and on the jug icon. Collect the icons and use them to create a class graph as shown.

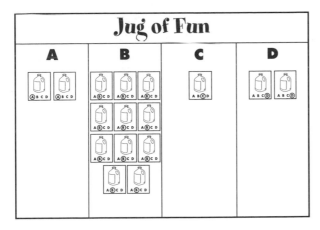

6. Fill the plastic jug with hot water and allow it to sit for one minute without the cap on. Then dump out the water and replace the cap. Tell students to observe the jug for several minutes. (As the air inside cools, the jug should begin to collapse slightly.) Have students record their observations on the investigation sheet.

7. Discuss with students what they observed. Encourage them to offer an explanation for why the jug collapsed. Once the class has had a chance to discuss their theories, introduce the idea that the warm water heated the jug. After the water was poured out, the warm jug heated the air inside it, causing it to expand and force some air to escape through the opening. When the jug was capped, it contained fewer air particles than it did before. Fewer air particles mean lower pressure. The higher pressure outside the jug then pressed on the jug, collapsing it slightly.

8. Have students answer the conclusion question on the investigation sheet. Finally, have them draw a picture of the experiment on the back of the sheet. Encourage them to label their drawing and provide a caption that explains what happened in the experiment.

Try this for fun:

Place the capped jug in an ice-water bath for a more dramatic effect.

Jug of Fun

Question

What do you think will happen to the plastic jug when it is heated with hot water, sealed, and then allowed to cool?

The jug will _____.

    A collapse

    B pop the cap off

    C expand

    D fall over

Procedure and Observations

1. Watch as your teacher fills the jug with hot water, lets it sit a minute, then dumps it out and puts the cap on.

2. Observe the jug for several minutes. What does it do?

_____

_____

Conclusion

How can you explain what happened to the jug in this experiment?

_____

_____

_____

On the back of this sheet, draw a picture showing what happened in your experiment. Label your drawing and write a sentence that describes what it is showing.

29

Materials:

- laminated graph chart
- page 124, reproduced for each student
- page 125, reproduced, one icon for each student
- plastic bottles
- glass eyedroppers
- corks
- water
- food coloring
- newspaper

Under Pressure

Objective: Students will demonstrate that pressure affects air volume.

Question: What will happen to an eyedropper in a bottle of water when you push the cork in the bottle?

Science Background: Volume is the amount of space an object or substance takes up. Air volume, or the amount of space taken up by a quantity of air, can change with an increase or decrease in pressure. At a constant temperature, volume decreases with an increase in pressure. Likewise, volume increases with a decrease in pressure.

Consider an eyedropper floating in a bottle of water. When a cork is pushed into the mouth of the bottle, the pressure on the air in the eyedropper increases, and so its volume decreases. Because the air inside the dropper now takes up less space, water enters the dropper. This water increases the overall weight of the dropper, and the dropper sinks to the bottom of the bottle. When the cork is released, pressure on the air in the dropper decreases, the air's volume increases, and the water is forced back out of the dropper. The larger volume of air makes the dropper buoyant and it floats to the top of the bottle again.

Teaching Procedure:

1. Post the laminated graph chart at the front of the class. Label the top of the graph "Under Pressure."

2. Have each group cover its work area with newspaper. Distribute an investigation sheet and an eyedropper icon to each student.

3. Show students the materials to be used in the experiment. Read aloud the question on the investigation sheet. Refer students to the picture of the experiment on the sheet and briefly explain how the experiment will be set up. Answer any questions students might have about the procedure.

4. Fill all the bottles to the top with water and place a few drops of food coloring in each. The color will help students distinguish the water from the air inside the eyedropper.

5. Distribute a plastic bottle full of colored water, a cork that fits the mouth of the bottle, and a glass eyedropper to each group. Instruct students to partially fill the eyedropper with

water from the bottle. Have them place the half full dropper into the bottle and watch where it goes. ***Tell students not to place the cork in the bottle yet.*** Have students record their observations on the investigation sheet.

6. Have students select an answer to the question posed on the investigation sheet about what they think will happen to the dropper when they place the cork in the bottle. Tell them to record their answer both on the sheet and on the eyedropper icon. Collect the icons and use them to create a class graph as shown.

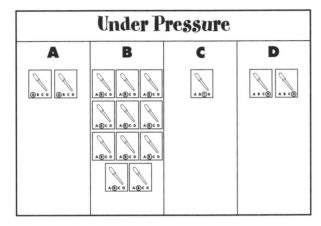

7. Now instruct students to place the cork in the bottle and record what happens to the eyedropper. (It sinks.) Have students remove and replace the cork several more times and note what happens to the dropper each time. Draw students' attention to the amount of air in the dropper before and after the bottle is corked. (Students may notice that the air takes up slightly more space when the cork is not in the bottle.)

8. Discuss with students what they observed. Encourage them to offer an explanation for why the eyedropper sank when the cork was inserted into the bottle. Once the class has had a chance to discuss their theories, introduce the idea that air volume changes when it is squeezed. When students stuck the cork in the bottle, they squeezed, or put pressure on, the air in the eyedropper. The pressure made the air volume shrink. Because the compressed air took up less space, more water could enter the eyedropper. The added weight of the water made the eyedropper sink. When students removed the cork, the air expanded (took up more space) in the dropper again and made the dropper float.

9. Have students answer the conclusion question on the investigation sheet. Finally, have them draw a picture of the experiment on the back of the sheet. Encourage them to label their drawing and provide a caption that explains what happened in the experiment.

Try this for fun:

Have students try the experiment again, this time with the bottle only partially filled with water. Do they get the same results? Why not? (The dropper will not fill with water and sink in a bottle that has a lot of air in it. Air is more easily compressed than water, so a bottle half full of air will "absorb" the pressure added by the cork and not transfer it as efficiently to the pocket of air in the dropper.

Under Pressure

Question

What do you think will happen to the eyedropper when you push the cork in the bottle?

The eyedropper will _____.

    A move in circles around the bottle

    B sink to the bottom of the bottle

    C come apart in two pieces

    D do nothing

Procedure and Observations

1. Place your partially filled eyedropper in your bottle of colored water. What happens to the dropper?

_____

_____

2. Push the cork into the top of the bottle. What happens to the eyedropper?

_____

_____

Conclusion

How can you explain what happened to the eyedropper?

_____

_____

_____

On the back of this sheet, draw a picture showing what happened in your experiment. Label your drawing and write a sentence that describes what it is showing.

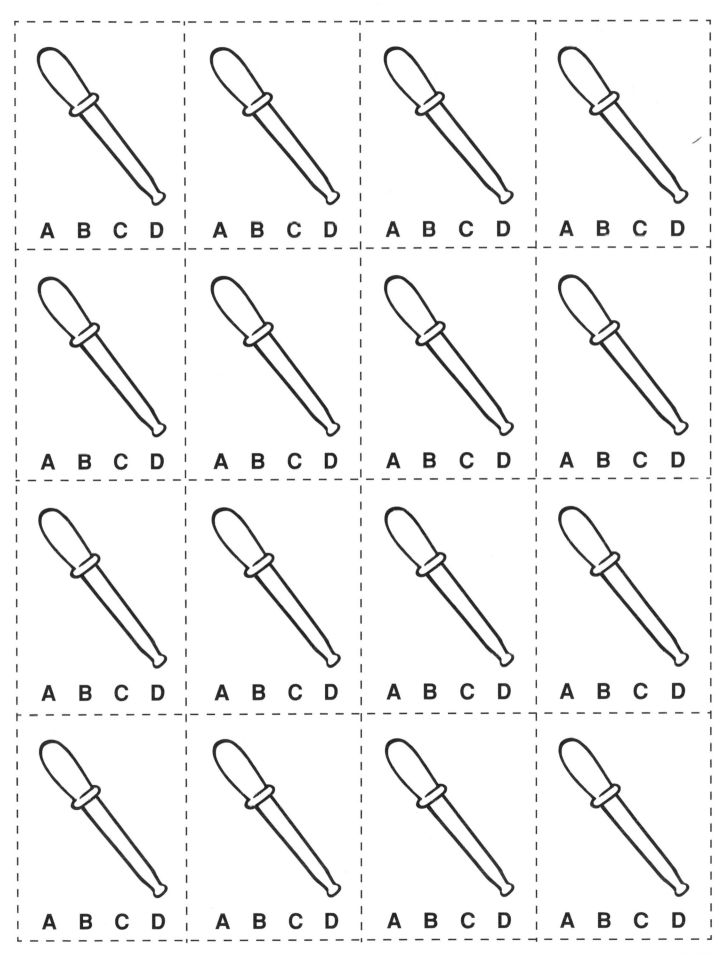

A B C D   A B C D   A B C D   A B C D

A B C D   A B C D   A B C D   A B C D

A B C D   A B C D   A B C D   A B C D

A B C D   A B C D   A B C D   A B C D

GASES

30

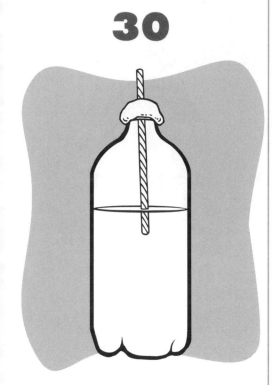

Materials:

- laminated graph chart
- page 128, reproduced for each student
- page 129, reproduced, one icon for each student
- plastic bottles
- drinking straws
- clay
- water
- newspaper

The Last Straw

Objective: Students will demonstrate that air moves from areas of higher pressure to areas of lower pressure.

Question: What will happen when you stop blowing through a straw that is sealed into a bottle of water?

Science Background: Fluids, including water and air, move from areas of higher pressure to areas of lower pressure. By blowing into the sealed bottle of water in this experiment, students increase the amount of air in the bottle. By increasing the amount of air in the bottle, they also increase the pressure inside the bottle. When they remove their mouth from the straw, the higher-pressure air inside the bottle forces the water up the straw as it attempts to move toward the lower-pressure area outside the bottle.

Teaching Procedure:

1. Post the laminated graph chart at the front of the class. Label the top of the graph "The Last Straw."

2. Have each group cover its work area with newspaper. Distribute an investigation sheet and a straw icon to each student.

3. Show students the materials to be used in the experiment. Read aloud the question at the top of the investigation sheet. Refer students to the picture of the experiment on the sheet and briefly explain how the experiment will be set up. Answer any questions students might have about the procedure.

4. Have students select an answer to the question posed on the investigation sheet about what they think will happen when they stop blowing through the straw. Tell them to record their answer both on the sheet and on the straw icon. Collect the icons and use them to create a class graph as shown.

The Last Straw

A	B	C	D

5. Distribute a drinking straw to each student. Distribute a small lump of clay and a plastic bottle three-quarters full with water to each group.

6. Tell students to take turns doing the following: Have them place the straw in the bottle and seal the opening as shown in the picture on the investigation sheet. Instruct them to blow into the bottle. (They should be able to blow only a few bubbles into the water. If they can blow more, have them readjust the clay to make a better seal.) Then have students observe what happens when they stop blowing through the straw and remove their mouth from it. (Water in the bottle moves up the straw and squirts out of the bottle.) Tell students to record their observations on the investigation sheet.

7. Discuss with students what they observed. Encourage them to offer an explanation for why the water moved up the straw when they stopped blowing into it. Once the class has had a chance to discuss their theories, introduce the idea that by blowing into the straw, students increased the amount of air and therefore the air pressure inside the bottle. When they removed their mouth from the straw, the higher-pressure air inside the bottle pushed the water up the straw as it tried to move to the lower-pressure area outside the bottle.

8. Have students answer the conclusion question on the investigation sheet. Finally, have them draw a picture of the experiment on the back of the sheet. Encourage them to label their drawing and provide a caption that explains what happened in the experiment.

Try this for fun:

Have students try the experiment again, this time without the clay. What happens? Why? (First, they are able to blow more than just a few bubbles into the water. Second, the water does not squirt out of the straw when they stop blowing. Without the seal, the air pressure inside the bottle does not increase. That's because the extra air they blow in just escapes the bottle at the opening.)

The Last Straw

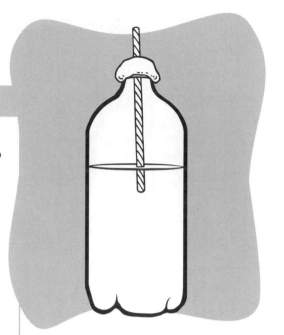

Question

What do you think will happen when you stop blowing through the straw that is sealed into the bottle of water?

A Nothing will happen.

B Air pressure will blow the straw out of the bottle.

C The straw will be sucked into the bottle.

D The water will squirt out the top of the straw.

Procedure and Observations

1. Place the straw in the bottle of water and seal the opening with clay. Make sure it's a tight seal.

2. Blow into the bottle. (You should only be able to blow in a few bubbles. If you can blow more, reseal the opening with clay.) What happened when you stopped blowing through the straw?

_____

_____

_____

Conclusion

How can you explain what happened when you stopped blowing through the straw?

_____

_____

_____

On the back of this sheet, draw a picture showing what happened in your experiment. Label your drawing and write a sentence that describes what it is showing.

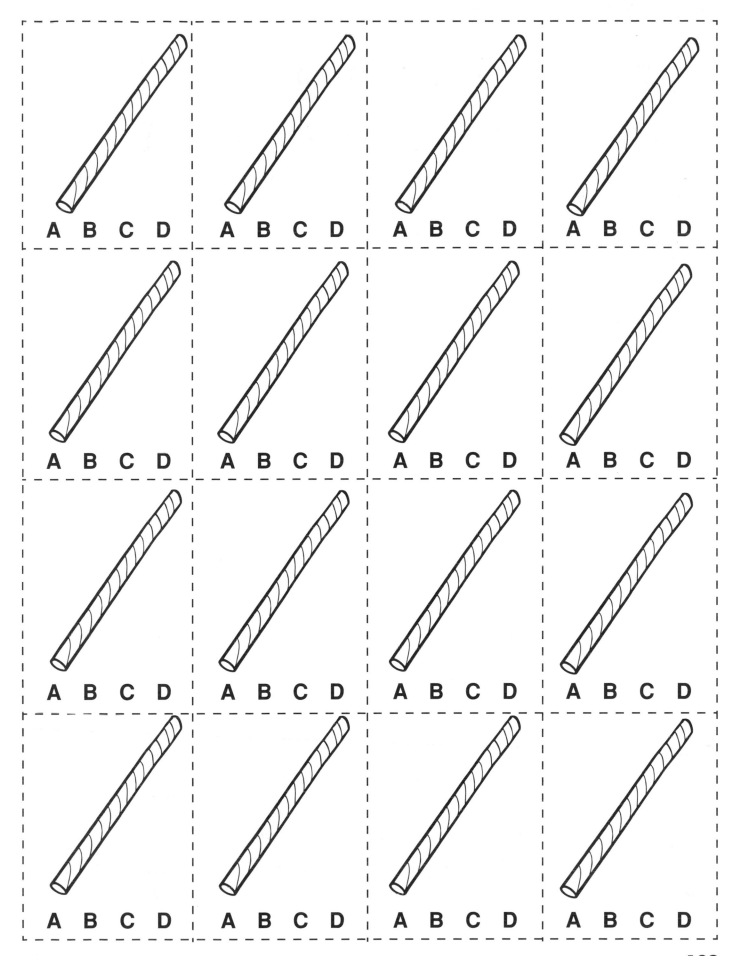

A B C D   A B C D   A B C D   A B C D

A B C D   A B C D   A B C D   A B C D

A B C D   A B C D   A B C D   A B C D

A B C D   A B C D   A B C D   A B C D

31

Double Trouble

Objective: Students will demonstrate that air moves from areas of higher pressure to areas of lower pressure.

Question: What will happen when you drink through two straws: one placed in a cup of water, and one placed outside the cup?

Science Background: Fluids, including water and air, move from areas of higher pressure to areas of lower pressure. When you suck on a straw that is sitting in water, you reduce the amount of air in the straw and in your mouth. Less air means lower air pressure. Because the air pressure in your mouth is now lower than the air pressure outside your mouth, the outside air presses down on the water as it attempts to move from an area of higher pressure to an area of lower pressure. The result: Water is forced up the straw and into your mouth.

When a second straw is held in the mouth and left to dangle beside the cup, no water can be sucked up through the first straw. Why? Because air can move freely through the second straw, the pressure inside and outside the mouth will be equalized. Since you can no longer lower the air pressure inside your mouth, the outside air cannot force the water up the straw.

Materials:

- laminated graph chart
- page 132, reproduced for each student
- page 133, reproduced, one icon for each student
- drinking straws
- plastic cups
- water
- newspaper

Teaching Procedure:

1. Post the laminated graph chart at the front of the class. Label the top of the graph "Double Trouble."

2. Have each group cover its work area with newspaper. Distribute an investigation sheet and a straws icon to each student.

3. Show students the materials to be used in the experiment. Read aloud the question on the investigation sheet. Refer students to the picture of the experiment on the sheet and briefly explain how the experiment will be set up. Answer any questions students might have about the procedure.

4. Distribute a cup of water and a straw to each student. Have them stick the straw in the water and drink a few sips. *Remind students that they are not to drink or eat anything in science class unless instructed to do so by their teacher.*

5. Now have students select an answer to the question posed on the investigation sheet about what they think will happen when they try to sip through two straws simultaneously, only one of which is in the water. Tell them to record their answer both on the sheet and on the straws icon. Collect the icons and use them to create a class graph as shown.

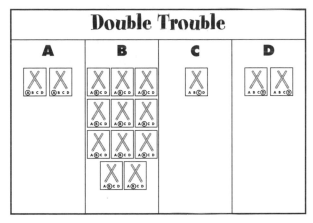

6. Distribute a second straw to each student. Have students place the second straw in their mouth next to the first, but let it dangle outside the cup of water as shown in the picture on the investigation sheet. Challenge them to take a sip of water as before. (They will not be able to suck up any liquid through the first straw.) Instruct students to record their observations.

7. Discuss with students what they observed. Encourage them to offer an explanation for why they were unable to suck up any water while the second straw was in their mouth. Once the class has had a chance to discuss their theories, introduce the idea that air moves from areas of higher pressure to areas of lower pressure. When they used just one straw, students were able to lower the pressure in their mouth by sucking on the straw. The air outside the water then pressed down on the water and moved it up the straw and into their mouth. The second straw made it impossible to lower the pressure in their mouth, as air could move freely through the straw. Without the lowered pressure in their mouth, the water could not be forced up the straw.

8. Have students answer the conclusion question on the investigation sheet. Finally, have them draw a picture of the experiment on the back of the sheet. Encourage them to label their drawing and provide a caption that explains what happened in the experiment.

Try this for fun:

Have students try the first part of the experiment again, this time with a longer straw. (The longer the straw, the less water they'll be able to suck up.)

Name _____

Double Trouble

Question

What do you think will happen when you drink through two straws: one placed in the cup of water, and one placed outside the cup?

I will be able to _____.

    A drink the water more quickly

    B suck water up one straw and spit it out the other

    C make bubbles as I drink

    D drink hardly any of the water

Procedure and Observations

1. Place your straw in your cup of water and take a sip.

2. Stick the other straw in your mouth and position it outside the cup of water as shown above. Try to drink a sip of water as before. What happens?

_____

_____

Conclusion

How can you explain what happened when you tried to drink the water with two straws in your mouth?

_____

_____

_____

On the back of this sheet, draw a picture showing what happened in your experiment. Label your drawing and write a sentence that describes what it is showing.

How to Do Science Experiments with Children • EMC 5001 • ©2003 by Evan-Moor Corp.

32

The Water Mystery

Objective: Students will observe that air moves from areas of higher pressure to areas of lower pressure.

Question: What will happen to water surrounding a candle under a jar when the candle begins to burn?

Science Background: Fluids, including water and air, move from areas of higher pressure to areas of lower pressure. In this experiment, a candle is burned inside a glass jar that is turned upside down and placed on two coins in a dish of shallow, colored water. Burning reduces the amount of oxygen in the jar (by using it up) and therefore reduces the pressure in the jar. When the pressure inside the jar becomes lower than the pressure outside the jar, the colored water is pushed into the jar by the higher-pressure air outside.

Materials:

- laminated graph chart
- page 136, reproduced for each student
- page 137, reproduced, one icon for each student
- flat dish
- two coins
- water
- food coloring
- glass jar
- short candle
- matches

Teaching Procedure:

1. Post the laminated graph chart at the front of the class. Label the top of the graph "The Water Mystery."

2. Perform this experiment as a demonstration at the front of the class.

3. Distribute an investigation sheet and a candle icon to each student.

4. Show students the materials to be used in the experiment. Read aloud the question on the investigation sheet. Refer students to the picture of the experiment on the sheet and briefly explain how the experiment will be set up. Answer any questions students might have about the procedure.

5. Set up the experiment as follows: Place two coins on a flat dish as shown on the investigation sheet. Add water tinted with a few drops of food coloring to the dish. The water level should be slightly above the coins. Place a candle between the coins and set the glass jar upside down over the candle so that it rests on both coins. The water level should be above the rim of the jar so that the candle is in a sealed environment.

6. Have students select an answer to the question posed on the investigation sheet about what they think will happen to the colored water when you light the candle. Tell them to record their answer both on the sheet and on the candle icon. Collect the icons and use them to create a class graph as shown.

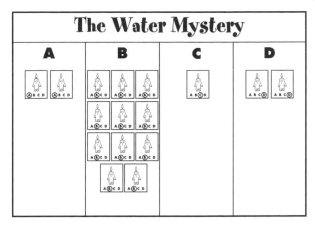

7. Lift the glass jar, light the candle, and replace the jar. (The candle will burn for a while and then go out. While it is burning, water will be drawn up into the jar.) Instruct students to record their observations.

8. Discuss with students what they observed. Encourage them to offer an explanation for why the water was drawn up into the jar. Once the class has had a chance to discuss their theories, introduce the idea that burning uses up some of the air in the jar. Less air means lower pressure, so burning decreased the air pressure in the jar. Higher-pressure air outside the jar then pushed the water up into the jar as it pressed down on the water from above. That's because air moves from areas of higher pressure to areas of lower pressure.

9. Have students answer the conclusion question on the investigation sheet. Finally, have them draw a picture of the experiment on the back of the sheet. Encourage them to label their drawing and provide a caption that explains what happened in the experiment.

Try this for fun:

Try different-sized jars and see how much water rises into each.

Name _____

The Water Mystery

Question

What do you think will happen to the colored water in the dish when your teacher lights the candle?

The water in the dish will _____.

    A do nothing

    B start to bubble

    C dry up

    D get sucked into the jar

Procedure and Observations

1. Watch as your teacher sets up the candle in the dish of water and covers it with a jar.

2. Watch as your teacher lights the candle. What happens to the water?

_____

_____

_____

Conclusion

How can you explain the behavior of the water in this experiment?

_____

_____

_____

On the back of this sheet, draw a picture showing what happened in your experiment. Label your drawing and write a sentence that describes what it is showing.

 How to Do Science Experiments with Children • EMC 5001 • ©2003 by Evan-Moor Corp.

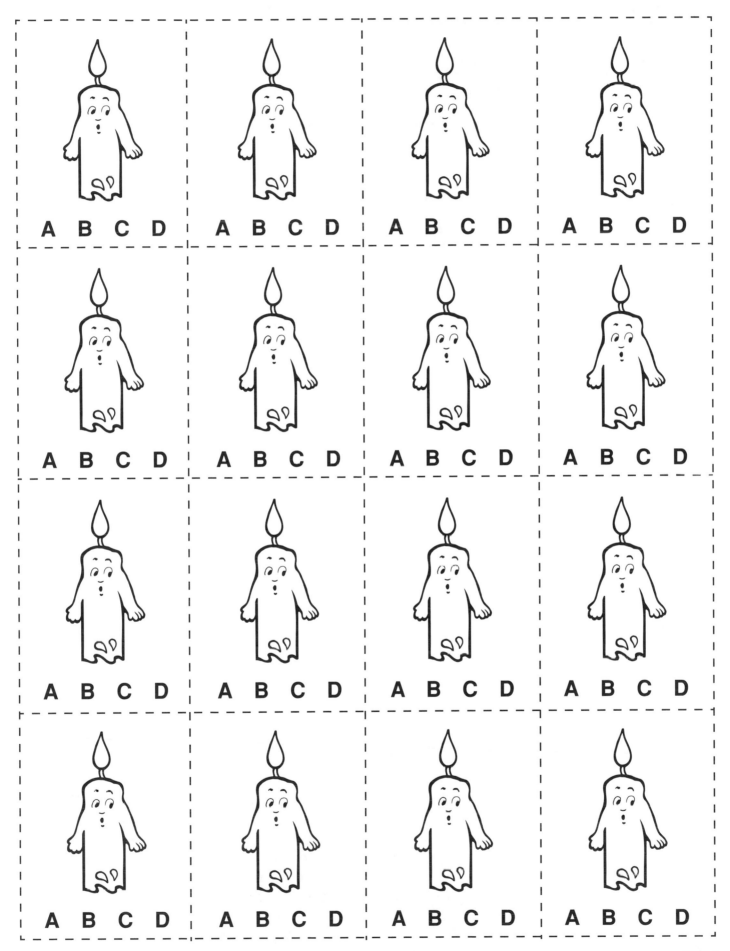

33

Follow the Bouncing Ball

Objective: Students will observe that moving air exerts less pressure than still air.

Question: What will happen to a Ping-Pong ball resting on the nozzle of a hair dryer when the dryer is turned on?

Science Background: Air particles are constantly bumping into objects around them and exerting pressure on the objects. Moving air actually exerts less pressure than still air. That's because the faster the air moves past an object, the less frequently the air particles can strike, or press on, the surface of the object. Thus, fast-moving air will actually create a low-pressure area relative to the still air around it.

Consider a hair dryer with its nozzle pointed toward the ceiling. When the dryer is turned on, a column of rapidly moving air shoots upward. The pressure within this column of air is actually lower than the pressure on either side of the column. How can we tell? A Ping-Pong ball placed in the column of air will be continually pushed back into the column by the higher-pressure air particles on either side of the column. That happens because air moves from areas of higher pressure to areas of lower pressure.

Materials:

- laminated graph chart
- page 140, reproduced for each student
- page 141, reproduced, one icon for each student
- Ping-Pong ball
- hair dryer

Teaching Procedure:

1. Post the laminated graph chart at the front of the class. Label the top of the graph "Follow the Bouncing Ball."

2. Perform this experiment as a class demonstration.

3. Distribute an investigation sheet and a Ping-Pong ball icon to each student.

4. Show students the hair dryer and the Ping-Pong ball. Read aloud the question at the top of the investigation sheet. Refer students to the picture of the experiment on the sheet and briefly explain how the experiment will be set up.

5. Have students select an answer to the question posed on the investigation sheet about what they think will happen to the Ping-Pong ball when you turn on the hair dryer. Tell them to record their answer both on the sheet and on the Ping-Pong ball icon. Collect the icons and use them to create a class graph as shown.

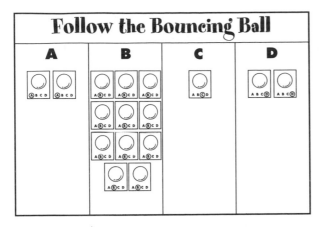

6. Hold the hair dryer so that the nozzle is pointing upward. Place the Ping-Pong ball on the nozzle opening and turn the dryer on. (The ball will bounce and bob in the column of air produced by the dryer.) Now move the dryer very slowly from side to side, or slowly walk with the dryer, so the ball "follows" the column of air. Instruct students to record their observations.

7. Discuss with students what they observed. Encourage them to offer an explanation for why the ball stayed in the stream of air. Once the class has had a chance to discuss their theories, introduce the idea that moving air exerts less pressure than still air. The moving column of air above the dryer had a lower pressure than the air surrounding the column. Now remind students that air moves from areas of higher pressure to areas of lower pressure. The higher-pressure surrounding air pushed against the ball whenever it veered to the sides of the column and steered it back into the column's center.

8. Have students answer the conclusion question on the investigation sheet. Finally, have them draw a picture of the experiment on the back of the sheet. Encourage them to label their drawing and provide a caption that explains what happened in the experiment.

Try this for fun:

Have students hold one end of a strip of paper to their mouth and let the other end hang down. Tell them to blow a stream of air straight out over the strip and watch what happens. (The strip will rise up to float parallel to the air stream as students blow.) Lead students to conclude that the fast-moving air above the strip created an area of lower pressure. The higher-pressure air particles beneath the strip then pushed the strip into that area. (Remember: Air moves from areas of higher pressure to areas of lower pressure.)

Name _____

Follow the Bouncing Ball

Question

What do you think will happen to a Ping-Pong ball resting on the nozzle of a hair dryer when the dryer is turned on?

The Ping-Pong ball will _____.

    A blow away

    B stay in the column of air above the dryer

    C be sucked into the dryer

    D melt

Procedure and Observations

Watch as your teacher turns the dryer on. What happens to the ball?

_____

_____

_____

Conclusion

How can you explain the behavior of the ball in this experiment?

_____

_____

_____

On the back of this sheet, draw a picture showing what happened in your experiment. Label your drawing and write a sentence that describes what it is showing.

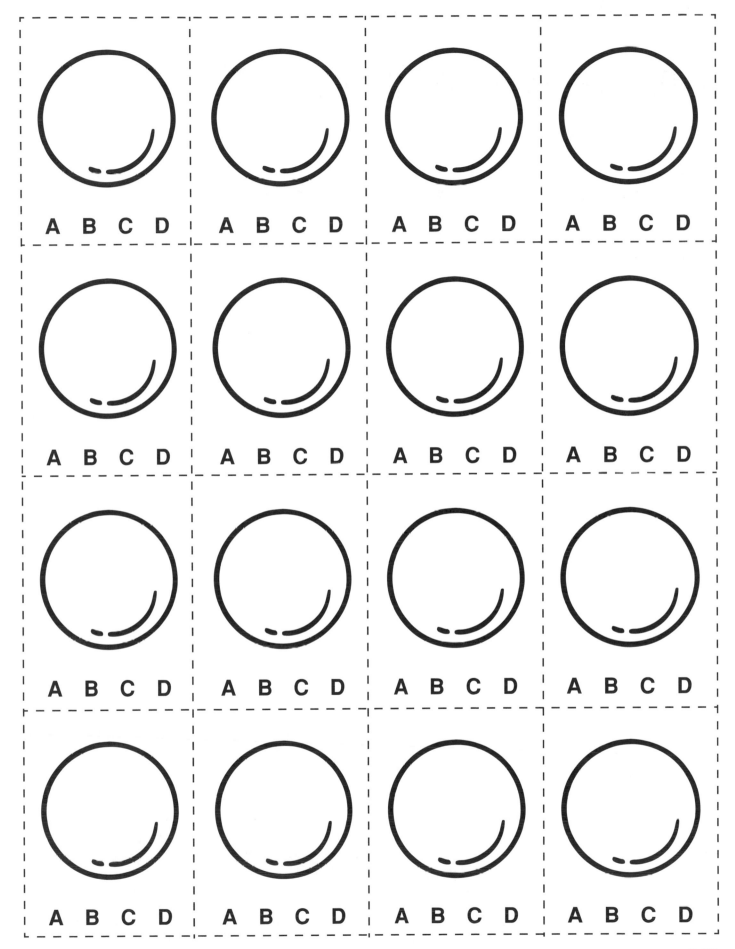

A B C D   A B C D   A B C D   A B C D

A B C D   A B C D   A B C D   A B C D

A B C D   A B C D   A B C D   A B C D

A B C D   A B C D   A B C D   A B C D

34

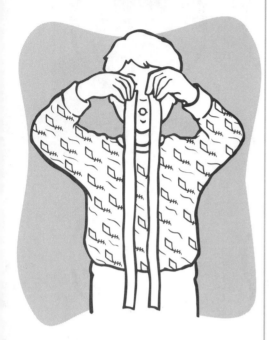

Materials:

- laminated graph chart
- page 144, reproduced for each student
- page 145, reproduced, one icon for each student
- paper
- scissors

Paper Play

Objective: Students will demonstrate that as air speed increases, air pressure decreases.

Question: What will happen to two long strips of paper when you blow air between them?

Science Background: Air particles are constantly bumping into objects around them and exerting pressure on the objects. Air pressure is affected by air speed. As the speed at which air moves across a surface increases, the frequency of hits by air particles decreases, and so does the pressure exerted by the air.

When students blow air between two strips of paper, they increase the speed of the air moving between the strips. As the air moves faster, its particles strike the inside surfaces of the strips less frequently. As a result, they exert less pressure on the strips than the relatively still air particles on the outside of the strips. Because air moves from areas of higher pressure to areas of lower pressure, the two strips get pushed into the low-pressure zone between them by the higher-pressure air outside the strips.

Teaching Procedure:

1. Cut two 3 cm × 30 cm strips of paper for each student.

2. Post the laminated graph chart at the front of the class. Label the top of the graph "Paper Play."

3. Distribute an investigation sheet and a paper strip icon to each student.

4. Show students the materials to be used in the experiment. Read aloud the question at the top of the investigation sheet. Refer students to the picture of the experiment on the sheet and briefly explain how the experiment will be set up. Answer any questions students might have about the procedure.

5. Have students select an answer to the question posed on the investigation sheet about what they think will happen to the two strips of paper when they blow air between them. Tell them to record their answer both on the sheet and on the paper strip icon. Collect the icons and use them to create a class graph as shown.

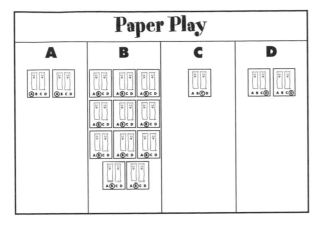

Paper Play

| **A** | **B** | **C** | **D** |

6. Distribute two strips of paper to each student. Have students grasp one end of each strip and hold up the strips about 3 cm apart. What do the strips do? (They hang straight down.) Have students record their observations on the investigation sheet.

7. Now have students blow gently between the strips and observe what happens. (The strips move closer together.) What happens when they stop blowing? (The strips hang straight down again.) Have students record their observations on the investigation sheet.

8. Discuss with students what they observed. Encourage them to offer an explanation for why the strips moved together when they blew air between them. Once the class has had a chance to discuss their theories, introduce the idea that air speed affects air pressure. The faster the air moves, the less pressure it exerts on things around it. Because the air moved quickly between the strips, a lower-pressure zone was created there, and the higher-pressure still air outside the strips pushed them inward. (Remind students that air moves from areas of higher pressure to areas of lower pressure.)

9. Have students answer the conclusion question on the investigation sheet. Finally, have them draw a picture of the experiment on the back of the sheet. Encourage them to label their drawing and provide a caption that explains what happened in the experiment.

Try this for fun:

Have students hold a single strip of paper next to running water from a faucet. What happens? (The strip is pulled near or into the water stream.) Explain that, like moving air, moving water also creates an area of lower pressure in the relatively still air around it, and the strip was pulled into this area.

Paper Play

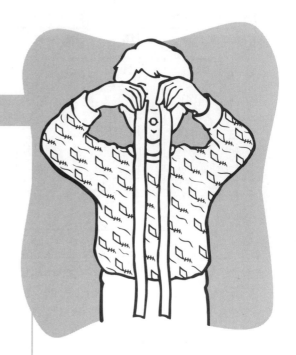

Question

What do you think will happen to two long strips of paper when you blow air between them?

The strips of paper will _____.

    A move apart

    B move toward each other

    C be ripped to pieces

    D make a whistling sound

Procedure and Observations

1. Hold up two strips of paper about 3 cm apart. What do the strips do?

_____

2. Blow gently between the strips. What do the strips do now? What happens to the strips when you stop blowing?

_____

_____

Conclusion

How can you explain what happened to the strips when you blew air between them?

_____

_____

_____

On the back of this sheet, draw a picture showing what happened in your experiment. Label your drawing and write a sentence that describes what it is showing.

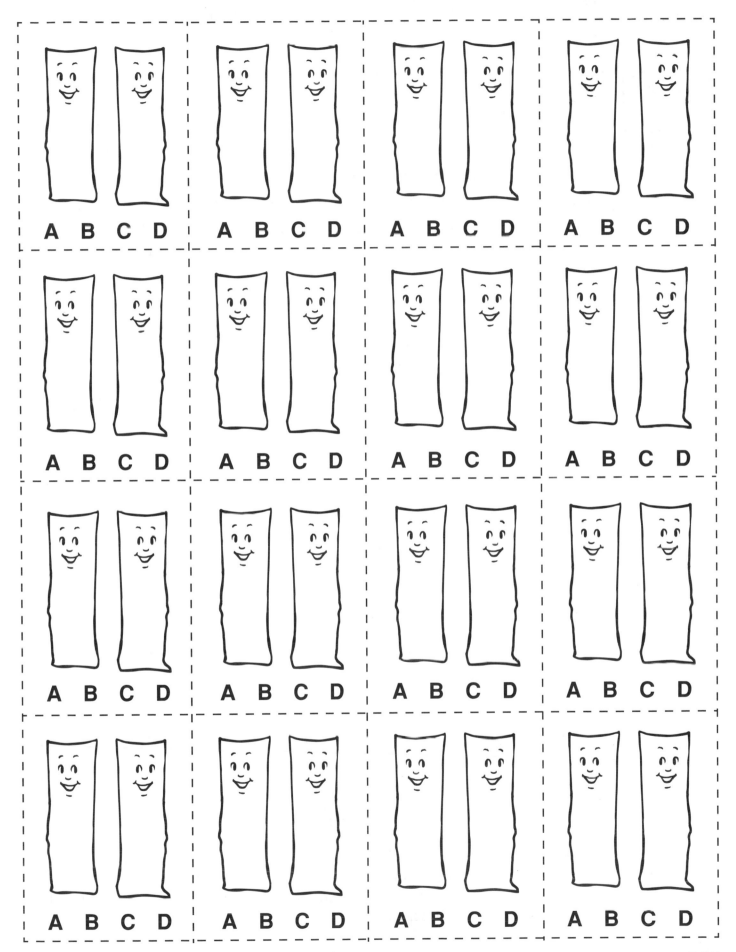

35

Materials:

- laminated graph chart
- page 148, reproduced for each student
- page 149, reproduced, one icon for each student
- plastic bottle
- balloon
- bowl
- hot water

Unbelievable Balloons

Objective: Students will observe that air volume increases as temperature increases.

Question: What will happen to a balloon stretched over the mouth of a bottle when the bottle is placed in hot water?

Science Background: Air takes up space. The amount of space that a quantity of air takes up is called **air volume**. Air volume is affected by temperature. Recall that air is made up of tiny particles that are constantly moving around. At higher temperatures, the particles move around more quickly and so are more spread out. Thus, as long as pressure remains constant, a given number of particles will have a greater volume (take up more space) when they are at a higher temperature than when they are at a lower temperature.

Consider a balloon stretched over the mouth of an "empty" bottle. (Remember, the bottle is full of air.) When you place the bottle in a hot water bath, the particles of air inside the bottle begin to move around more quickly and spread out. As they spread out, they inflate the balloon.

Teaching Procedure:

1. Post the laminated graph chart at the front of the class. Label the top of the graph "Unbelievable Balloons."

2. Perform this experiment as a demonstration, as it uses hot water that could burn students.

3. Distribute an investigation sheet and a balloon icon to each student.

4. Show students the materials to be used in the experiment. Read aloud the question at the top of the investigation sheet. Refer students to the picture of the experiment on the sheet and briefly explain how the experiment will be set up. Answer any questions students might have about the procedure.

5. Have students select an answer to the question posed on the investigation sheet about what they think will happen to the balloon when the bottle is placed in hot water. Tell them to record their answer both on the sheet and on the balloon icon. Collect the icons and use them to create a class graph as shown.

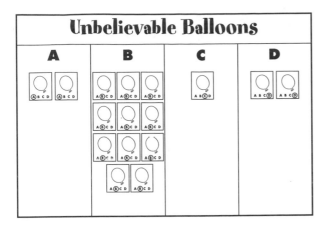

6. Stretch the neck of the balloon over the mouth of the bottle. Have students record on the investigation sheet what the balloon looks like at this point.

7. Now place the bottle with attached balloon in the bowl of hot water and hold it there. Tell students to observe the balloon for several minutes. (The balloon will begin to inflate as the air inside the bottle heats up and expands.) Instruct students to record their observations.

8. Discuss with students what they observed. Encourage them to offer an explanation for why the balloon inflated in the hot water bath. Once the class has had a chance to discuss their theories, introduce the idea that air volume is affected by temperature. As air heats up, it expands and takes up more space. As the hot water heated up the air inside the bottle, the air expanded and moved into the balloon, inflating it.

9. Have students answer the conclusion question on the investigation sheet. Finally, have them draw a picture of the experiment on the back of the sheet. Encourage them to label their drawing and provide a caption that explains what happened in the experiment.

Try this for fun:

Try the experiment again, using cold water instead of hot water. (The balloon will not inflate because the cold water bath does not heat up the air particles inside the bottle. In fact, if the water is cold enough, the balloon may collapse further as the small amount of air inside it contracts.)

Unbelievable Balloons

Question

What do you think will happen to a balloon stretched over the mouth of a bottle when the bottle is placed in hot water? The balloon will _____.

    A pop

    B fly off the top of the bottle

    C be sucked into the bottle

    D fill with air

Procedure and Observations

1. Look at the balloon that your teacher has stretched over the mouth of the bottle. Describe what the balloon looks like.

_____

_____

2. Now watch as your teacher puts the bottle into the bowl of hot water. Observe the balloon for several minutes. What happens to the balloon?

_____

_____

Conclusion

How can you explain what happened to the balloon?

_____

_____

_____

On the back of this sheet, draw a picture showing what happened in your experiment. Label your drawing and write a sentence that describes what it is showing.

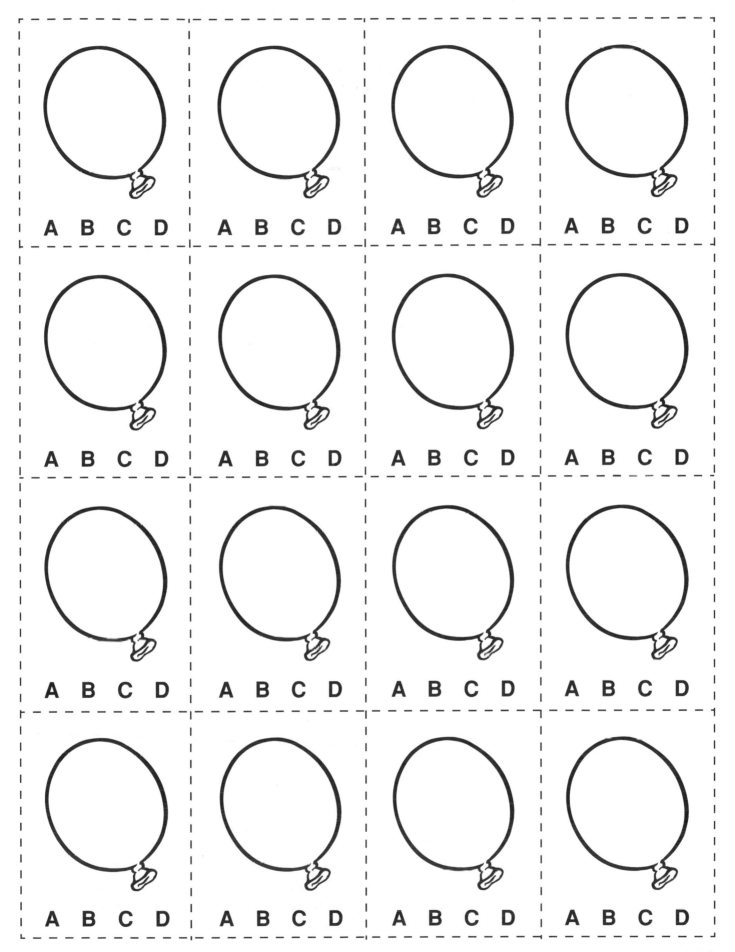

A B C D   A B C D   A B C D   A B C D

A B C D   A B C D   A B C D   A B C D

A B C D   A B C D   A B C D   A B C D

A B C D   A B C D   A B C D   A B C D

36

It's Cold in Here!

Objective: Students will demonstrate that air volume decreases as temperature decreases.

Question: What will happen to an inflated balloon when it is placed in the refrigerator?

Science Background: Air volume is affected by temperature. Remember that air is made up of tiny particles that are constantly moving around. At higher temperatures, the particles move around more quickly and, as a result, take up more space. The opposite happens at lower temperatures: The particles move around more slowly and so are less spread out. Thus, as long as pressure remains constant, a given number of particles will have a smaller volume (take up less space) when they are at a lower temperature than when they are at a higher temperature.

An inflated balloon at room temperature has a certain volume. That volume depends on the number of air particles in the balloon and how spread out they are. When you cool the air inside the balloon by placing it in the refrigerator, the air particles in the balloon slow down and take up less space. How can you tell? As the air volume decreases, the circumference of the balloon shrinks.

Materials:

- laminated graph chart

- page 152, reproduced for each student

- page 153, reproduced, one icon for each student

- balloons (inflated by teacher)

- measuring tape

- access to a refrigerator

Teaching Procedure:

1. Post the laminated graph chart at the front of the class. Label the top of the graph "It's Cold in Here!"

2. Distribute an investigation sheet and a balloon icon to each student.

3. Show students the materials to be used in the experiment. Read aloud the question at the top of the investigation sheet. Refer students to the picture of the experiment on the sheet and briefly explain how the experiment will be set up. Answer any questions students might have about the procedure.

4. Have students select an answer to the question posed on the investigation sheet about what they think will happen to the balloon when it is placed in the refrigerator. Tell them to record their answer both on the sheet and on the balloon icon. Collect the icons and use them to create a class graph as shown.

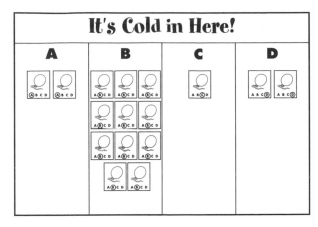

5. Distribute an inflated balloon and a measuring tape to each group. (If you don't have measuring tapes, pass out lengths of string and rulers. Students can wrap the string around the balloon and then measure the length of the string to determine the circumference of the balloon.) Show students how to use the measuring tape to measure the distance around the balloon. Have students record the distance on the investigation sheet.

6. Now have students place the balloon in the refrigerator. An hour later, have them remove the balloon and observe it. (The balloon will have shrunk.) Instruct students to take and record new measurements for the distance around the middle of their balloon.

7. Discuss with students what they observed. Encourage them to offer an explanation for why the balloon shrunk after sitting in the refrigerator. Once the class has had a chance to discuss their theories, introduce the idea that air volume is affected by temperature. The colder temperatures in the refrigerator slowed down the particles of air in the balloon. As a result, they took up less space, so the balloon shrunk.

8. Have students answer the conclusion question on the investigation sheet. Finally, have them draw a picture of the experiment on the back of the sheet. Encourage them to label their drawing and provide a caption that explains what happened in the experiment.

Try this for fun:

Have students try placing one balloon in the freezer and one in the refrigerator for the same amount of time. What difference do they notice? (The balloon in the freezer shrinks even more than the one in the refrigerator.)

Name _____

It's Cold in Here!

Question

What do you think will happen to the inflated balloon when it is placed in the refrigerator?

The balloon will _____.

    A pop

    B become larger

    C become smaller

    D not change

Procedure and Observations

1. Use the measuring tape to measure the distance around the middle of your balloon. Record the distance below.

   Before refrigerator—distance around middle of balloon: _____ cm

2. Put the balloon in the refrigerator for an hour. Then take it out and observe it. What is the distance around the middle of the balloon now?

   After refrigerator—distance around middle of balloon: _____ cm

Conclusion

How can you explain what happened to the balloon?

_____

_____

_____

On the back of this sheet, draw a picture showing what happened in your experiment. Label your drawing and write a sentence that describes what it is showing.

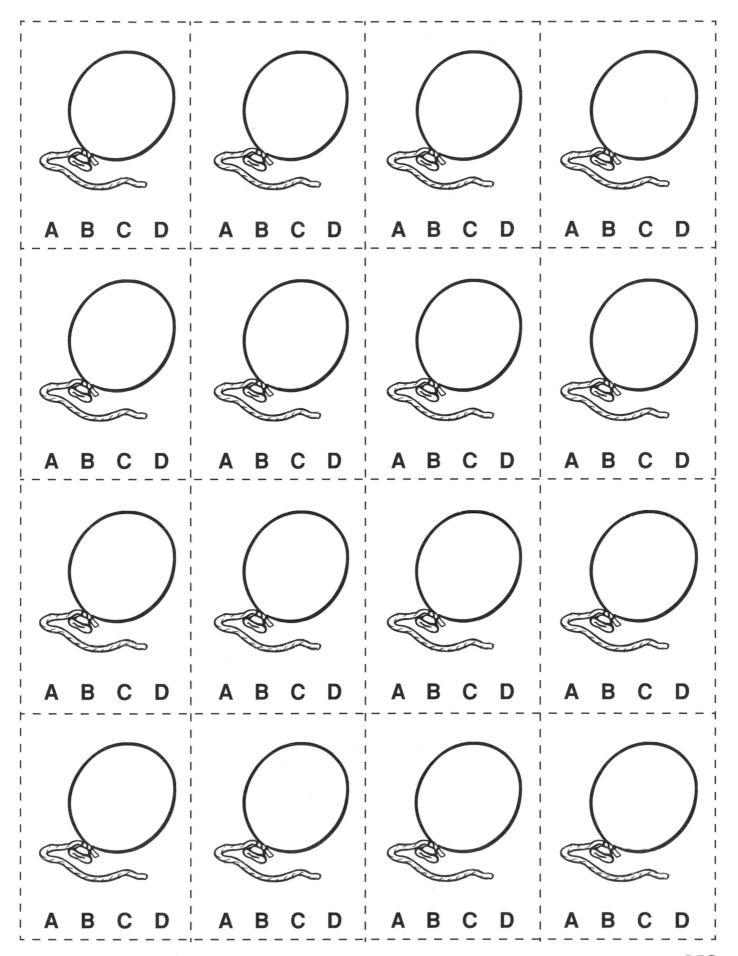

37

Materials:

- laminated graph chart
- page 156, reproduced for each student
- page 157, reproduced, one icon for each student
- plastic bottles
- small paper or plastic cups
- nickels
- water

Funny Money

Objective: Students will demonstrate that air pressure increases as temperature increases.

Question: What will happen to a nickel when it is placed on a plastic bottle that has just come out of the freezer?

Science Background: Air pressure is affected by temperature. Remember that air is made up of tiny particles that are constantly moving around. At higher temperatures, the particles move around more quickly and therefore make more hits on the objects around them. More hits results in higher pressure. Thus, the pressure of a given volume of air will increase as temperature increases.

In this activity, an "empty" bottle is "overstuffed" with air particles by placing it uncapped in a freezer. (You can fit more cold air particles in a bottle than warm air particles because cold air is more compact.) The bottle is then removed from the freezer, "capped" with a nickel, and allowed to warm up. As the air inside the bottle warms, its pressure increases. When the pressure inside the bottle becomes higher than the pressure outside the bottle, the air particles push up on the nickel and escape. This happens over and over again until the pressure of the air inside and outside the bottle is the same again.

Teaching Procedure:

1. Place a plastic bottle for each group in the freezer at least 15 minutes before the experiment begins.

2. Post the laminated graph chart at the front of the class. Label the top of the graph "Funny Money."

3. Distribute an investigation sheet and a nickel icon to each student.

4. Show students the materials to be used in the experiment. Read aloud the question at the top of the investigation sheet. Refer students to the picture of the experiment on the sheet and briefly explain how the experiment will be set up. Answer any questions students might have about the procedure.

5. Have students select an answer to the question posed on the investigation sheet about what they think will happen to the nickel when it is placed on the bottle of cold air. Tell them to record their answer both on the sheet and on the nickel icon. Collect the icons and use them to create a class graph as shown.

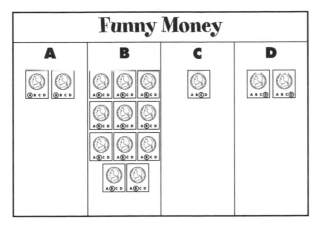

6. Distribute a plastic bottle fresh from the freezer, a small cup of water, and a nickel to each group. Point out to students that the bottles are filled with cold air. Then have students moisten their nickel with water, place it on the top of the bottle, and observe what happens. (The nickel will lift and drop a number of times.) Instruct students to record their observations.

7. Discuss with students what they observed. Encourage them to offer an explanation for why the nickel lifted up and down. Once the class has had a chance to discuss their theories, introduce the idea that air pressure is affected by temperature. As the temperature of the air in the bottle increased, the air particles moved around faster and made more hits on the inside walls of the container. More hits means higher pressure. When the pressure inside the bottle became greater than the pressure outside the bottle, some air particles escaped the bottle by lifting the nickel. Each time the nickel rose and air escaped, the pressures were equalized and the nickel fell. This process repeated itself until the temperature and the pressure of the air inside the bottle were the same as the air outside the bottle.

8. Have students answer the conclusion question on the investigation sheet. Finally, have them draw a picture of the experiment on the back of the sheet. Encourage them to label their drawing and provide a caption that explains what happened in the experiment.

Try this for fun:

Have students try the experiment in reverse, placing a glass bottle in a hot water bath, topping it with a wet coin, and then allowing the bottle to cool. (The coin will stick to the bottle top as the pressure inside the bottle decreases.)

Name _____

Funny Money

What do you think will happen to the nickel when it is placed on a plastic bottle that has just come out of the freezer?

The nickel will _____.

    A turn on its side and spin

    B fly off the top of the bottle

    C get sucked into the bottle

    D lift and fall, over and over again

Procedure and Observations

1. Dip the nickel in the cup of water. Then place the nickel on top of the cold bottle. Dribble a little more water around the opening of the bottle.

2. Watch the nickel carefully for several minutes. What does the nickel do?

_____

_____

_____

Conclusion

How can you explain the behavior of the nickel?

_____

_____

_____

On the back of this sheet, draw a picture showing what happened in your experiment. Label your drawing and write a sentence that describes what it is showing.

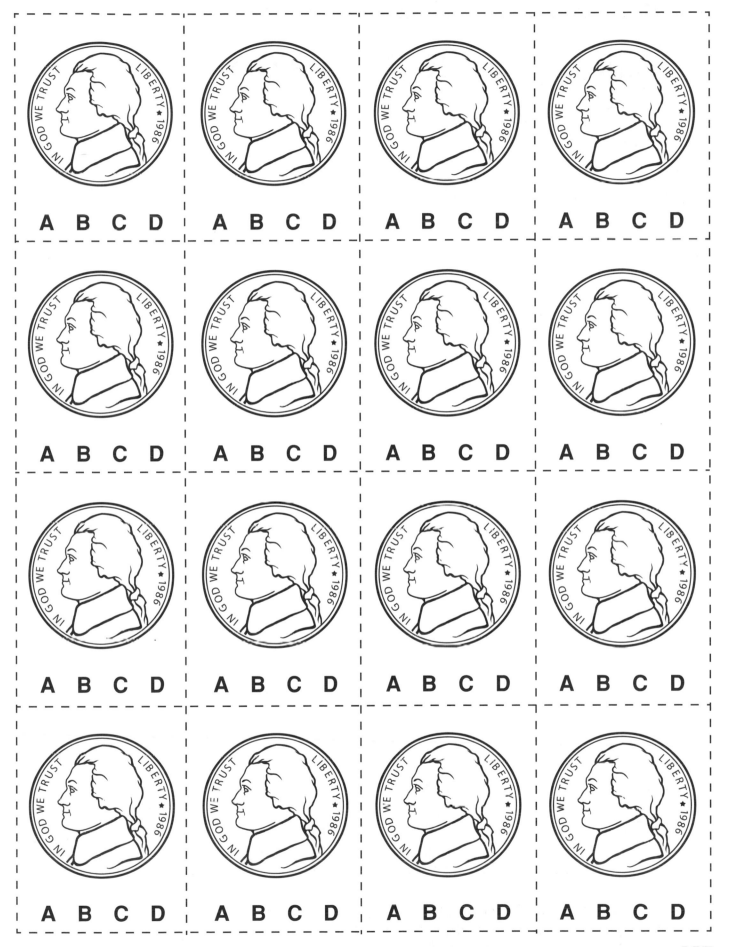

38

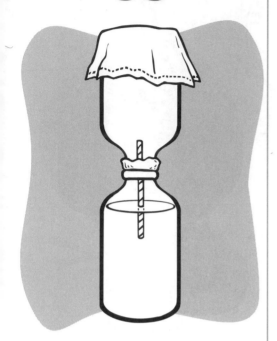

Materials:

- laminated graph chart
- page 160, reproduced for each student
- page 161, reproduced, one icon for each student
- plastic bottles
- drinking straws
- clay
- rags
- food coloring
- bowl
- water
- ice cubes
- newspaper

A Real Cool Experiment

Objective: Students will demonstrate that air pressure decreases as temperature decreases.

Question: What will happen when a cold rag is placed on an empty bottle inverted on top of a bottle of colored water?

Science Background: Air pressure is affected by temperature. Remember that air is made up of tiny particles that are constantly moving around. At lower temperatures, the particles move around more slowly and therefore make fewer hits on the objects around them. Fewer hits results in lower pressure. Thus, the pressure of a given volume of air will decrease as its temperature decreases.

When a cold rag is draped over the empty, inverted bottle in this activity, it cools the air in the bottle, reducing its pressure. When the pressure inside the empty bottle becomes lower than the pressure of the air pocket above the water in the bottom bottle, the higher-pressure air pocket pushes on the water, causing it to rise up through the straw and enter the inverted bottle.

Teaching Procedure:

1. Soak several rags in a bowl of ice water. Each group will need one rag.

2. Post the laminated graph chart at the front of the class. Label the top of the graph "A Real Cool Experiment."

3. Have each group cover its work area with newspaper. Distribute an investigation sheet and a bottle icon to each student.

4. Show students the materials to be used in the experiment. Read aloud the question at the top of the investigation sheet. Refer students to the picture of the experiment on the sheet and briefly explain how the experiment will be set up. Answer any questions students might have about the procedure.

5. Distribute an empty plastic bottle, a plastic bottle filled most of the way with colored water, a straw, and a lump of clay to each group. Have students set up the bottles as shown in the picture on the investigation sheet.

6. Have students select an answer to the question posed on the investigation sheet about what they think will happen when they place the cold rag over the inverted bottle. Tell them to record their answer both on the sheet and on the bottle icon. Collect the icons and use them to create a class graph as shown.

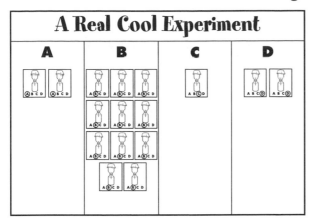

7. Distribute a cold, wet rag to each group. Have students drape the rag over the inverted bottle and watch what happens. (The water in the lower bottle will rise up through the straw and enter the inverted bottle.) Have students record their observations on the investigation sheet.

8. Discuss with students what they observed. Encourage them to offer an explanation for why the water rose up through the straw. Once the class has had a chance to discuss their theories, introduce the idea that air pressure is affected by temperature. The cold rag cooled the air in the inverted bottle, causing the air particles in that bottle to move around more slowly. The more slowly they moved, the fewer hits they made on the inside walls of the bottle. Fewer hits means lower pressure. When the pressure in the inverted bottle became lower than the pressure of the air pocket above the water in the lower bottle, the higher-pressure air in the lower bottle forced the water up the straw and into the inverted bottle.

9. Have students answer the conclusion question on the investigation sheet. Finally, have them draw a picture of the experiment on the back of the sheet. Encourage them to label their drawing and provide a caption that explains what happened in the experiment.

Try this for fun:

Have students try placing a hot, wet rag rather than a cold one on the inverted bottle. (The heat from the rag will increase the air pressure in the inverted bottle. This increased pressure will push down on any water in the straw, causing the water level in the bottom bottle to rise slightly.)

Name _____

A Real Cool Experiment

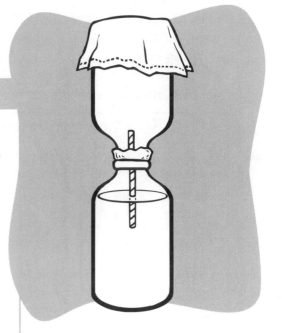

Question

What do you think will happen when the cold rag is placed on the empty bottle inverted on top of the bottle of colored water?

The water will _____.

A start to bubble

B move up through the straw

C change color

D fill up more of the bottom bottle

Procedure and Observations

1. Use clay to seal the straw into the mouth of the empty bottle. Place the empty bottle on top of the bottle of water as shown in the picture above.

2. Now place a cold rag over the empty bottle. What happens?

_____

_____

Conclusion

How can you explain what happened in the experiment?

_____

_____

_____

On the back of this sheet, draw a picture showing what happened in your experiment. Label your drawing and write a sentence that describes what it is showing.

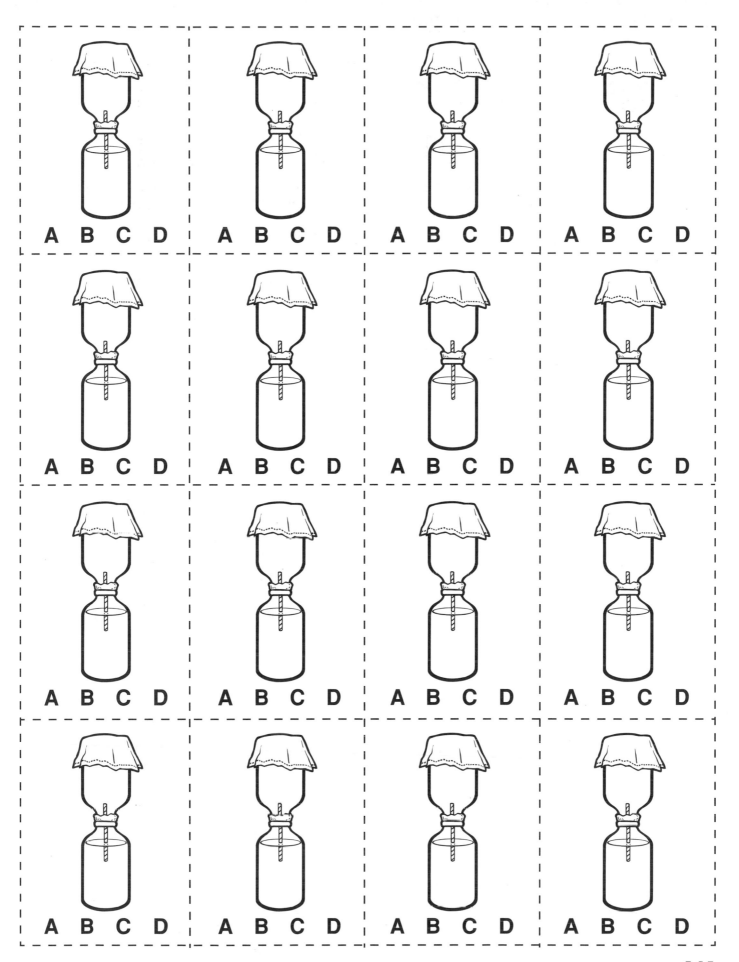

A B C D | A B C D | A B C D | A B C D

A B C D | A B C D | A B C D | A B C D

A B C D | A B C D | A B C D | A B C D

A B C D | A B C D | A B C D | A B C D

39

Materials:

- laminated graph chart
- page 164, reproduced for each student
- page 165, reproduced, one icon for each student
- glass or plastic bottle
- cork
- vinegar
- baking soda
- measuring spoon (Tbsp.)
- tissue

Cork Caper

Objective: Students will observe that substances can combine chemically to produce new substances.

Question: What will happen to the cork on a bottle when vinegar and baking soda are mixed inside the bottle?

Science Background: Vinegar (CH_3COOH) and baking soda ($NaHCO_3$) combine chemically to produce carbon dioxide gas (CO_2). This gas fills up the bottle. When enough gas is produced, the force it exerts on the cork causes the cork to fly out of the bottle with a "pop"!

Teaching Procedure:

1. Post the laminated graph chart at the front of the class. Label the top of the graph "Cork Caper."

2. Perform this experiment outside as a demonstration for the class. Make sure the cork you are using fits snugly in the top of the bottle.

3. Distribute an investigation sheet and a cork icon to each student.

4. Show students the materials to be used in the experiment. Read aloud the question at the top of the investigation sheet. Refer students to the picture of the experiment on the sheet and briefly explain how the experiment will be set up. Answer any questions students might have about the procedure.

5. Have students select an answer to the question posed on the investigation sheet about what they think will happen to the cork on the bottle when vinegar and baking soda are mixed inside. Tell them to record their answer both on the sheet and on the cork icon. Collect the icons and use them to create a class graph as shown.

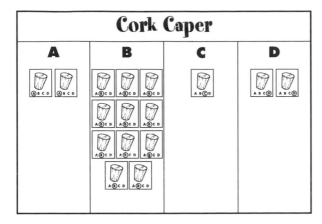

6. Bring all the materials outside. Gather students around.

7. Pour about 1 cup of vinegar into the bottle. Wrap 1 to 2 tablespoons of baking soda in a tissue and drop it into the bottle. Quickly place the cork in the bottle and point the top of the bottle away from students. (The vinegar and baking soda will fizz inside the bottle. After a few seconds, the cork will fly off the bottle.) Have students record their observations on the investigation sheet.

8. Discuss with students what they observed. Encourage them to offer an explanation for why the cork flew off the bottle. Once the class has had a chance to discuss their theories, introduce the idea that some substances, when mixed together, react chemically, producing a brand new substance. In this case, the vinegar and the baking soda combined to produce a gas that filled up the bottle and put pressure on the cork. Eventually, the pressure was strong enough to blow the cork off the bottle.

9. Have students answer the conclusion question on the investigation sheet. Finally, have them draw a picture of the experiment on the back of the sheet. Encourage them to label their drawing and provide a caption that explains what happened in the experiment.

Try this for fun:

Try different quantities of baking soda and see what effect they have on how far the cork flies.

Cork Caper

Question

What do you think will happen to the cork on the bottle when vinegar and baking soda are mixed inside the bottle?

The cork will _____.

    A get sucked into the bottle

    B do nothing

    C fly off

    D change color

Procedure and Observations

1. Watch as your teacher adds vinegar and baking soda to the bottle and plugs it with a cork.

2. What happens to the cork after a few seconds?

_____

_____

Conclusion

How can you explain what happened in the experiment?

_____

_____

_____

On the back of this sheet, draw a picture showing what happened in your experiment. Label your drawing and write a sentence that describes what it is showing.

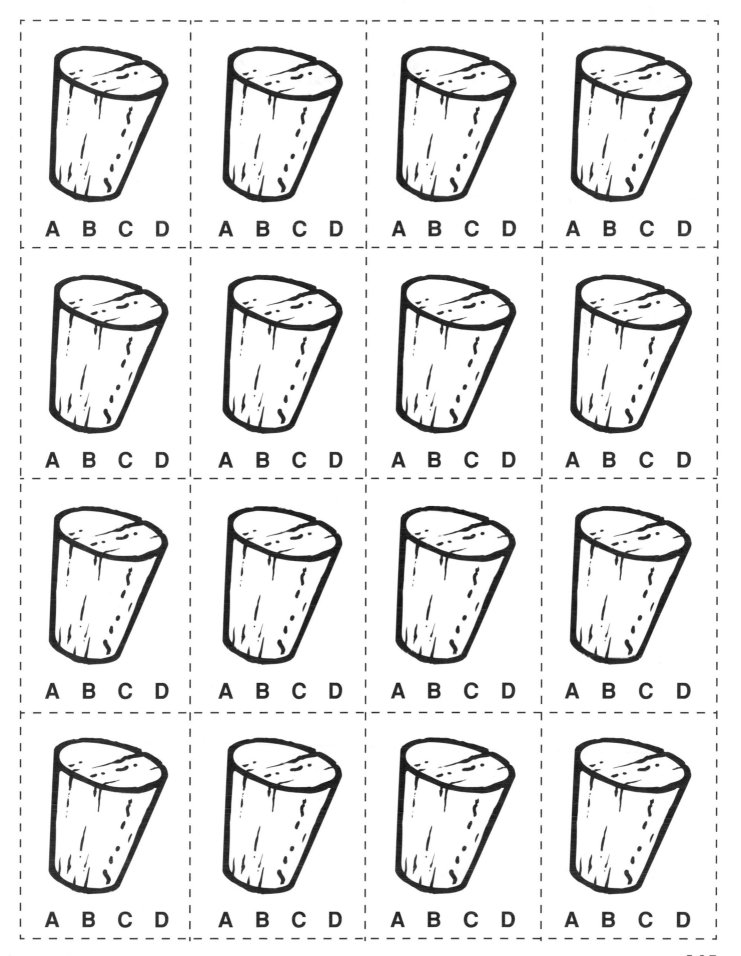

40

Materials:

- laminated graph chart
- page 168, reproduced for each student
- page 169, reproduced, one icon for each student
- plastic bottles
- balloons
- vinegar
- baking soda
- funnels
- measuring spoons (Tbsp.)
- newspaper

Chemical

The Big Balloon Takeoff

Objective: Students will demonstrate that substances can combine chemically to produce new substances.

Question: What will happen when vinegar and baking soda are mixed in a bottle that has a balloon stretched over the top?

Science Background: Vinegar (CH_3COOH) and baking soda ($NaHCO_3$) combine chemically to produce carbon dioxide gas (CO_2). This gas fills up the bottle and inflates the balloon.

Teaching Procedure:

1. Post the laminated graph chart at the front of the class. Label the top of the graph "The Big Balloon Takeoff."

2. Have each group cover its work area with newspaper. Distribute an investigation sheet and a balloon icon to each student.

3. Show students the materials to be used in the experiment. Read aloud the question at the top of the investigation sheet. Refer students to the picture of the experiment on the sheet and briefly explain how the experiment will be set up. Answer any questions students might have about the procedure.

4. Have students select an answer to the question posed on the investigation sheet about what they think will happen to a balloon stretched over the top of a bottle in which vinegar and baking soda are being mixed. Tell them to record their answer both on the sheet and on the balloon icon. Collect the icons and use them to create a class graph as shown.

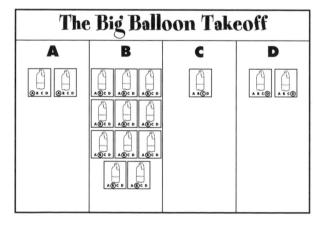

How to Do Science Experiments with Children • EMC 5001 • ©2003 by Evan-Moor Corp.

5. Have groups use one of the funnels to put 2 tablespoons of baking soda in their balloon. Have them use a different funnel to put about 8 tablespoons of vinegar in their bottle.

6. When all groups have prepared their bottles and balloons, instruct them to stretch the neck of their balloon over the opening of the bottle and hold the balloon up straight so that the baking soda pours into the bottle. What happens? (When the vinegar and baking soda combine, they will fizz in the bottle. After a few seconds, the balloon will begin to inflate.) Have students record their observations on the instruction sheet.

7. Discuss with students what they observed. Encourage them to offer an explanation for why the balloon inflated. Once the class has had a chance to discuss their theories, introduce the idea that some substances, when mixed together, react chemically, producing a brand new substance. In this case, the vinegar and the baking soda combined to produce a gas called carbon dioxide, which inflated the balloon.

8. Have students answer the conclusion question on the investigation sheet. Finally, have them draw a picture of the experiment on the back of the sheet. Encourage them to label their drawing and provide a caption that explains what happened in the experiment.

Try this for fun:

Try different quantities of baking soda and see what effect they have on how big the balloon gets.

The Big Balloon Takeoff

Question

What do you think will happen when vinegar and baking soda are mixed in a bottle that has a balloon stretched over the top?

A Nothing will happen.

B A loud explosion will happen.

C The balloon will inflate.

D The balloon will get sucked into the bottle.

Procedure and Observations

1. Use a funnel to add 2 tablespoons of baking soda to your balloon. Use a different funnel to add 8 tablespoons of vinegar to your bottle.

2. Stretch the neck of the balloon over the bottle and dump the baking soda into the bottle. What happens?

_____

_____

_____

Conclusion

How can you explain what happened in the experiment?

_____

_____

_____

On the back of this sheet, draw a picture showing what happened in your experiment. Label your drawing and write a sentence that describes what it is showing.

How to Do Science Experiments with Children • EMC 5001 • ©2003 by Evan-Moor Corp.

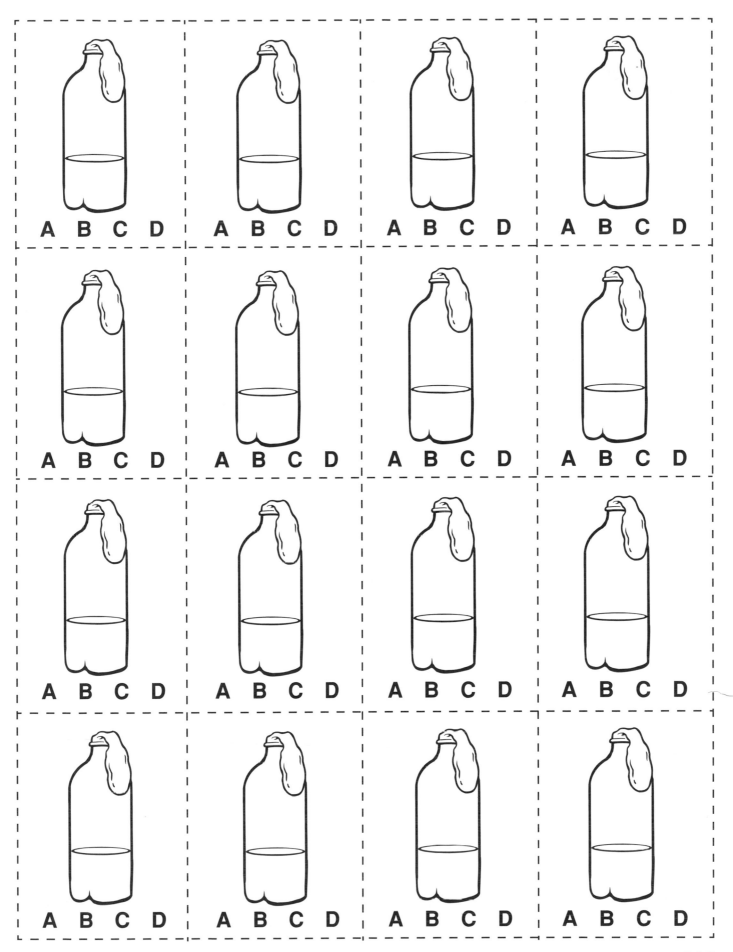

A B C D   A B C D   A B C D   A B C D

A B C D   A B C D   A B C D   A B C D

A B C D   A B C D   A B C D   A B C D

A B C D   A B C D   A B C D   A B C D

Chemical

41

Penny Bath

Objective: Students will demonstrate a chemical reaction.

Question: What will happen to dull pennies when they are washed in a mixture of vinegar and salt?

Science Background: A **chemical reaction** occurs when two or more substances combine chemically to form a new substance. The dull film on pennies forms when oxygen atoms from the air combine with copper atoms in the pennies. Vinegar (CH_3COOH) and salt ($NaCl$) combine to form hydrochloric acid (HCl). Hydrochloric acid, in turn, combines with oxygen atoms on the surface of dull pennies, leaving them shiny like new.

Teaching Procedure:

1. Post the laminated graph chart at the front of the class. Label the top of the graph "Penny Bath."

2. Have each group cover its work area with newspaper. Distribute an investigation sheet and a penny icon to each student.

3. Show students the materials to be used in the experiment. Read aloud the question at the top of the investigation sheet. Refer students to the picture of the experiment on the sheet and briefly explain how the experiment will be set up. Answer any questions students might have about the procedure.

4. Have students select an answer to the question posed on the investigation sheet about what they think will happen to the pennies when they are washed with vinegar and salt. Tell them to record their answer both on the sheet and on the penny icon. Collect the icons and use them to create a class graph as shown.

Materials:

- laminated graph chart
- page 172, reproduced for each student
- page 173, reproduced, one icon for each student
- glass jars
- dull pennies
- white vinegar
- salt
- small paper or plastic cups
- water
- measuring spoons (Tbsp.)
- plastic spoons
- paper towels
- newspaper

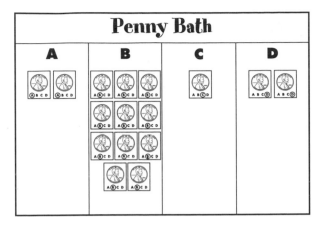

5. Distribute two pennies, a glass jar, a cup filled with water, a plastic spoon, and a paper towel to each group. Groups will also need access to the salt, vinegar, and measuring spoons. Have students pour some salt on one penny and a few drops of vinegar on the other. What happened? (nothing) Have them record their observations on the investigation sheet.

6. Now have students mix 6 tablespoons of vinegar and 2 tablespoons of salt in the glass jar. Have them put the pennies in the jar and stir them around for a few minutes. Then have them remove the pennies, rinse them in water, and dry them with a paper towel. What happened to the pennies? (They are now shiny.) Tell students to record their observations on the investigation sheet.

7. Discuss with students what they observed. Encourage them to offer an explanation for why the pennies became shiny. Once the class has had a chance to discuss their theories, introduce the idea that a chemical reaction took place between the vinegar, the salt, and the pennies. Explain that the vinegar and salt combined to form a new chemical that was able to clean the pennies.

8. Have students answer the conclusion question on the investigation sheet. Finally, have them draw a picture of the experiment on the back of the sheet. Encourage them to label their drawing and provide a caption that explains what happened in the experiment.

Try this for fun:

Have students try to restore other copper objects to their original luster using the vinegar and salt bath.

Penny Bath

Question

What do you think will happen to dull pennies when they are washed in a mixture of vinegar and salt?

The pennies will _____.

    A make a sizzling sound

    B turn black

    C begin to bounce up and down

    D become shiny

Procedure and Observations

1. Place some salt on one penny and some vinegar on another. What happened?

_____

2. Mix 6 tablespoons of vinegar and 2 tablespoons of salt in a jar. Add the pennies and stir for several minutes. Then remove the pennies, rinse them in water, and dry them. What happened to the pennies?

_____

_____

Conclusion

How can you explain what happened in the experiment?

_____

_____

_____

On the back of this sheet, draw a picture showing what happened in your experiment. Label your drawing and write a sentence that describes what it is showing.

How to Do Science Experiments with Children • EMC 5001 • ©2003 by Evan-Moor Corp.

42

Materials:

- laminated graph chart
- page 176, reproduced for each student
- page 177, reproduced, one icon for each student
- plastic cups
- uncooked eggs
- vinegar
- paper towels
- newspaper

Chemical

The Yolk's on You

Objective: Students will demonstrate a chemical reaction.

Question: What will happen to an egg when it is soaked in vinegar for two days?

Science Background: A **chemical reaction** occurs when two or more substances combine chemically to form a new substance. Calcium carbonate ($CaCO_3$) is the chief component in the shell of a chicken egg. The calcium carbonate makes the eggshell hard so that the developing chick is protected from the weight of the parent during incubation. Vinegar (CH_3COOH) is an acid that reacts chemically with calcium. When an egg is soaked in vinegar, the vinegar will dissolve the calcium in the eggshell, rendering the shell rubbery.

Teaching Procedure:

1. Post the laminated graph chart at the front of the class. Label the top of the graph "The Yolk's on You."

2. Have each group cover its work area with newspaper. Distribute an investigation sheet and an egg icon to each student.

3. Show students the materials to be used in the experiment. Read aloud the question on the investigation sheet. Refer students to the picture of the experiment on the sheet and briefly explain how the experiment will be set up. Answer any questions students might have about the procedure.

4. Distribute an uncooked egg and a cup filled with vinegar to each group. Have students examine and feel the egg and record their observations on the investigation sheet. Then instruct them to place the egg in the cup of vinegar. Tell them they will leave the egg in the vinegar for two days.

5. Have students select an answer to the question posed on the investigation sheet about what they think will happen to the egg after soaking in vinegar for two days. Tell them to record their answer both on the sheet and on the egg icon. Collect the icons and use them to create a class graph as shown.

The Yolk's on You

| A | B | C | D |

6. After two days, have students remove the egg from the cup of vinegar and wipe it with a paper towel. How has the egg changed? (The shell is now rubbery rather than hard.) Have students record their observations on the investigation sheet.

7. Discuss with students what they observed. Encourage them to offer an explanation for why the eggshell turned rubbery. Once the class has had a chance to discuss their theories, introduce the idea that a chemical reaction took place between the vinegar and the eggshell. That chemical reaction turned the shell rubbery. You might want to explain that the vinegar dissolved the chemical (calcium) in the shell that made it hard.

8. Have students answer the conclusion question on the investigation sheet. Finally, have them draw a picture of the experiment on the back of the sheet. Encourage them to label their drawing and provide a caption that explains what happened in the experiment.

Try this for fun:

Have students try soaking chicken bones in vinegar for several days. Like the eggshells, the bones will eventually become rubbery as the calcium in them dissolves.

Name _____

The Yolk's on You

Question

What do you think will happen to the egg when it is soaked in vinegar for two days?

The egg will _____.

    A turn black

    B become rubbery

    C harden on the inside

    D break open

Procedure and Observations

1. Observe your egg. Describe how it feels.

_____

_____

2. Place the egg in a cup of vinegar and let it sit for two days. Then remove the egg and wipe it off with a paper towel. Describe the egg again.

_____

_____

Conclusion

How can you explain what happened to the egg in the experiment?

_____

_____

_____

On the back of this sheet, draw a picture showing what happened in your experiment. Label your drawing and write a sentence that describes what it is showing.

 How to Do Science Experiments with Children • EMC 5001 • ©2003 by Evan-Moor Corp.

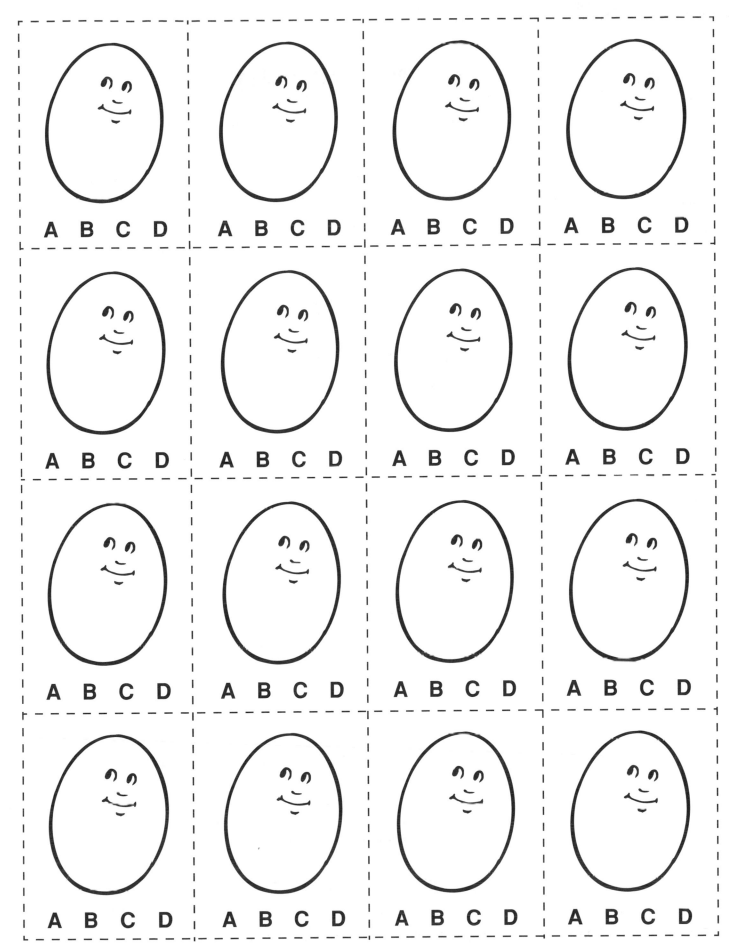

43

Chemical

Mystery Messages

Objective: Students will observe a chemical reaction caused by heat.

Question: What will happen to a mystery message when it is heated over a candle flame?

Science Background: Heat from the candle flame causes paper to undergo a chemical reaction and turn brown. Lemon juice on the paper also undergoes a chemical reaction and turns brown—but does so at a lower temperature than the paper. As a result, a secret message written in lemon juice on paper will become visible as the paper is slowly heated above a flame.

Teaching Procedure:

1. Post the laminated graph chart at the front of the class. Label the top of the graph "Mystery Messages."

2. Cut the lemons and squeeze a few tablespoons of lemon juice into a cup for each group.

3. Have each group cover its work area with newspaper. Distribute an investigation sheet and a secret paper icon to each student.

4. Show students the materials to be used in the experiment. Read aloud the question on the investigation sheet. Refer students to the picture of the experiment on the sheet and briefly explain how the experiment will be set up. Answer any questions students might have about the procedure.

5. Distribute a small cup of lemon juice, several toothpicks, and several pieces of paper to each group. Have each student dip a toothpick into the juice and write a secret message on a piece of paper.

6. Have students select an answer to the question posed on the investigation sheet about what they think will happen when their paper is heated over a candle flame. Tell them to record their answer both on the sheet and on the secret paper icon. Collect the icons and use them to create a class graph as shown.

Materials:

- laminated graph sheet
- page 180, reproduced for each student
- page 181, reproduced, one icon for each student
- candle
- matches
- lemons
- knife
- small plastic cups
- toothpicks
- paper
- newspaper

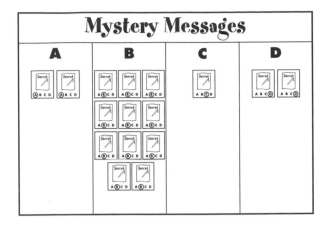

Mystery Messages

7. Light the candle at the front of the room. Have students bring you their secret message papers, one at a time. Hold each paper above the candle flame until the message appears on the paper. Instruct students to record their observations.

8. Discuss with students what they observed. Encourage them to offer an explanation for why their message appeared when held over the candle flame. Once the class has had a chance to discuss their theories, introduce the idea that the heat of the flame caused a chemical reaction to take place between the lemon juice on the paper and the air. This chemical reaction turned the lemon-soaked parts of the paper brown, revealing the secret message.

9. Have students answer the conclusion question on the investigation sheet. Finally, have them draw a picture of the experiment on the back of the sheet. Encourage them to label their drawing and provide a caption that explains what happened in the experiment.

Try this for fun:

Have students try creating secret messages using other liquids, like vinegar or milk. You might want to have students hold the messages over an uncovered light bulb instead of an open flame.

Mystery Messages

Question

What do you think will happen to your mystery message when it is heated over a candle flame?

The message will _____.

    A stay a mystery

    B suddenly appear

    C burn up

    D appear backward

Procedure and Observations

1. Use a toothpick and some lemon juice to write a secret message on a piece of paper.

    _____

    _____

2. Give your paper to your teacher. Watch as he or she holds it over the candle flame. What happens?

    _____

    _____

Conclusion

How can you explain what happened in the experiment?

_____

_____

_____

On the back of this sheet, draw a picture showing what happened in your experiment. Label your drawing and write a sentence that describes what it is showing.

44

Chemical

Woolly Wonder

Objective: Students will demonstrate that rusting (a chemical reaction) uses up oxygen from the air.

Question: What will happen to a balloon stretched over the mouth of a bottle when steel wool inside the bottle begins to rust?

Science Background: Oxidation is a chemical reaction that occurs when a substance combines with oxygen to produce a new substance. For example, iron combines with oxygen in the air to form iron oxide—the reddish material we know as rust. Rust is a product of oxidation.

Steel wool contains iron. In this activity, a steel wool pad is placed in a bottle and the bottle is sealed by stretching a balloon over the top. The steel wool rusts as it combines with oxygen in the air inside the bottle. As the oxygen gas in the bottle gets "used up," the pressure in the bottle decreases. The decreased pressure forms a vacuum in the bottle, which causes the balloon stretched over the bottle opening to get sucked inside.

Teaching Procedure:

1. Post the laminated graph chart at the front of the class. Label the top of the graph "Woolly Wonder."

2. Soak the steel wool pads in vinegar the night before the experiment. The vinegar dissolves the protective covering on the strands of steel in the pad, allowing them to rust faster.

3. Have each group cover its work area with newspaper. Distribute an investigation sheet and a steel wool pad icon to each student.

4. Show students the materials to be used in the experiment. Read aloud the question on the investigation sheet. Refer students to the picture of the experiment on the sheet and briefly explain how the experiment will be set up. Answer any questions students might have about the procedure.

Materials:

- laminated graph chart
- page 184, reproduced for each student
- page 185, reproduced, one icon for each student
- plastic bottles
- steel wool pads (plain)
- balloons
- small plastic cups
- vinegar
- water
- pencils
- newspaper

5. Distribute a plastic bottle, a balloon, a pad of steel wool that has soaked overnight in vinegar, and a small cup of water to each group. Have students use a pencil to poke the steel wool pad into the bottle. Have them add 5 drops of water to the bottle (oxygen in the water speeds up the rusting process), and then stretch the neck of the balloon over the top of the bottle. Tell students they are going to leave the bottle like this overnight.

6. Have students select an answer to the question posed on the investigation sheet about what they think will happen to the balloon overnight. Tell them to record their answer both on the sheet and on the steel wool pad icon. Collect the icons and use them to create a class graph as shown.

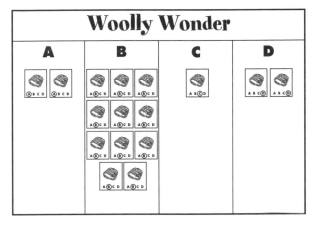

7. The next day, have students observe their bottle and balloon. (The balloon will have been sucked inside the bottle and inflated inside out. If the balloon has not been sucked inside the bottle yet, let it stand another night.) Instruct students to record their observations.

8. Discuss with students what they observed. Encourage them to offer an explanation for why the balloon was sucked into the bottle. Once the class has had a chance to discuss their theories, introduce the idea that as the steel wool rusted, it drew oxygen gas out of the air. Less gas means less pressure inside the bottle. The higher pressure outside the bottle then forced the balloon inside. (For more experiments on air pressure, see pages 94–145.)

9. Have students answer the conclusion question on the investigation sheet. Finally, have them draw a picture of the experiment on the back of the sheet. Encourage them to label their drawing and provide a caption that explains what happened in the experiment.

Try this for fun:

Have students continue to observe the bottles and balloons for a week.

Woolly Wonder

Question

What do you think will happen to the balloon when the steel wool inside the bottle begins to rust?

The balloon will _____.

   A inflate

   B fly off the top of the bottle

   C change color

   D get sucked into the bottle and inflate inside out

Procedure and Observations

1. Push the steel wool pad into your bottle, add a few drops of water, and stretch the balloon over the mouth of the bottle.

2. Observe your bottle the next day. What happened to the balloon?

_____

_____

Conclusion

How can you explain what happened in the experiment?

_____

_____

_____

On the back of this sheet, draw a picture showing what happened in your experiment. Label your drawing and write a sentence that describes what it is showing.

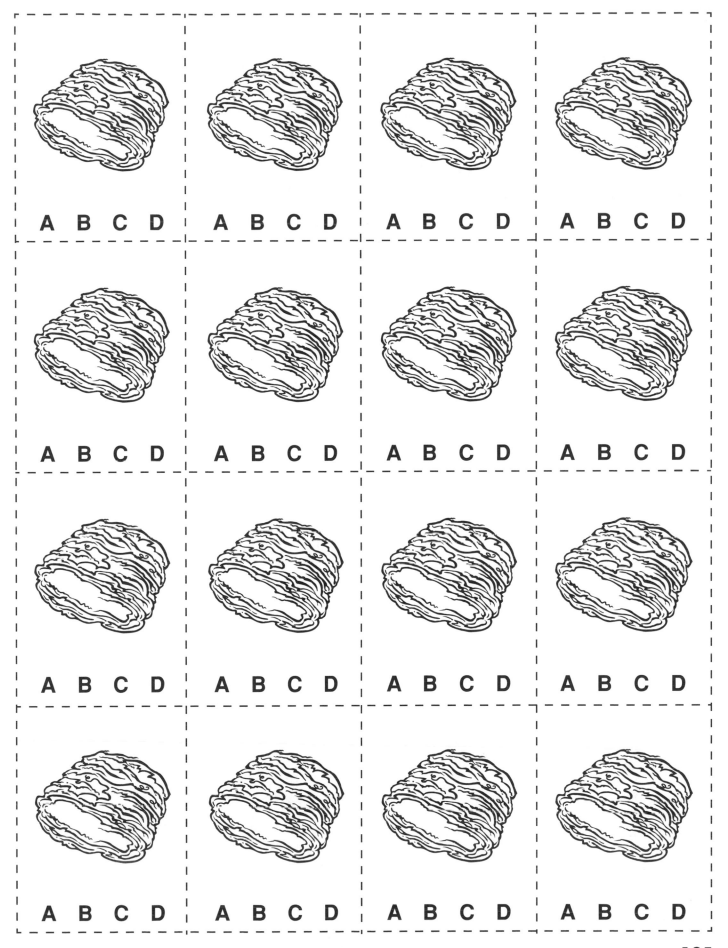

A B C D   A B C D   A B C D   A B C D

A B C D   A B C D   A B C D   A B C D

A B C D   A B C D   A B C D   A B C D

A B C D   A B C D   A B C D   A B C D

45

Materials:

- laminated graph chart
- page 188, reproduced for each student
- page 189, reproduced, one icon for each student
- drinking glass
- red or pink rose
- sulfur powder
- matches
- aluminum foil
- masking tape
- hydrogen peroxide
- newspaper

Chemical

Science in Full Bloom

Objective: Students will recognize that a chemical reaction can produce a physical change.

Question: What will happen to a rose when it is exposed to burning sulfur and then dipped into hydrogen peroxide?

Science Background: Chemical reactions can produce changes in the physical properties of matter. In this activity, a rose is placed in a glass filled with foul-smelling sulfur dioxide gas. (The gas is produced by burning sulfur.) The gas combines with oxygen from the colored part of the flower, leaving the flower bleached white. The bleached flower is then dipped in hydrogen peroxide (H_2O_2). The hydrogen peroxide provides oxygen to the flower, restoring its color.

Teaching Procedure:

1. Post the laminated graph chart at the front of the class. Label the top of the graph "Science in Full Bloom."

2. Perform this experiment as a demonstration for the class.

3. Cover your work area with newspaper. Distribute an investigation sheet and a flower icon to each student.

4. Show students the materials to be used in the experiment. Read aloud the question at the top of the investigation sheet. Refer students to the picture of the experiment on the sheet and briefly explain how the experiment will be set up. Answer any questions students might have about the procedure.

5. Have students select an answer to the question posed on the investigation sheet about what they think will happen to the rose in the experiment. They should record their answer both on the sheet and on the flower icon. Collect the icons and use them to create a class graph as shown.

Science in Full Bloom

A	B	C	D

6. Tape the rose head to the inside of the drinking glass as shown in the picture. Place a small amount of sulfur on a piece of aluminum foil. Light a match and hold it to the sulfur. When it begins to burn, invert the drinking glass over the pile of burning sulfur. Ask students to record what happens to the rose. (It loses its color and turns white.)

7. Now take the rose out of the glass. Fill the glass halfway with hydrogen peroxide and dip the rose into it. Have students record what happens to the rose. (It regains its original color.)

8. Discuss with students what they observed. Encourage them to offer an explanation for why the rose turned white and then regained its color. Once the class has had a chance to discuss their theories, introduce the idea that the burning sulfur produced sulfur dioxide gas. The sulfur dioxide gas reacted chemically with the rose, removing oxygen from it and turning it white. When the rose was dipped into hydrogen peroxide, the oxygen was restored to the rose and the rose returned to its original color.

9. Have students answer the conclusion question on their investigation sheet. Finally, have them draw a picture of the experiment on the back of their sheet. Encourage them to label their drawing and provide a caption that explains what happened in the experiment.

Try this for fun:

Try the experiment again, using different flowers.

Science in Full Bloom

Question

What do you think will happen to the rose when it is exposed to burning sulfur and then dipped into hydrogen peroxide?

The rose will _____.

    A wilt and die

    B harden and crack into pieces

    C burn and then dissolve

    D turn white and then go back to its original color

Procedure and Observations

1. Watch as your teacher places the glass containing the rose over the burning sulfur. What happens to the rose?

_____

_____

2. Next, watch as your teacher dips the rose into hydrogen peroxide. What happens to the rose now?

_____

_____

Conclusion

How can you explain what happened in the experiment?

_____

_____

_____

On the back of this sheet, draw a picture showing what happened in your experiment. Label your drawing and write a sentence that describes what it is showing.

46

Materials:

- laminated graph chart
- page 192, reproduced for each student
- page 193, reproduced, one icon for each student
- large pumpkin
- carving knife
- candle
- matches
- newspaper

Chemical

Jack-O'-Light

Objective: Students will recognize that fire needs oxygen to burn.

Question: What will happen to a lighted candle inside a pumpkin when the pumpkin lid is replaced?

Science Background: Fire is the rapid combination of oxygen with other substances. The three conditions necessary for fire are 1) a combustible material, 2) a temperature high enough to cause ignition, and 3) enough oxygen. The candle in the pumpkin will burn as long as there is enough oxygen. After the lid is placed on the pumpkin, the oxygen supply is cut off. Once all the oxygen inside the pumpkin is used up, the candle flame will go out.

Teaching Procedure:

1. Post the laminated graph chart at the front of the class. Label the top of the graph "Jack-O'-Light."

2. Perform this experiment as a demonstration for the class.

3. Cover your work area with newspaper. Carve a lid out of the top of the pumpkin and hollow out the insides. Make sure the lid fits snugly. Do not carve a face or make any other holes in the pumpkin.

4. Distribute an investigation sheet and a candle icon to each student.

5. Show students the materials to be used in the experiment. Read aloud the question at the top of the investigation sheet. Refer students to the picture of the experiment on the sheet and briefly explain how the experiment will be set up. Answer any questions students might have about the procedure.

6. Have students select an answer to the question posed on the investigation sheet about what they think will happen to the burning candle when the lid is put back on the pumpkin. Tell them to record their answer both on the sheet and on the candle icon. Collect the icons and use them to create a class graph as shown.

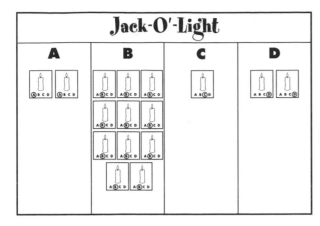

7. Place the candle in the pumpkin and light it. Have students watch it burn for a minute. Then place the lid on the pumpkin.

8. After one minute, remove the lid. Have students record what happened to the candle. (It will have burned out.)

9. Discuss with students what they observed. Encourage them to offer an explanation for why the candle burned out. Once the class has had a chance to discuss their theories, introduce the idea that fire needs oxygen to burn. Once the lid was placed on the pumpkin, no more oxygen could enter. After all the oxygen inside the pumpkin was used up, the flame went out.

10. Have students answer the conclusion question on the investigation sheet. Finally, have them draw a picture of the experiment on the back of the sheet. Encourage them to label their drawing and provide a caption that explains what happened in the experiment.

Try this for fun:

Carve a face in the pumpkin walls and repeat the experiment. Why doesn't the candle go out this time? (The carved holes allow oxygen to enter the pumpkin and fuel the fire continuously.)

Name _____

Jack-O'-Light

Question

What do you think will happen to the lighted candle inside the pumpkin when the pumpkin lid is replaced?

The candle will _____.

    A burn up the pumpkin

    B make the top pop off

    C go out

    D melt completely

Procedure and Observations

1. Watch as your teacher places the lid on the pumpkin with the burning candle inside.

2. Now watch as your teacher removes the lid a minute later. What happened to the candle?

_____

_____

Conclusion

How can you explain what happened in the experiment?

_____

_____

_____

On the back of this sheet, draw a picture showing what happened in your experiment. Label your drawing and write a sentence that describes what it is showing.

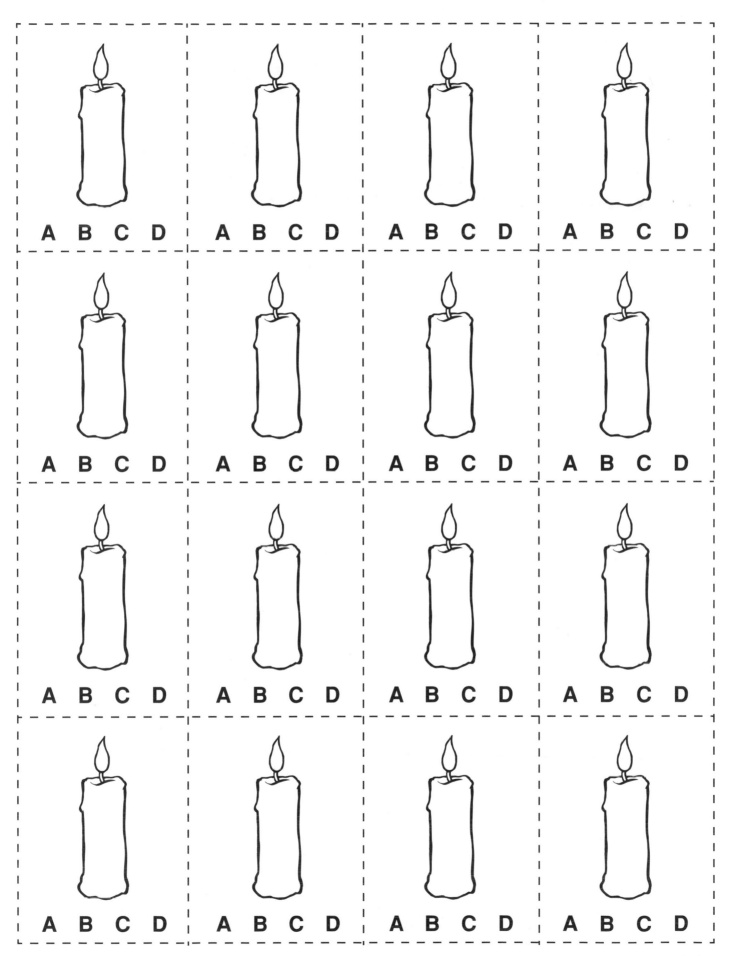

Chemical

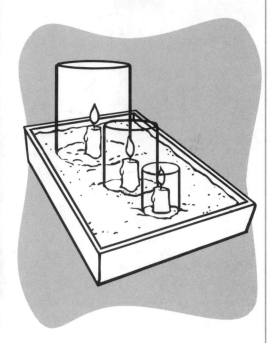

47

Festival of Lights

Objective: Students will recognize that fire needs oxygen to burn.

Question: In which jar will a candle burn longest: a small jar, a medium-size jar, or a large jar?

Science Background: Fire is the rapid combination of oxygen with other substances. The three conditions necessary for fire are 1) a combustible material, 2) a temperature high enough to cause ignition, and 3) enough oxygen. In this experiment, the largest jar contains the most oxygen and therefore will allow the candle to burn the longest. The candle will burn for the shortest length of time in the small jar.

Materials:

- laminated graph chart
- page 196, reproduced for each student
- page 197, reproduced, one icon for each student
- aluminum turkey roasting pan
- sand
- glass jars, three sizes
- candles, votive (same size)
- matches

Teaching Procedure:

1. Post the laminated graph chart at the front of the class. Label the top of the graph "Festival of Lights."

2. Perform this experiment as a demonstration for the class.

3. Distribute an investigation sheet and a candle icon to each student.

4. Show students the materials to be used in the experiment. Read aloud the question at the top of the investigation sheet. Refer students to the picture of the experiment on the sheet and briefly explain how the experiment will be set up. Answer any questions students might have about the procedure.

5. Have students select an answer to the question posed on the investigation sheet about which jar they think a candle will burn longest in. Tell them to record their answer both on the sheet and on the candle icon. Collect the icons and use them to create a class graph as shown.

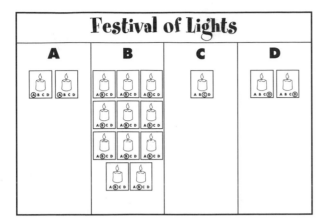

6. Arrange three candles in a pan of sand as shown in the picture. Light the candles and place a jar over each one. Have students observe the candles until all three have gone out. Which candle burned the longest? Which burned the shortest? (The candle in the largest jar burned the longest; the candle in the smallest jar burned the shortest.) Instruct students to record their observations.

7. Discuss with students what they observed. Encourage them to offer an explanation for why the candle in the largest jar burned for the longest length of time. Once the class has had a chance to discuss their theories, introduce the idea that fire needs oxygen to burn. Once all the oxygen has been used up, the fire goes out. Since the largest jar contained the most oxygen, it allowed the candle inside to burn for the longest length of time.

8. Have students answer the conclusion question on the investigation sheet. Finally, have them draw a picture of the experiment on the back of the sheet. Encourage them to label their drawing and provide a caption that explains what happened in the experiment.

Try this for fun:

Have students use stopwatches to time how long each candle burns.

Festival of Lights

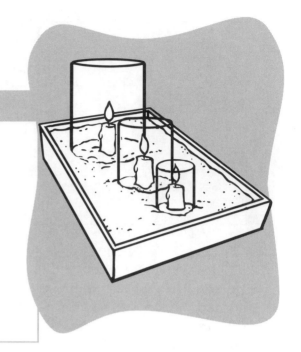

Question

In which jar do you think a candle will burn longest:
a small jar, a medium-size jar, or a large jar?

    A   a small jar

    B   a medium-size jar

    C   a large jar

    D   All the candles will burn for the
        same length of time.

Procedure and Observations

1. Watch as your teacher lights the three candles in the pan of sand and places a different-sized jar over each one. Watch the candles until all three have gone out.

2. In which jar did the candle burn the longest? The shortest?

_____

_____

Conclusion

How can you explain what happened in the experiment?

_____

_____

_____

On the back of this sheet, draw a picture showing what happened in your experiment. Label your drawing and write a sentence that describes what it is showing.

48

Materials:

- laminated graph chart
- page 200, reproduced for each student
- page 201, reproduced, one icon for each student
- paper cup
- laboratory tongs
- candle
- candle holder, if necessary
- water
- matches

Physical

Heating Up

Objective: Students will recognize that heat can be transferred from one object to another.

Question: What will happen to a paper cup of water when it is held over an open flame?

Science Background: The three conditions necessary for fire are 1) a combustible material, 2) a temperature high enough to cause ignition, and 3) enough oxygen. A paper cup of water held over an open flame will not burn because the heat from the flame transfers from the cup to the water. Thus, the paper never gets hot enough to ignite. Instead, the transferred heat causes the water to boil. The ability to conduct or transmit energy (including heat) is called **conductivity**. Conductivity is a physical property of matter.

Teaching Procedure:

1. Post the laminated graph chart at the front of the class. Label the top of the graph "Heating Up."

2. Perform this experiment as a demonstration for the class.

3. Distribute an investigation sheet and a paper cup icon to each student.

4. Show students the materials to be used in the experiment. Read aloud the question at the top of the investigation sheet. Refer students to the picture of the experiment on the sheet and briefly explain how the experiment will be set up. Answer any questions students might have about the procedure.

5. Have students select an answer to the question posed on the investigation sheet about what they think will happen to the paper cup of water when it is held over a flame. Tell them to record their answer both on the sheet and on the paper cup icon. Collect the icons and use them to create a class graph as shown.

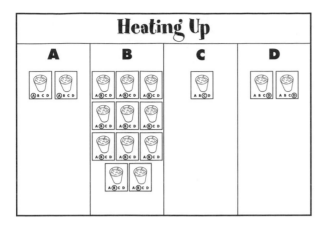

Heating Up

6. Fill the paper cup three-quarters full with water. Light the candle. Then pick up the cup using the tongs. Hold the cup a few centimeters above the candle flame. Have students observe what happens over the next several minutes and then record their observations. (Eventually, the water will begin to boil. The cup will not burn.)

7. Discuss with students what they observed. Encourage them to offer an explanation for why the paper cup did not burn. Once the class has had a chance to discuss their theories, introduce the idea that the water in the cup absorbed the heat from the candle flame and took it away from the cup. So the cup never got hot enough to burn.

8. Have students answer the conclusion question on the investigation sheet. Finally, have them draw a picture of the experiment on the back of the sheet. Encourage them to label their drawing and provide a caption that explains what happened in the experiment.

Try this for fun:

Try the experiment again using milk or another nonflammable liquid. (Results will be the same.)

Heating Up

Question

What do you think will happen to a paper cup of water when it is held over an open flame?

The cup of water will _____.

    A catch fire

    B start to boil

    C put the candle out

    D not change in any way

Procedure and Observations

Watch as your teacher holds the paper cup of water over the candle flame. What happens over the next several minutes?

_____

_____

Conclusion

How can you explain what happened in the experiment?

_____

_____

_____

On the back of this sheet, draw a picture showing what happened in your experiment. Label your drawing and write a sentence that describes what it is showing.

     How to Do Science Experiments with Children • EMC 5001 • ©2003 by Evan-Moor Corp.

A B C D   A B C D   A B C D   A B C D

A B C D   A B C D   A B C D   A B C D

A B C D   A B C D   A B C D   A B C D

A B C D   A B C D   A B C D   A B C D

49

Materials:

- laminated graph chart
- page 204, reproduced for each student
- page 205, reproduced, one icon for each student
- quarter
- piece of cotton cloth
- candle
- candle holder, if necessary
- pencil
- matches

Hot Stuff

Objective: Students will recognize that heat can be transferred from one object to another.

Question: What will happen to a piece of cloth wrapped around a quarter when it is touched with a heated pencil?

Science Background: A piece of cloth wrapped around a quarter will not burn when touched with a hot object because the heat is immediately transferred away from the cloth to the quarter. Metals are very good conductors of energy (including heat). **Conductivity** is a physical property of matter.

Teaching Procedure:

1. Post the laminated graph chart at the front of the class. Label the top of the graph "Hot Stuff."

2. Perform this experiment as a demonstration for the class.

3. Distribute an investigation sheet and a quarter icon to each student.

4. Show students the materials to be used in the experiment. Read aloud the question at the top of the investigation sheet. Refer students to the picture of the experiment on the sheet and briefly explain how the experiment will be set up. Answer any questions students might have about the procedure.

5. Have students select an answer to the question posed on the investigation sheet about what they think will happen to the cloth wrapped around the quarter when it is touched with a heated pencil. Tell them to record their answer both on the sheet and on the quarter icon. Collect the icons and use them to create a class graph as shown.

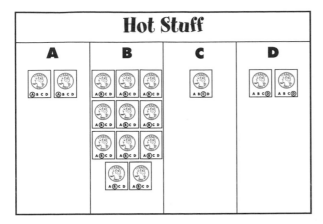

6. Light the candle. Wrap the cloth tightly around the quarter. (The quarter must be wrapped tightly in order for the experiment to work.) Hold the pencil tip in the candle flame until it is very hot. Touch the point of the pencil to the cloth. Have students observe and record what happens. (The cloth does not burn.)

7. Discuss with students what they observed. Encourage them to offer an explanation for why the cloth did not burn. Once the class has had a chance to discuss their theories, introduce the idea that the quarter absorbed the heat of the pencil tip, pulling it away from the cloth and preventing the cloth from burning.

8. Have students answer the conclusion question on the investigation sheet. Finally, have them draw a picture of the experiment on the back of the sheet. Encourage them to label their drawing and provide a caption that explains what happened in the experiment.

Try this for fun:

Try the experiment again using different types of cloth.

Hot Stuff

Question

What do you think will happen to the piece of cloth wrapped around the quarter when it is touched with a heated pencil?

The cloth will _____.

    A burn

    B do nothing

    C tear

    D smoke

Procedure and Observations

Watch as your teacher touches the hot pencil tip to the cloth wrapped around the quarter. What happens to the cloth?

_____

_____

_____

Conclusion

How can you explain what happened in the experiment?

_____

_____

_____

_____

On the back of this sheet, draw a picture showing what happened in your experiment. Label your drawing and write a sentence that describes what it is showing.

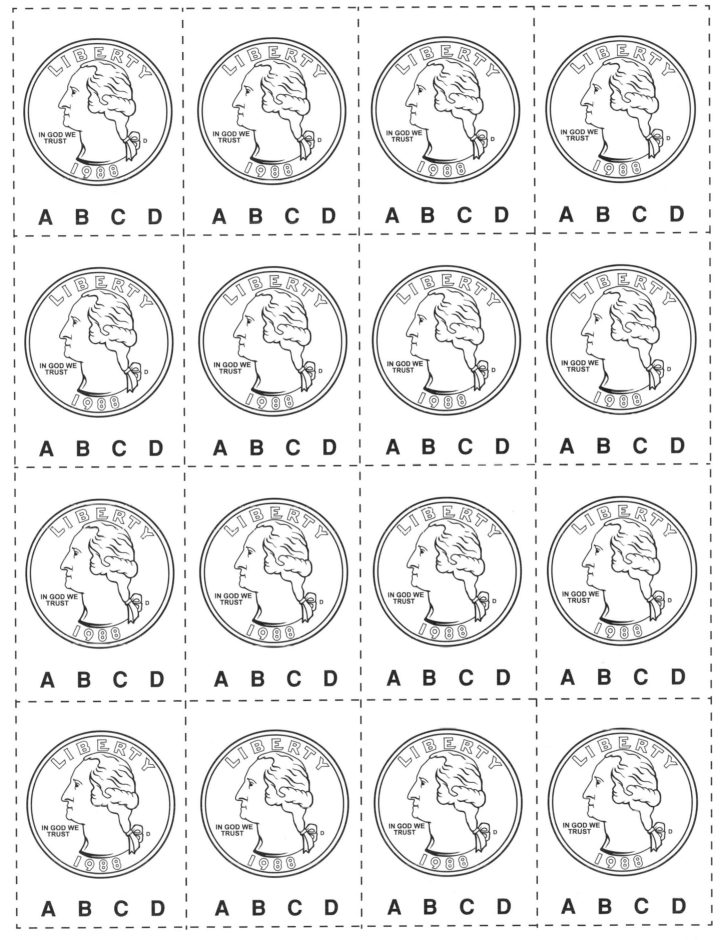

Physical

50

Inka-Dinka-Do

Objective: Students will demonstrate that parts of a mixture can be separated out by physical means.

Question: What will happen to a dot of purple ink on paper when the end of the paper is dipped into water and left there for 15 minutes?

Science Background: **Solubility**, the ability to dissolve in another substance, is a physical property of matter. Different substances have different solubilities. Some substances, like salt, are very soluble in water. Others, like talcum powder, are not.

Differences in solubility can be used to separate out the different parts of a mixture. Consider the various colors that are mixed together to make the ink in a purple marker. When a purple dot is drawn on a strip of absorbent paper and the paper is dipped into water, the colors that make up the purple ink (red, blue, and maybe others) will separate out according to their solubility. The more soluble colors will rise higher on the strip than the less soluble colors.

Teaching Procedure:

1. Post the laminated graph chart at the front of the class. Label the top of the graph "Inka-Dinka-Do."

2. Cut the blotter paper or coffee filters into 3 cm x 15 cm strips. Each group will need one strip.

3. Have each group cover its work area with newspaper. Distribute an investigation sheet and an ink icon to each student.

4. Show students the materials to be used in the experiment. Read aloud the question at the top of the investigation sheet. Refer students to the picture of the experiment on the sheet and briefly explain how the experiment will be set up. Answer any questions students might have about the procedure.

5. Have students select an answer to the question posed on the investigation sheet about what they think will happen to the purple dot when the end of the paper is dipped into water for 15 minutes. Tell them to record their answer both on the sheet and on the ink icon. Collect the icons and use them to create a class graph as shown.

Materials:

- laminated graph chart
- page 208, reproduced for each student
- page 209, reproduced, one icon for each student
- plastic cups
- blotter paper or coffee filters
- scissors
- water
- purple marker (water-soluble)
- pencils
- newspaper

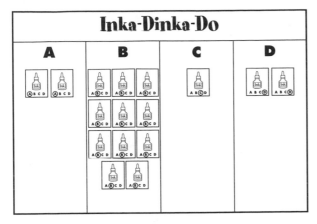

6. Distribute a plastic cup with a small amount of water in it and a strip of blotting paper to each group. Have groups take turns using the purple marker to draw a dot a few centimeters from the bottom of the strip. Tell them to poke the pencil through the top of the strip and set the pencil on the cup rim so that the strip hangs down and touches the water in the bottom of the cup. (The ink dot should be above the water level. See picture.)

7. Instruct students to leave the strip of paper undisturbed for about 15 minutes. Then have them look at the strip and record their observations. (Several individual colors, including red and blue, will have separated out along the length of the strip.)

8. Discuss with students what they observed. Encourage them to offer an explanation for why there are now several different colors along the length of the strip. Once the class has had a chance to discuss their theories, introduce the idea that the purple ink is actually a mixture of several different colors of ink. As the paper strip absorbed water and the water came into contact with the purple ink dot, each color in the mixture dissolved in the water and moved up the strip. More soluble colors moved farther up the strip than less soluble colors.

9. Have students answer the conclusion question on the investigation sheet. Finally, have them draw a picture of the experiment on the back of the sheet. Encourage them to label their drawing and provide a caption that explains what happened in the experiment.

Try this for fun:

Try the experiment again using different colors of ink, including black.

Name _____

Inka-Dinka-Do

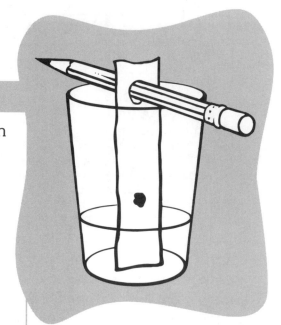

Question

What do you think will happen to the purple ink dot on the paper strip when the end of the paper is dipped into water and left there for 15 minutes?

The purple ink dot will _____.

    A disappear

    B make the water purple

    C stay the same color

    D separate into different colors

Procedure and Observations

1. Draw a purple dot near the bottom of the strip of paper as shown in the picture. Poke a pencil through the top of the paper and set the pencil on the cup rim. Let the paper strip hang down and dip in the water. Wait 15 minutes.

2. Look at the strip of paper and the water. What do you see?

_____

_____

_____

Conclusion

How can you explain what happened in the experiment?

_____

_____

_____

On the back of this sheet, draw a picture showing what happened in your experiment. Label your drawing and write a sentence that describes what it is showing.

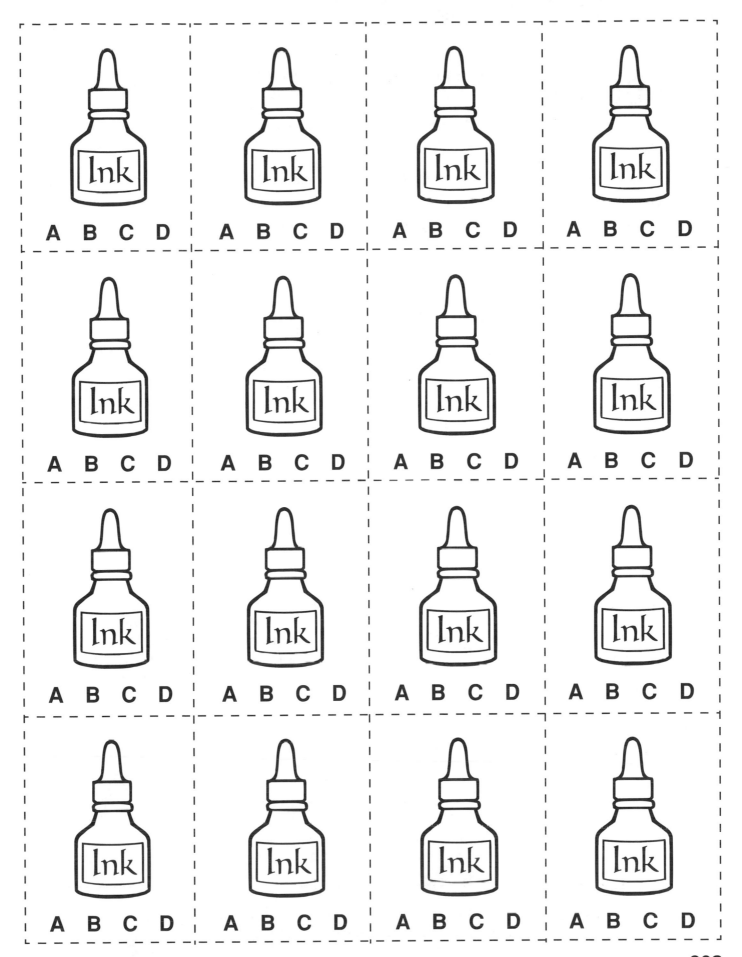

51

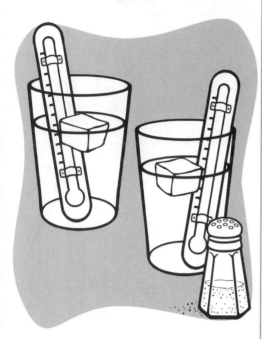

Cool Cubes

Objective: Students will demonstrate that salt can change the freezing point of water/melting point of ice.

Question: Will an ice cube melt faster in plain water or salty water?

Science Background: The **freezing point** of a liquid is the temperature at which it freezes. The **melting point** of a solid is the temperature at which it melts. The freezing point of pure water is 32°F (0°C), the same as the melting point of pure ice. When salt is added to water, its freezing point is lowered to a colder temperature. Likewise, when ice comes into contact with salt, the melting point of the ice is lowered. Thus, an ice cube in salty water will melt faster than an ice cube in plain water, not because the salty water is warmer, but because the salty water allows the cube to be in a liquid state where it would normally be in a solid state at the same temperature.

Materials:

- laminated graph chart
- page 212, reproduced for each student
- page 213, reproduced, one icon for each student
- plastic cups
- ice cubes, equal-sized
- thermometers
- salt
- plastic spoons
- cold water
- newspaper

Teaching Procedure:

1. Post the laminated graph chart at the front of the class. Label the top of the graph "Cool Cubes."

2. Have each group cover its work area with newspaper. Distribute an investigation sheet and an ice cube icon to each student.

3. Show students the materials to be used in the experiment. Read aloud the question at the top of the investigation sheet. Refer students to the picture of the experiment on the sheet and briefly explain how the experiment will be set up. Answer any questions students might have about the procedure.

4. Have students select an answer to the question posed on the investigation sheet about whether they think the ice cube will melt faster in plain or salty water. Tell them to record their answer both on the sheet and on the ice cube icon. Collect the icons and use them to create a class graph as shown.

Cool Cubes

A	B	C	D

5. Distribute two plastic cups half-filled with cold water, two equal-sized ice cubes, two thermometers, and a plastic spoon to each group. Have students place one ice cube and one thermometer in each cup.

6. Now have students add about a tablespoon of salt to one of the cups and stir. Instruct them to measure the temperature of the water in each cup and record it on the investigation sheet.

7. Have students watch what happens to the cubes over the next several minutes. (The cube in the salt water should begin to melt more quickly than the cube in the plain water.) Have them also note the temperature of the water in each cup. (They should be about the same.)

8. Discuss with students what they observed. Encourage them to offer an explanation for why the ice cube in the salt water melted faster than the ice cube in the plain water. Once the class has had a chance to discuss their theories, introduce the idea that ice cubes melt at a certain temperature. Adding salt to the water in which an ice cube is floating lowers the temperature at which the ice cube will melt. Thus, it takes less heat, and therefore less time, to melt the cube.

9. Have students answer the conclusion question on the investigation sheet. Finally, have them draw a picture of the experiment on the back of the sheet. Encourage them to label their drawing and provide a caption that explains what happened in the experiment.

Try this for fun:

Try the experiment again, but instead of salt, use additives like baking soda, baking powder, sugar, and so on.

Name _____

Cool Cubes

Question

Do you think an ice cube will melt faster in plain water or in salty water?

An ice cube will _____.

    A melt faster in plain water

    B melt faster in salty water

    C melt at the same rate in each

    D not melt in either

Procedure and Observations

1. Drop an ice cube in each cup of water. Place a thermometer in each cup.

2. Add about a tablespoon of salt to one cup and stir. Then record the temperature of the water in each cup.

    plain water temperature: _____°F   **salty water temperature:** _____°F

3. Observe the ice cubes for several minutes. What do you notice?

_____

_____

Conclusion

How can you explain what happened in the experiment?

_____

_____

_____

On the back of this sheet, draw a picture showing what happened in your experiment. Label your drawing and write a sentence that describes what it is showing.

    How to Do Science Experiments with Children • EMC 5001 • ©2003 by Evan-Moor Corp.

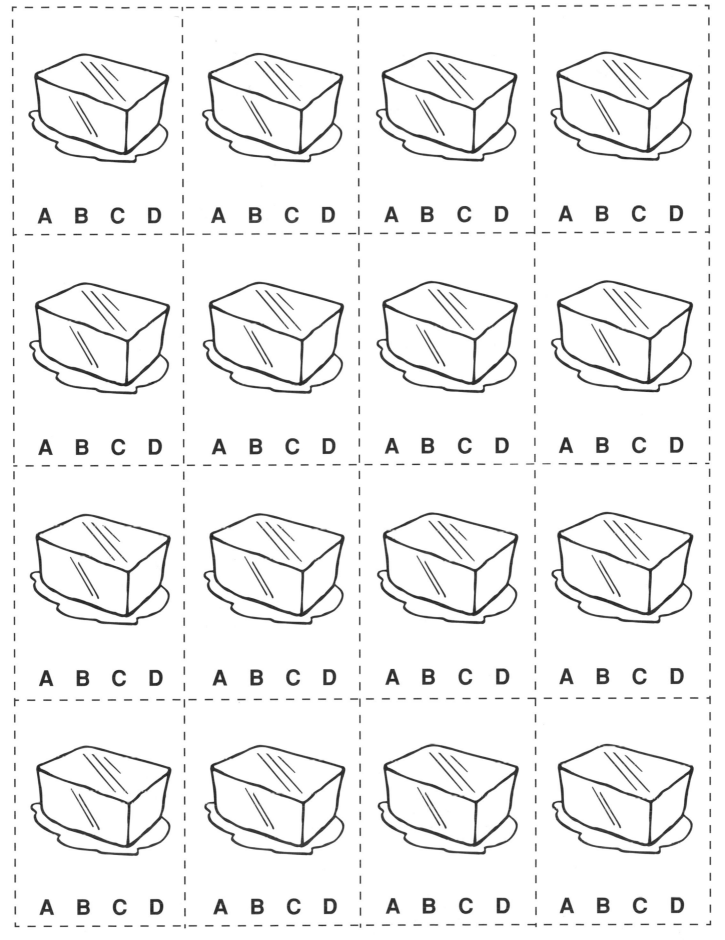

52

Materials:

- laminated graph chart
- page 216, reproduced for each student
- page 217, reproduced, one icon for each student
- plastic cups
- string
- scissors
- ice cubes
- salt
- cold water
- newspaper

Presto Change-O

Objective: Students will demonstrate that salt can change the freezing point of water/melting point of ice.

Question: What will happen when salt is sprinkled on an ice cube that has a piece of string lying across it?

Science Background: The **freezing point** of a liquid is the temperature at which it freezes. The **melting point** of a solid is the temperature at which it melts. The freezing point of pure water is 32°F (0°C), the same as the melting point of pure ice. When salt is sprinkled on the ice cube, its melting point is lowered. Thus, the ice melts a little where the salt hits it, forming a small pool of water. This water soon refreezes around the string as the salt is diluted by the melted water. As a result, the string becomes attached to the ice cube.

Teaching Procedure:

1. Post the laminated graph chart at the front of the class. Label the top of the graph "Presto Change-O."

2. Have each group cover its work area with newspaper. Distribute an investigation sheet and an ice cube icon to each student.

3. Show students the materials to be used in the experiment. Read aloud the question on the investigation sheet. Refer students to the picture of the experiment on the sheet and briefly explain how the experiment will be set up. Answer any questions students might have about the procedure.

4. Distribute a plastic cup filled with cold water, an ice cube, and a 10-cm length of string to each group. Have students place the ice cube in the cup of water and lay the piece of string over the ice cube.

5. Have students select an answer to the question posed on the investigation sheet about what they think will happen when they sprinkle salt over the ice cube. Tell them to record their answer both on the sheet and on the ice cube icon. Collect the icons and use them to create a class graph as shown.

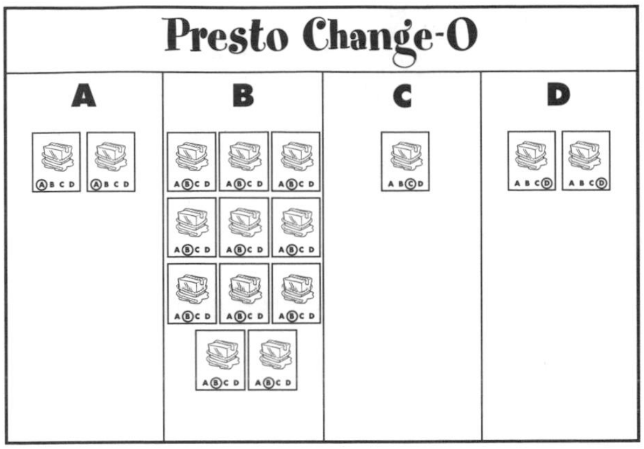

Presto Change-O

6. Have students sprinkle salt over the ice cube, wait a few seconds, and then tug on the piece of string. (The string should be stuck to the cube.) Instruct them to record their observations on the investigation sheet.

7. Discuss with students what they observed. Encourage them to offer an explanation for why the string stuck to the ice cube after salt was sprinkled on the ice. Once the class has had a chance to discuss their theories, introduce the idea that the salt lowered the melting point of the ice, so some of it melted. It then refroze as the salt became diluted. The string stuck to the cube as the water around it refroze.

8. Have students answer the conclusion question on the investigation sheet. Finally, have them draw a picture of the experiment on the back of the sheet. Encourage them to label their drawing and provide a caption that explains what happened in the experiment.

Try this for fun:

Try the experiment again using objects other than string. Which ones stick to the ice cube?

Presto Change-O

Question

What do you think will happen when salt is sprinkled on an ice cube that has a piece of string lying across it?

The ice cube and string will _____.

    A disappear

    B do nothing

    C freeze together

    D sink

Procedure and Observations

1. Place an ice cube in your cup of water. Lay a piece of string across the ice cube.

2. Sprinkle salt on the ice cube and then count to 10. Pull lightly on the string. What do you notice?

_____

_____

Conclusion

How can you explain what happened in the experiment?

_____

_____

_____

On the back of this sheet, draw a picture showing what happened in your experiment. Label your drawing and write a sentence that describes what it is showing.

A B C D   A B C D   A B C D   A B C D

A B C D   A B C D   A B C D   A B C D

A B C D   A B C D   A B C D   A B C D

A B C D   A B C D   A B C D   A B C D

53

Materials:

- laminated graph chart
- page 220, reproduced for each student
- page 221, reproduced, one icon for each student
- clear glass jar, heat-proof with cap
- hot plate
- oven mitt
- ice cube
- water

Water Magic

Objective: Students will recognize that air pressure affects boiling point.

Question: What will happen to a jar of just-boiled water when the jar is capped and an ice cube is placed on top?

Science Background: A liquid's **boiling point** is the temperature at which it boils. The boiling point of pure water is 212°F (100°C). **Air pressure** pushing downward acts to keep water from boiling. As the air pressure above a body of water increases, its boiling point increases. Conversely, as the air pressure above water decreases, so does its boiling point.

When water is boiled in an open heat-proof jar, the water vapor escapes out the top of the jar. When the jar is capped, water vapor is trapped in the space above the water and below the cap. When an ice cube is set on top of the cap, the ice cools the water vapor in the jar, causing it to condense. As the water vapor condenses, the pressure inside the jar decreases, and the water begins to boil again. Even though the temperature of the water is lower than 212°F, the pressure above the water is also lower, so the water boils.

Teaching Procedure:

1. Post the laminated graph chart at the front of the class. Label the top of the graph "Water Magic."

2. Perform this experiment as a demonstration for the class.

3. Distribute an investigation sheet and an ice cube icon to each student.

4. Show students the materials to be used in the experiment. Read aloud the question on the investigation sheet. Refer students to the picture of the experiment on the sheet and briefly explain how the experiment will be set up. Answer any questions students might have about the procedure.

5. Fill the heat-proof jar halfway with water and place it on the hot plate. Turn on the heat and allow the water to boil for one minute.

6. Have students select an answer to the question posed on the investigation sheet about what they think will happen when you take the jar off the heat, put its cap on, and place an ice cube on the cap. Tell them to record their answer both on the sheet and on the ice cube icon. Collect the icons and use them to create a class graph as shown.

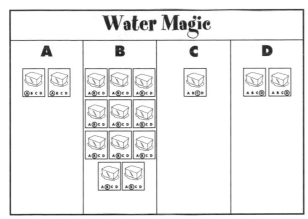

7. Put on the oven mitt and take the jar off the heat. Have students note that the water has stopped boiling. Immediately place the cap on the jar. Now set an ice cube on top of the cap. Have students observe and record what happens next. (The water will begin to boil again.)

8. Discuss with students what they observed. Encourage them to offer an explanation for why the water started boiling again after the ice cube was placed on top of the jar. Once the class has had a chance to discuss their theories, introduce the idea that boiling point is the temperature at which a liquid boils, and that the boiling point of pure water is 212°F (100°C). Add that boiling point is affected by air pressure. When you removed the jar of water from the heat, its temperature dropped and it stopped boiling. But when you capped the jar and set the ice cube on it, the coldness condensed the water vapor inside the jar, and lowered the air pressure above the water. As the air pressure decreased, so did the boiling point of the water. So the water started boiling again, even though it was lower than 212°F.

9. Have students answer the conclusion question on the investigation sheet. Finally, have them draw a picture of the experiment on the back of the sheet. Encourage them to label their drawing and provide a caption that explains what happened in the experiment.

Try this for fun:

Remove the ice cube and have students watch as the water stops boiling. Then replace the cube and have them watch as the water begins to boil again. This may be repeated several times.

Name _____

Water Magic

Question

What do you think will happen to the jar of boiling water when it is removed from the heat, capped, and topped with an ice cube?

The water in the jar will _____.

    A freeze

    B crack the jar

    C evaporate

    D begin to boil again

Procedure and Observations

1. Watch as your teacher places the jar of water on the hot plate and brings the water to a boil.

2. Watch as your teacher removes the jar from the heat, caps it, and places an ice cube on top. What happens to the water in the jar?

_____

_____

Conclusion

How can you explain what happened to the water in the jar?

_____

_____

_____

On the back of this sheet, draw a picture showing what happened in your experiment. Label your drawing and write a sentence that describes what it is showing.

    How to Do Science Experiments with Children • EMC 5001 • ©2003 by Evan-Moor Corp.

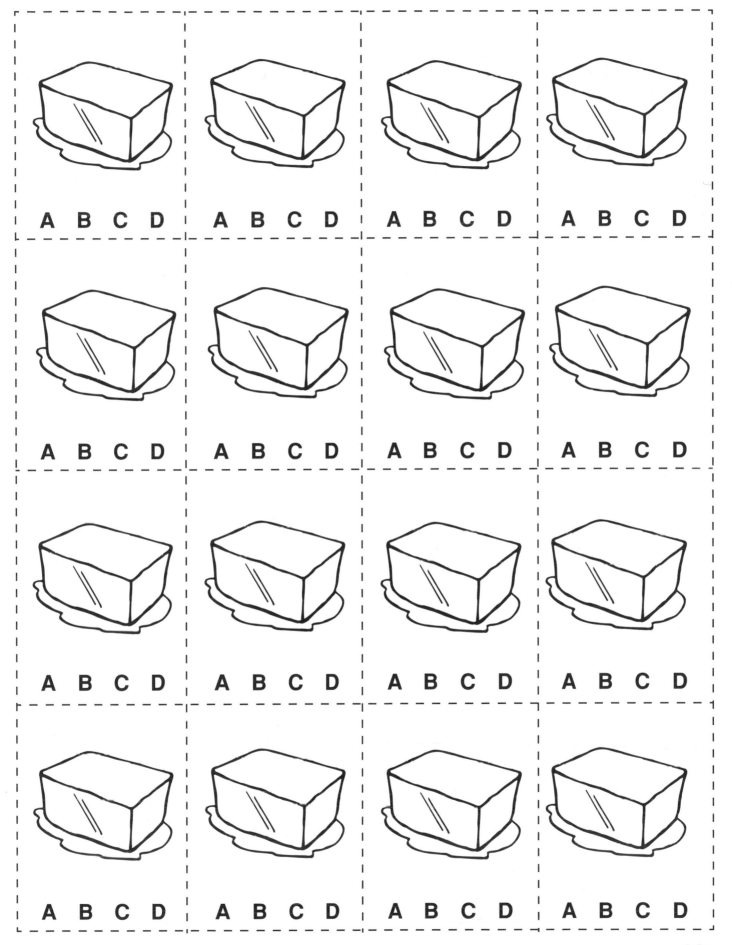

A B C D   A B C D   A B C D   A B C D

A B C D   A B C D   A B C D   A B C D

A B C D   A B C D   A B C D   A B C D

A B C D   A B C D   A B C D   A B C D

54

Materials:

- laminated graph chart
- page 224, reproduced for each student
- page 225, reproduced, one icon for each student
- cauldron or large pot
- dry ice
- plate
- tongs
- oven mitt
- water

Mystery Brew

Objective: Students will recognize that matter can change directly from a solid to a gas.

Question: What will happen when dry ice is placed in a cauldron of water?

Science Background: Matter exists in one of three **states**—solid, liquid, or gas. Substances typically change from one state to the next as heat is added or removed from the substance. Thus, ice melts when warmed (solid to liquid), and water boils when heated on a stove (liquid to gas). Likewise, water vapor condenses (gas to liquid) and liquid water freezes (liquid to solid) when cooled.

Dry ice is not ice at all. Rather, it is carbon dioxide (CO_2) in a solid state. Unlike ice made from water, which melts at 32°F, dry ice must be kept below –110°F in order to stay a solid. Dry ice is also unique in that it exists only very briefly in a liquid state, moving almost immediately from a solid state to a gaseous state. When chunks of dry ice are placed in a pot of water, heat from the water is transferred to the "ice," warming it and causing it to change to a gas. The effect is dramatic: steam rises from the pot without ever having heated the water.

Teaching Procedure:

1. Post the laminated graph chart at the front of the class. Label the top of the graph "Mystery Brew."

2. Perform this experiment as a demonstration for the class. **Warn students that they must never touch dry ice, as it can "burn" their skin.**

3. Distribute an investigation sheet and a cauldron icon to each student.

4. Show students the materials to be used in the experiment. Read aloud the question on the investigation sheet. Refer students to the picture of the experiment on the sheet and briefly explain how the experiment will be set up. Answer any questions students might have about the procedure.

5. Use tongs to place a chunk of dry ice on a plate. Use the oven mitt to carry the plate of dry ice around the room for students to see. **Do not allow students to touch the ice.** Also show students the cauldron of water.

6. Have students select an answer to the question posed on the investigation sheet about what they think will happen when you place the dry ice in the cauldron of water. Tell them to record their answer both on the sheet and on the cauldron icon. Collect the icons and use them to create a class graph as shown.

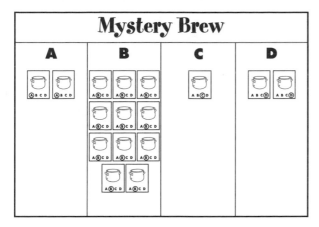

7. Use the tongs to place several pieces of dry ice in the cauldron of water. Have students observe and record what happens. (Lots of steam will rise up from the cauldron.)

8. Discuss with students what they observed. Encourage them to offer an explanation for why the cauldron produced steam even though you didn't heat it. Once the class has had a chance to discuss their theories, introduce the idea that dry ice is not really ice. It isn't frozen water; it's frozen carbon dioxide (CO_2). Because dry ice is so cold, it doesn't take much heat (only that contained in room temperature water) to make the dry ice change from a solid to a gaseous state. The steam students saw was the dry ice in its gaseous form. It passed through its liquid state so quickly that they couldn't even see it!

9. Have students answer the conclusion question on the investigation sheet. Finally, have them draw a picture of the experiment on the back of the sheet. Encourage them to label their drawing and provide a caption that explains what happened in the experiment.

Try this for fun:

Have students place a chunk of regular ice (H_2O) on one plate and a chunk of dry ice (CO_2) on another and compare how the two different ices "melt."

Mystery Brew

Question

What do you think will happen when the dry ice is placed in the cauldron of water?

    A Nothing will happen.

    B The dry ice will explode.

    C A spooky fog will form over the cauldron.

    D The water will change color.

Procedure and Observations

1. Observe the dry ice, but don't touch it!

2. Watch as your teacher places the dry ice in the water. What happens?

_____

_____

_____

Conclusion

How can you explain what happened to the dry ice?

_____

_____

_____

_____

On the back of this sheet, draw a picture showing what happened in your experiment. Label your drawing and write a sentence that describes what it is showing.

55

Materials:

- laminated graph chart
- page 228, reproduced for each student
- page 229, reproduced, one icon for each student
- plastic cups
- hot water
- cold water
- bouillon cubes
- newspaper

Hot Bath-Cold Bath

Objective: Students will recognize that solubility is affected by temperature.

Question: Will a bouillon cube dissolve more quickly in a cup of cold water or a cup of hot water?

Science Background: Solubility, the ability to dissolve in another substance, is a physical property of matter. The **solute** is the material that is dissolved into another substance. The **solvent** is the substance into which the solute dissolves. Together, the solute and solvent form a **solution**. Generally speaking, solutes are solids and solvents are liquids. Solutions are usually liquid but can also be gases (air) or solids (steel). Many substances are soluble in water. Hence, water is known as the "universal solvent."

Solubility is affected by the temperature of the solvent. In most cases, solubility increases with temperature. Consider two bouillon cubes: one in a cup of hot water and the other in a cup of cold water. Thermal energy in the hot water acts to break apart the bouillon cube and separate its individual particles, moving them into solution. Particles of cold water move around less, and so are less able to break up the bouillon cube. Thus, a bouillon cube will dissolve faster in hot water than in cold water.

Teaching Procedure:

1. Post the laminated graph chart at the front of the class. Label the top of the graph "Hot Bath–Cold Bath."

2. Have each group cover its work area with newspaper. Distribute an investigation sheet and a bouillon cube icon to each student.

3. Show students the materials to be used in the experiment. Read aloud the question at the top of the investigation sheet. Refer students to the picture of the experiment on the sheet and briefly explain how the experiment will be set up. Answer any questions students might have about the procedure.

4. Have students select an answer to the question posed on the investigation sheet about whether they think the bouillon cube will dissolve more quickly in hot or in cold water. Tell them to record their answer both on the sheet and on the bouillon cube icon. Collect the icons and use them to create a class graph as shown.

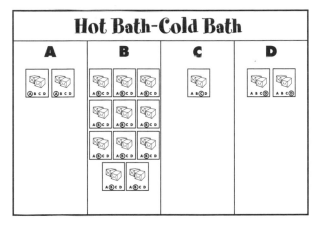

5. Distribute a cup of hot water (not too hot), a cup of cold water, and two bouillon cubes to each group. Have students place one cube in each cup and let them sit. After one minute, have students gently swirl their cups. What do they notice about the bouillon cubes? (The cube in the hot water will have mostly dissolved. The cube in the cold water will have hardly dissolved at all.) Have students record their observations on the investigation sheet.

6. Discuss with students what they observed. Encourage them to offer an explanation for why the bouillon cube dissolved more quickly in the hot water than in the cold water. Once the class has had a chance to discuss their theories, introduce the idea that the particles of hot water have more energy and therefore move around more quickly than the particles of cold water. As the hot water particles move around and bump into the bouillon cube, they help to break it apart. Thus, the cube in hot water disintegrates and goes into solution more quickly than the cube in cold water.

7. Have students answer the conclusion question on the investigation sheet. Finally, have them draw a picture of the experiment on the back of the sheet. Encourage them to label their drawing and provide a caption that explains what happened in the experiment.

Try this for fun:

Have students try the experiment again, this time with sugar cubes. (Results will be similar.)

Hot Bath-Cold Bath

Question

Do you think a bouillon cube will dissolve faster in a cup of cold water or in a cup of hot water?

A The bouillon cube will dissolve faster in the cold water.

B The bouillon cube will dissolve faster in the hot water.

C The bouillon cube will dissolve at the same speed in both cups.

D The bouillon cube will not dissolve in either cup.

Procedure and Observations

1. Place one bouillon cube in the cup of cold water. Place the other bouillon cube in the cup of hot water. Leave the cups alone for one minute.

2. Observe the cube in each cup. Gently swirl the water in each cup. What do you notice?

_____

_____

Conclusion

How can you explain what happened in this experiment?

_____

_____

_____

On the back of this sheet, draw a picture showing what happened in your experiment. Label your drawing and write a sentence that describes what it is showing.

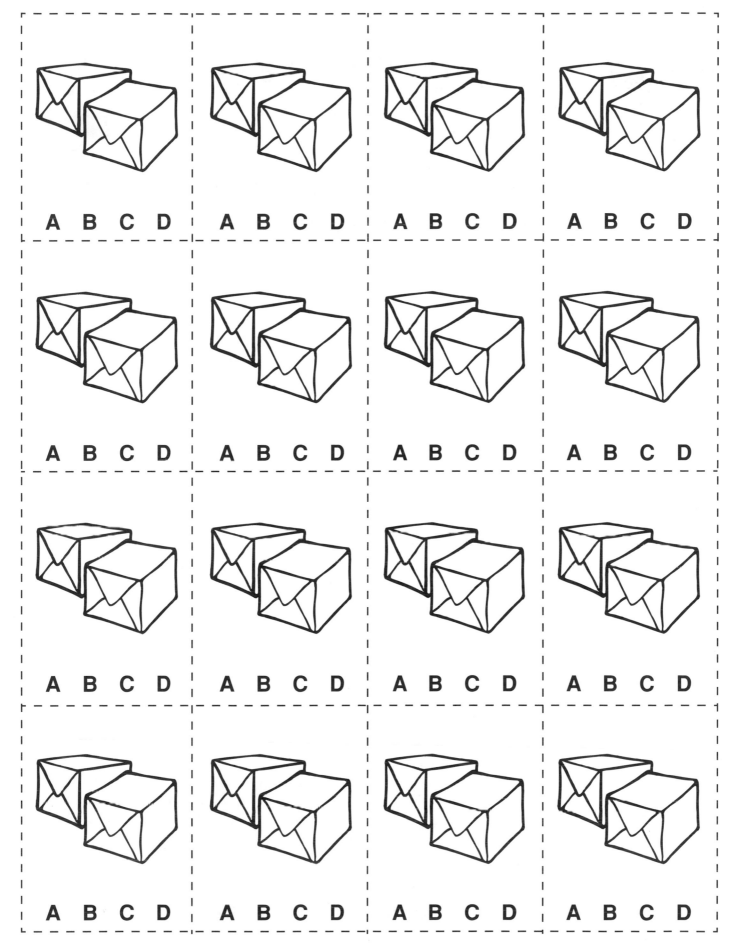

A B C D   A B C D   A B C D   A B C D

A B C D   A B C D   A B C D   A B C D

A B C D   A B C D   A B C D   A B C D

A B C D   A B C D   A B C D   A B C D

56

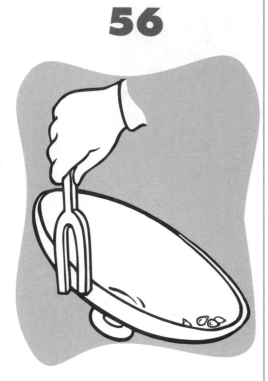

Materials:

- laminated graph chart
- page 232, reproduced for each student
- page 233, reproduced, one icon for each student
- metal pot lids
- popcorn kernels
- tuning forks

Crazy Kernels

Objective: Students will demonstrate that sound is produced by vibrations.

Question: What will happen to popcorn kernels inside a metal lid when the lid is touched by a vibrating tuning fork?

Science Background: All sound is created by vibration. As an object (such as a radio speaker) vibrates, it pushes the air particles around it in pulses, forming areas where the air particles are closer together (compressions) and areas where they are farther apart (rarefactions). These compressions and rarefactions move away from the vibrating object in all directions. When they enter our ears, they cause our eardrums to vibrate. Electrical signals are sent from our eardrums to our brain, where the vibrations are interpreted as sounds.

A tuning fork produces sound as it is struck and begins to vibrate. The vibrating motion of the tuning fork is not always obvious to students, but can be made more obvious by touching the fork to a metal surface on which small, light objects are resting. The vibrations of the fork will travel through the metal and cause the objects to start bouncing.

Teaching Procedure:

1. Post the laminated graph chart at the front of the class. Label the top of the graph "Crazy Kernels."

2. Distribute an investigation sheet and a crazy kernel icon to each student.

3. Show students the materials to be used in the experiment. Read aloud the question on the investigation sheet. Refer students to the picture of the experiment on the sheet and briefly explain how the experiment will be set up. Answer any questions students might have about the procedure.

4. Distribute a tuning fork to each group. Show students how to strike the fork on the palms of their hands to get it humming. Have students note the sound the fork makes. Tell students to record their observations on the investigation sheet.

5. Now have students select an answer to the question posed on the investigation sheet about what they think will happen when they strike the tuning fork and then touch it to a metal lid with popcorn kernels inside. Tell them to record their answer both on the sheet and on the crazy kernel icon. Collect the icons and use them to create a class graph as shown.

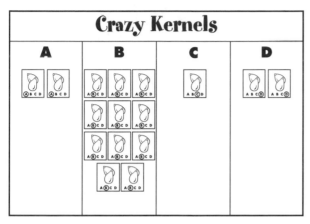

6. Distribute a metal lid and a handful of popcorn kernels to each group. Have students place the kernels in the inverted pot lid. Then have them strike the tuning fork as before and touch it to the inside of the lid. What happens? (The kernels begin to hop and dance.) Have students record their observations on the investigation sheet.

7. Discuss with students what they observed. Encourage them to offer an explanation for why the kernels began to dance when the lid was touched with the tuning fork. Once the class has had a chance to discuss their theories, introduce the idea that the tuning fork began to vibrate when they struck it. These vibrations were transferred to the lid and then the kernels when the tuning fork touched the lid. Point out to students that vibrations create sounds. We hear the humming of the tuning fork as it vibrates and causes the air around it to vibrate. When the vibrating air reaches our ears, we hear sound.

8. Have students answer the conclusion question on the investigation sheet. Finally, have them draw a picture of the experiment on the back of the sheet. Encourage them to label their drawing and provide a caption that explains what happened in the experiment.

Try this for fun:

Try the experiment again using rice grains on a drum. Touch the tuning fork to the drum head and watch the rice grains dance!

Name _____

Crazy Kernels

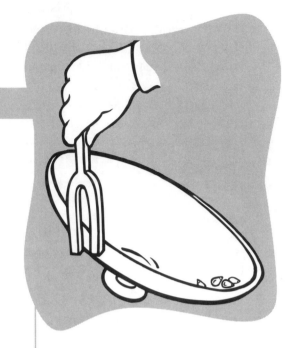

Question

What do you think will happen to popcorn kernels inside a metal lid when the lid is touched by the vibrating tuning fork?

The popcorn kernels will _____.

    A dance

    B do nothing

    C pop into white puffs

    D change color

Procedure and Observations

1. Strike the tuning fork against your palm. What do you hear?

_____

_____

2. Strike the tuning fork against your palm again. Now touch it to the lid with the kernels inside. What happens to the kernels?

_____

_____

Conclusion

How can you explain what happened to the kernels?

_____

_____

_____

On the back of this sheet, draw a picture showing what happened in your experiment. Label your drawing and write a sentence that describes what it is showing.

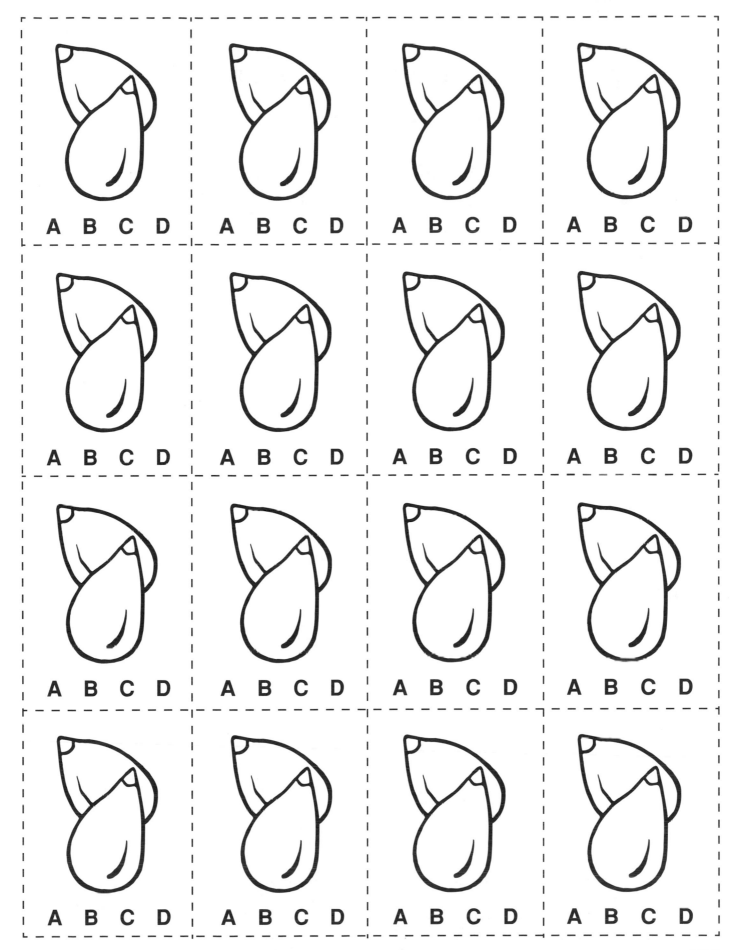

57

Materials:

- laminated graph chart
- page 236, reproduced for each student
- page 237, reproduced, one icon for each student

A Real Humdinger

Objective: Students will demonstrate that vocal sounds are produced when air passes over and vibrates the vocal cords.

Question: How can you stop a friend from humming?

Science Background: All sound is created by vibration. As an object vibrates, it pushes the air particles around it in pulses, forming areas where the air particles are closer together (compressions) and areas where they are farther apart (rarefactions). These compressions and rarefactions move away from the vibrating object in all directions. When they enter our ears, they cause our eardrums to vibrate. Electrical signals are sent from our eardrums to our brain, where the vibrations are interpreted as sounds.

Vocalizations are also produced by vibrations. Air moving up from the lungs passes over the vocal cords at the top of the windpipe, causing them to vibrate and create the sounds we make as we talk, sing, and laugh. Humming is achieved by moving air up through the lungs, over the vocal cords, and out the nose. (The mouth is closed.) If the nose is plugged, the air cannot flow up and over the vocal cords, and no sound can be produced.

Teaching Procedure:

1. Post the laminated graph chart at the front of the class. Label the top of the graph "A Real Humdinger."

2. Distribute an investigation sheet and a musical note icon to each student. Read aloud the question on the investigation sheet. Answer any questions students might have about the procedure.

3. Invite students to start humming. Tell them that in this experiment, you'd like them to hum with their mouth closed. Demonstrate how, if necessary.

4. Instruct students to place their fingers on their throat as they hum and note what they feel. (They will feel their vocal cords vibrating.) Have students record their observations on the investigation sheet.

5. Now have students select an answer to the question posed on the investigation sheet about how they think they can prevent a friend from humming. Tell them to record their answer both on the sheet and on the musical note icon. Collect the icons and use them to create a class graph as shown.

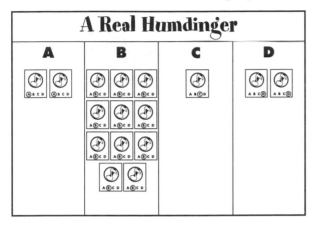

6. Have students pick a partner and try each of the suggestions on the investigation sheet for how to make him or her stop humming. (Gently pinching the person's nose shut will stop the humming as long as the hummer's mouth is also closed.) Have students record the method that worked.

7. Discuss with students what they observed. Encourage them to offer an explanation for why gently pinching their partner's nose shut stopped the humming. Once the class has had a chance to discuss their theories, introduce the idea that vibrations of the vocal cords produced the humming sound. The vocal cords vibrate as air moves up from the lungs and passes over them. By gently pinching the hummer's nose shut, students were preventing the movement of air from the lungs out through the nose. Since the hummer's mouth was also closed, air could not flow. Without airflow, no vibration occurred and no sound was produced.

8. Have students answer the conclusion question on the investigation sheet. Finally, have them draw a picture of the experiment on the back of the sheet. Encourage them to label their drawing and provide a caption that explains what happened in the experiment.

Try this for fun:

Have students try to stop themselves from singing by holding their hands over their mouth. What happens? (Sound is still produced, although it is muffled. That's because even with the mouth covered, air can still move up from the lungs, over the vocal cords, and out the nose. As long as air has a place to exit, it can vibrate the vocal cords and produce sound.)

Name _____

A Real Humdinger

Question

How do you think you can stop a friend from humming?

    A by gently covering his or her eyes

    B by gently covering his or her mouth

    C by gently pinching his or her nose shut

    D by gently covering his or her ears

Procedure and Observations

1. Hum a little tune with your mouth closed. Place your fingers on your throat as you hum. What do you feel?

_____

_____

2. Try each of the four ideas above. Which one worked?

_____

_____

Conclusion

How can you explain why your partner stopped humming?

_____

_____

_____

On the back of this sheet, draw a picture showing what happened in your experiment. Label your drawing and write a sentence that describes what it is showing.

    How to Do Science Experiments with Children • EMC 5001 • ©2003 by Evan-Moor Corp.

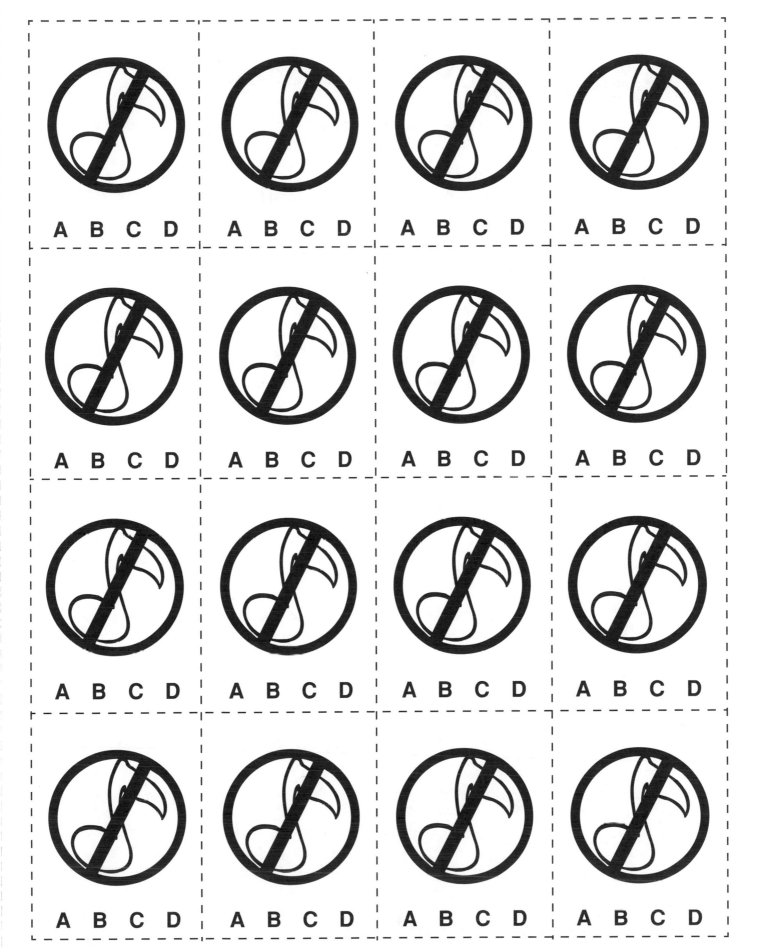

58

Materials:

- laminated graph chart
- page 240, reproduced for each student
- page 241, reproduced, one icon for each student
- pencils

A Scratching Sound

Objective: Students will demonstrate that vibrations travel better through some mediums than through others.

Question: What will you hear when you hold the end of a pencil between your teeth and then scratch it?

Science Background: All sound is created by vibration. As an object (such as a radio speaker) vibrates, it pushes the air particles around it in pulses, forming areas where the air particles are closer together (compressions) and areas where they are farther apart (rarefactions). These compressions and rarefactions move away from the vibrating object in all directions. When they enter our ears, they cause our eardrums to vibrate. Electrical signals are sent from our eardrums to our brain, where the vibrations are interpreted as sounds.

But vibrations don't travel just through air. They can also travel through solid objects, creating compressions and rarefactions of the particles that make up the solid. (Note that vibrations also travel through liquids.) And because the particles in a solid object are so much closer together than the particles in a gas, sound actually travels faster through solids than it does through air.

When a solid object like a pencil is held between the teeth and is then scratched, the vibrations travel through the pencil and into the teeth and head of the person holding the pencil. The sound actually seems louder and more resonant than if it had been received through the air. That's because the person's whole head—and not just their eardrums—is vibrating.

Teaching Procedure:

1. Post the laminated graph chart at the front of the class. Label the top of the graph "A Scratching Sound."

2. Distribute an investigation sheet and a mouth icon to each student.

3. Read aloud the question on the investigation sheet. Refer students to the picture of the experiment on the sheet and briefly explain how the experiment will be set up. Answer any questions students might have about the procedure.

4. Distribute a pencil to each student. Have them hold the pencil in one hand and scratch it with the other. What do they hear? (a very faint scratching sound) Have them record their observations on the investigation sheet.

5. Now have students select an answer to the question posed on the investigation sheet about what they think they will hear when they hold their pencil between their teeth and scratch it. Tell them to record the answer both on the sheet and on the mouth icon. Collect the icons and use them to create a class graph as shown.

A Scratching Sound

6. Have students place the eraser end of the pencil between their teeth and scratch the pencil like before. What do they notice? (The scratching sound is much louder this time.) Have students record their observations on the investigation sheet.

7. Discuss with students what they observed. Encourage them to offer an explanation for why the scratching sound was so much louder when they held the pencil between their teeth. Once the class has had a chance to discuss their theories, introduce the idea that when they held the pencil in their hand and scratched it, the vibrations traveled through the air to their ears. But when they held the pencil between their teeth, the vibrations traveled along the pencil and into their teeth and head. Point out that because their whole head felt the vibrations, not just their eardrums, the sound seemed louder.

8. Have students answer the conclusion question on the investigation sheet. Finally, have them draw a picture of the experiment on the back of the sheet. Encourage them to label their drawing and provide a caption that explains what happened in the experiment.

Try this for fun:

Have students try the experiment again, this time holding the pencil between their lips rather than their teeth. What do they notice? (The sound won't be as loud or as resonant as it was when the pencil was held between the teeth.) Explain that vibrations travel better through rigid objects (like teeth) than through soft objects (like lips).

Name _____

A Scratching Sound

Question

What do you think you will hear when you hold the pencil between your teeth and scratch it?

I will hear _____.

    A nothing

    B a softer scratching sound

    C a louder scratching sound

    D a loud popping sound

Procedure and Observations

1. Hold the pencil in one hand and scratch it with the other. What do you hear?

_____

_____

2. Hold the eraser end of the pencil between your teeth and scratch it like before. What do you hear?

_____

_____

Conclusion

How can you explain the difference between what you heard when you held the pencil in your teeth, and what you heard when you held it in your hand?

_____

_____

_____

On the back of this sheet, draw a picture showing what happened in your experiment. Label your drawing and write a sentence that describes what it is showing.

 How to Do Science Experiments with Children • EMC 5001 • ©2003 by Evan-Moor Corp.

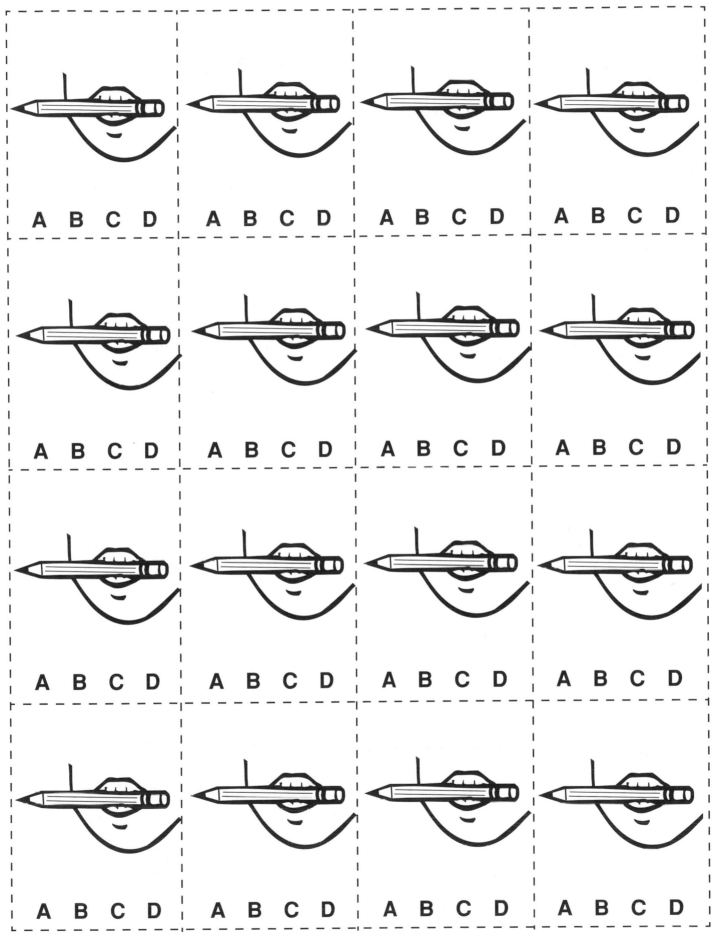

59

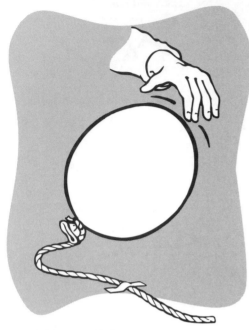

Materials:

- laminated graph chart
- page 244, reproduced for each student
- page 245, reproduced, one icon for each student
- string
- tape
- balloons

"I Get a Charge Out of You"

Objective: Students will demonstrate that objects can pick up static charges that make them either repellent or attractive to other objects.

Question: What will happen when you rub a balloon against your hair, and then move your hand near the balloon?

Science Background: Matter is made up of atoms. Atoms consist of a positively charged center of protons surrounded by negatively charged clouds of electrons. Most atoms are neutrally charged, as the number of protons equals the number of electrons.

Objects can become **electrically charged** (obtain an overall positive or negative charge) when they are rubbed together and the electrons from one object are transferred to the other. (Some objects lose electrons more readily than others.) The object that loses electrons becomes positively charged. The object that gains electrons becomes negatively charged.

When a balloon is rubbed against a student's hair, electrons from the hair are transferred to the balloon. This surplus of electrons gives the balloon an overall negative charge. This negative charge induces a positive charge in the student's approaching hand as electrons move away from the balloon. Since unlike charges attract, the balloon will move toward the student's hand.

Teaching Procedure:

1. Perform this activity on a cold, dry day, as humidity interferes with the transfer of electrons.

2. Post the laminated graph chart at the front of the class. Label the top of the graph "I Get a Charge Out of You."

3. Distribute an investigation sheet and a balloon icon to each student.

4. Show students the materials to be used in the experiment. Read aloud the question at the top of the investigation sheet. Refer students to the picture of the experiment on the sheet and briefly explain how the experiment will be set up. Answer any questions students might have about the procedure.

5. Have students select an answer to the question posed on the

investigation sheet about what they think will happen when they rub the balloon against their hair, and then hold their hand near the balloon. Tell them to record their answer both on the sheet and on the balloon icon. Collect the icons and use them to create a class graph as shown.

"I Get a Charge Out of You"

6. Distribute an inflated balloon, a 15-cm piece of string, and a piece of tape to each group. Tell students to tie the end of the string to the neck of the balloon as shown in the picture on the investigation sheet.

7. Have students rub the balloon against their hair for several seconds and then tape the free end of the string to their desk. Instruct students to move their hand near the balloon without touching it. What happens? (The balloon will move toward their hand.) Have students record their observations.

8. Discuss with students what they observed. Encourage them to offer an explanation for why the balloon moved toward their hand. Once the class has had a chance to discuss their theories, introduce the idea that rubbing the balloon against their hair gave the balloon a negative electric (or static) charge. As their hands moved toward the balloon, positive charges in their hands were attracted to the negatively charged balloon.

9. Have students answer the conclusion question on the investigation sheet. Finally, have them draw a picture of the experiment on the back of the sheet. Encourage them to label their drawing and provide a caption that explains what happened in the experiment.

Try this for fun:

Have students find out what happens when their hand touches the balloon. (The built-up charges on the balloon move to their hand. This action, known as static discharge, may produce a small shock. Once the charges have discharged, the balloon will no longer be attracted to their hand unless it is recharged by rubbing against their hair again.)

"I Get a Charge Out of You"

Question

What do you think will happen when you rub a balloon against your hair, and then move your hand near the balloon?

The balloon will _____.

    A pop

    B move away from my hand

    C move toward my hand

    D do nothing

Procedure and Observations

1. Tie one end of the string around the neck of the balloon. Rub the balloon against your hair. Now tape the free end of the string to your desk.

2. Move your hand near the balloon, but don't touch it. What happens?

_____

_____

_____

Conclusion

How can you explain what happened in the experiment?

_____

_____

_____

On the back of this sheet, draw a picture showing what happened in your experiment. Label your drawing and write a sentence that describes what it is showing.

How to Do Science Experiments with Children • EMC 5001 • ©2003 by Evan-Moor Corp.

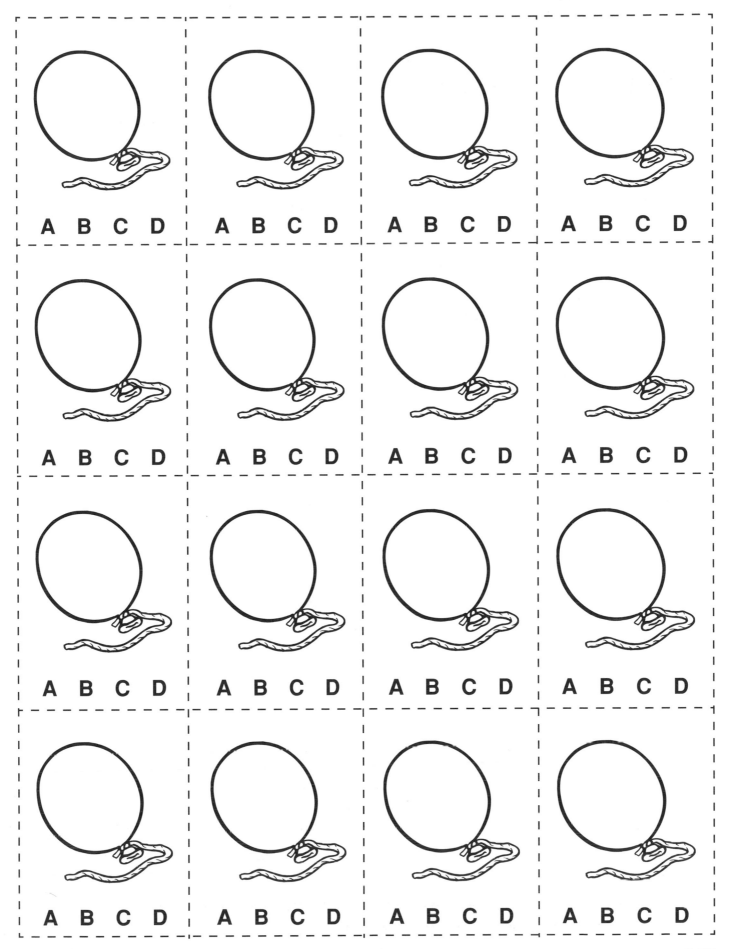

60

Materials:

- laminated graph chart
- page 248, reproduced for each student
- page 249, reproduced, one icon for each student
- tissue paper
- cardboard
- scissors
- glue
- balloons

Springtime Science

Objective: Students will demonstrate that objects can pick up static charges that make them either repellent or attractive to other objects.

Question: What will happen to the wings of a paper butterfly when a charged balloon is held near the butterfly and then moved up and down?

Science Background: Matter is made up of atoms. Atoms consist of a positively charged center of protons surrounded by negatively charged clouds of electrons. Most atoms are neutrally charged, as the number of protons equal the number of electrons. However, objects can become **electrically charged** when they are rubbed together and the electrons from one object are transferred to the other. The object that loses electrons becomes positively charged. The object that gains electrons becomes negatively charged.

When a balloon is rubbed against a student's hair, electrons from the hair are transferred to the balloon, giving the balloon an overall negative charge. When the balloon is held near the wings of a paper butterfly, the negative charge of the balloon induces a positive charge in the butterfly wings, as electrons in the wings move away from the balloon. This leaves a surplus of positive charges on the part of the wing closest to the balloon. Because unlike charges attract, the wings lift up toward the balloon. As the balloon is pulled away, the charges no longer interact and the wings drop again. If the balloon is moved above the butterfly just right, its wings will appear to be fluttering.

Teaching Procedure:

1. Perform this activity on a cold, dry day, as humidity interferes with the transfer of electrons.

2. Prepare the paper butterflies as follows: Use a large butterfly icon as a template to draw and cut out one tissue paper butterfly for each group. Glue the narrow body of each butterfly to a piece of cardboard. When the body is dry, crease the wings so that they will move freely up and down.

3. Post the laminated graph chart at the front of the class. Label the top of the graph "Springtime Science."

4. Distribute an investigation sheet and a butterfly icon to each student.

5. Show students the materials to be used in the experiment. Read aloud the question at the top of the investigation sheet. Refer students to the picture of the experiment on the sheet and briefly explain how the experiment will be set up. Answer any questions students might have about the procedure.

6. Have students select an answer to the question posed on the investigation sheet about what they think will happen when they bring the charged balloon near the butterfly and then move the balloon up and down. Tell them to record their answer both on the sheet and on the butterfly icon. Collect the icons and use them to create a class graph as shown.

Springtime Science

A	B	C	D

Try this for fun:

Have students try to charge the balloon by rubbing it on objects other than their hair (such as clothing, a wall, etc.).

7. Distribute a prepared butterfly and an inflated balloon to each group. Have students hold the butterfly by the cardboard glued to the body. Tell students to rub the balloon against their hair for several seconds. Then tell them to bring the balloon toward the butterfly and move it away again. What happens? (The butterfly wings flutter as the balloon approaches and moves away.) Have students record their observations.

8. Discuss with students what they observed. Encourage them to offer an explanation for why the butterfly wings fluttered when they brought the charged balloon near the butterfly and moved the balloon up and down. Once the class has had a chance to discuss their theories, introduce the idea that rubbing the balloon against their hair gave the balloon a negative electric (or static) charge. As the butterfly moved toward the balloon, positive charges in the butterfly wings were attracted to the negatively charged balloon. Then the wings fell as the balloon moved away again. These actions made the wings look as though they were "fluttering."

9. Have students answer the conclusion question on the investigation sheet. Finally, have them draw a picture of the experiment on the back of the sheet. Encourage them to label their drawing and provide a caption that explains what happened in the experiment.

Name _____

Springtime Science

What do you think will happen to the wings of a paper butterfly when a charged balloon is held near the butterfly and then moved up and down?

The wings will _____.

    A   do nothing

    B   make a humming sound

    C   move away from the balloon

    D   flutter back and forth

Procedure and Observations

Rub the balloon against your hair. Now hold the balloon just above the butterfly and move it up and down. What happens?

_____

_____

_____

Conclusion

How can you explain what happened to the butterfly wings in the experiment?

_____

_____

_____

On the back of this sheet, draw a picture showing what happened in your experiment. Label your drawing and write a sentence that describes what it is showing.

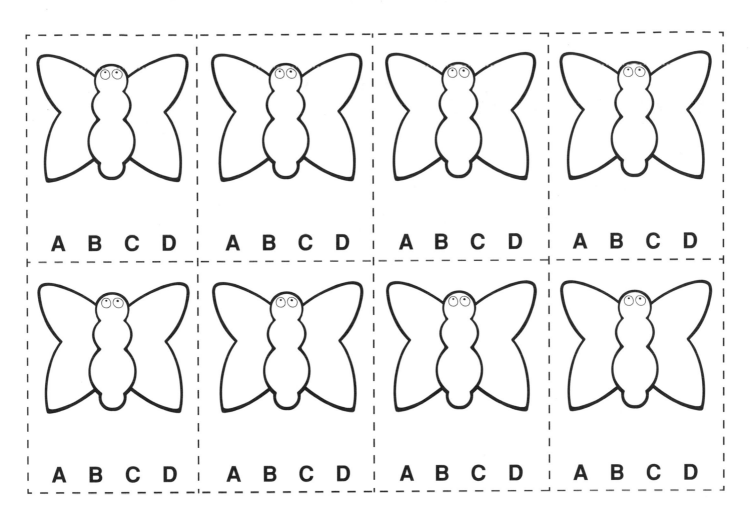

A B C D | A B C D | A B C D | A B C D

A B C D | A B C D | A B C D | A B C D

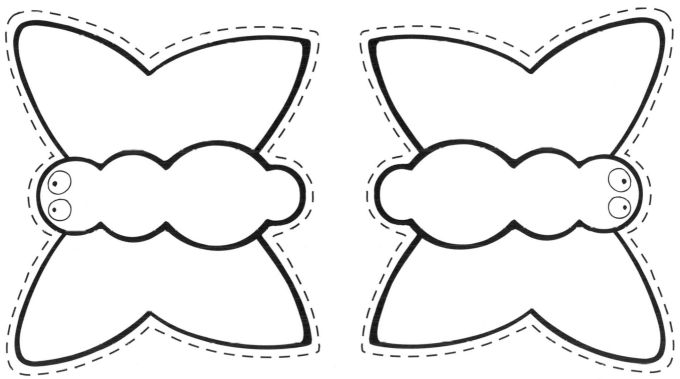

61

Materials:

- laminated graph chart
- page 252, reproduced for each student
- page 253, reproduced, one icon for each student
- string
- tape
- balloons

Balloon Chase

Objective: Students will demonstrate that objects can pick up static charges that make them either repellent or attractive to other objects.

Question: What will happen when you rub two balloons against your hair, then move the balloons close together?

Science Background: Matter is made up of atoms. Atoms consist of a positively charged center of protons surrounded by negatively charged clouds of electrons. Most atoms are neutrally charged, as the number of protons equal the number of electrons.

Objects can become **electrically charged** when they are rubbed together and the electrons from one object are transferred to the other. The object that loses electrons becomes positively charged. The object that gains electrons becomes negatively charged.

When two balloons are rubbed against a student's hair, electrons from the hair are transferred to the balloons. This surplus of electrons gives each balloon an overall negative charge. Since like charges repel, the balloons will move away from each other when you try to bring them together.

Teaching Procedure:

1. Perform this activity on a cold, dry day, as humidity interferes with the transfer of electrons.

2. Post the laminated graph chart at the front of the class. Label the top of the graph "Balloon Chase."

3. Distribute an investigation sheet and a double balloon icon to each student.

4. Show students the materials to be used in the experiment. Read aloud the question at the top of the investigation sheet. Refer students to the picture of the experiment on the sheet and briefly explain how the experiment will be set up. Answer any questions students might have about the procedure.

5. Have students select an answer to the question posed on the investigation sheet about what they think will happen when they rub two balloons against their hair, and then move the balloons near each other. Tell them to record their answer both on the sheet and on the double balloon icon. Collect the icons and use them to create a class graph as shown.

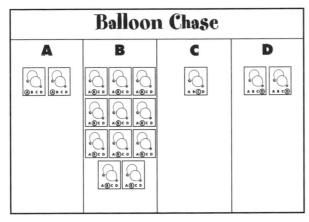

6. Distribute two inflated balloons, a 15-cm piece of string, and a piece of tape to each group. Tell students to tie the end of the string to the neck of one of the balloons.

7. Have students rub both balloons against their hair for several seconds and then tape the balloon with the string to their desk. Instruct students to move the free balloon near the tethered balloon without touching it. What happens? (The tethered balloon moves away from the free balloon every time it comes near.) Have students record their observations.

8. Discuss with students what they observed. Encourage them to offer an explanation for why the tethered balloon moved away. Once the class has had a chance to discuss their theories, introduce the idea that rubbing the balloons against their hair gave both balloons a negative electric (or static) charge. Because like charges repel, the balloons pushed away from each other.

9. Have students answer the conclusion question on the investigation sheet. Finally, have them draw a picture of the experiment on the back of the sheet. Encourage them to label their drawing and provide a caption that explains what happened in the experiment.

Try this for fun:

Have students repeat the experiment by rubbing one of the balloons against a material other than hair. (The balloons will repel or attract each other, depending on what material students choose.)

Balloon Chase

Question

What do you think will happen when you rub two balloons against your hair, then move the balloons close together?

The balloons will _____.

    A pop

    B move toward each other

    C move away from each other

    D do nothing

Procedure and Observations

1. Tie a string to the neck of one of the balloons. Rub both balloons against your hair. Now tape the balloon with the string to your desk.

2. Move the free balloon near the tethered balloon, but don't let them touch. What happens?

_____

_____

_____

Conclusion

How can you explain what happened in the experiment?

_____

_____

_____

On the back of this sheet, draw a picture showing what happened in your experiment. Label your drawing and write a sentence that describes what it is showing.

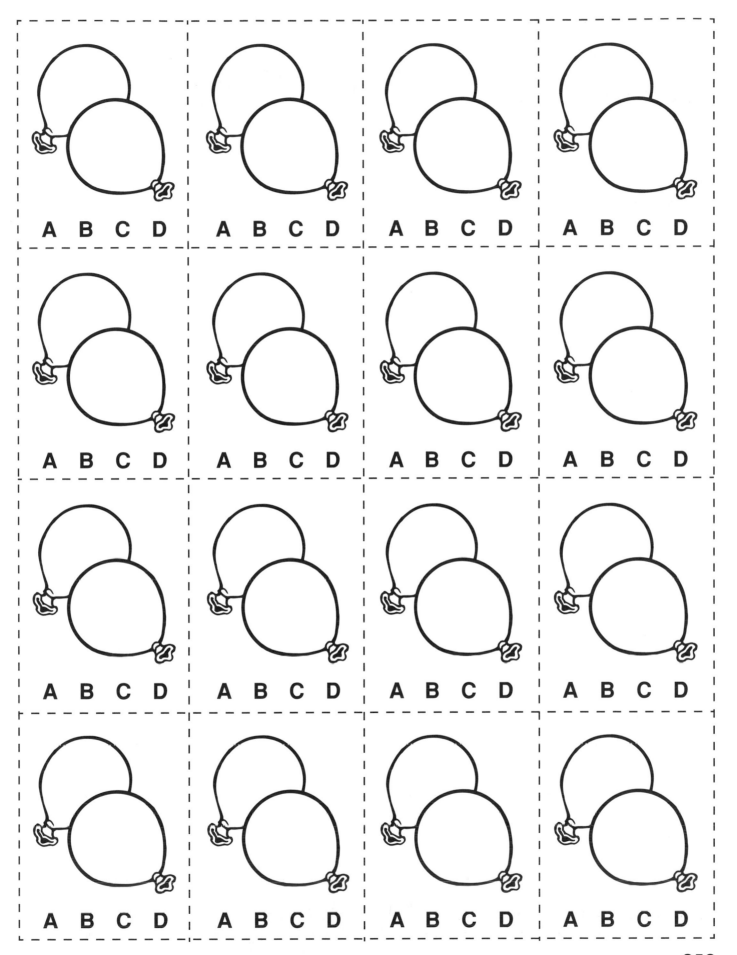

A B C D | A B C D | A B C D | A B C D

A B C D | A B C D | A B C D | A B C D

A B C D | A B C D | A B C D | A B C D

A B C D | A B C D | A B C D | A B C D

62

Materials:

- laminated graph chart

- page 256, reproduced for each student

- page 257, reproduced, one icon for each student

- decks of playing cards (slightly used work best)

House of Cards

Objective: Students will demonstrate that unbalanced forces produce a change in motion.

Question: What will happen to a card house when a card near the middle is removed?

Science Background: A **force** is a push or a pull. A force can set an object in motion or change the speed or direction of a moving object. Objects can exert forces on each other. If the force exerted by one object is equal to the force exerted by the other, the forces will cancel each other out and neither object will move. Forces that produce no change in the motion of an object are said to be **balanced**. However, if the force exerted by one object is greater than the force exerted by the other, the objects will move in the direction of the stronger force. Forces that produce a change in the motion of an object are said to be **unbalanced**.

Card houses rely on carefully balanced forces in order to remain standing. A card house usually starts with two cards positioned in a "tepee" shape. Because the cards exert equal forces on each other (they balance each other out), there is no change in the motion of the cards and they stay put. Several such tepees and other shapes combine to form the structure of the house. But if just one load-bearing card is removed, the forces become unbalanced and the house collapses.

Teaching Procedure:

1. Post the laminated graph chart at the front of the class. Label the top of the graph "House of Cards."

2. Distribute an investigation sheet and a playing cards icon to each student.

3. Show students the playing cards. Read aloud the question at the top of the investigation sheet. Refer students to the picture of the card house on the sheet and briefly explain how the experiment will be set up.

4. Have students select an answer to the question posed on the investigation sheet about what they think will happen when they remove one card from their card house. Tell them to record their answer both on the sheet and on the playing cards icon. Collect the icons and use them to create a class graph as shown.

House of Cards

5. Distribute a deck of playing cards to each group. Show students how to lean two cards against each other to form a sort of tepee shape. Offer help as needed to those who have never built card houses before. (The houses do not need to be elaborate.)

6. Once the houses are completed, have students try to remove one card from the center of their house (i.e., a load-bearing card). What happens? (Most or all of the house collapses.) Have students record their observations on the investigation sheet.

7. Discuss with students what they observed. Encourage them to offer an explanation for why the house collapsed when one card was removed. Once the class has had a chance to discuss their theories, introduce the idea that the leaning cards exerted a force on one another. When these forces were balanced, the cards did not move. But when students removed a card, the forces became unbalanced, making one card, and then other cards, fall.

8. Have students answer the conclusion question on the investigation sheet. Finally, have them draw a picture of the experiment on the back of the sheet. Encourage them to label their drawing and provide a caption that explains what happened in the experiment.

Try this for fun:

Challenge students to build the biggest card houses they can using combinations of four-sided "boxes" and three-sided "tepees."

House of Cards

Question

What do you think will happen to the card house when a card near the middle is removed?

    A The house will not move.

    B The house will collapse.

    C The house will lean to one side.

    D The house will grow higher.

Procedure and Observations

1. Work with your group to make a house out of playing cards.

2. Now remove one card from the middle of the house. What happens?

_____

_____

_____

Conclusion

How can you explain what happened to the house when you removed one card from the middle?

_____

_____

_____

On the back of this sheet, draw a picture showing what happened in your experiment. Label your drawing and write a sentence that describes what it is showing.

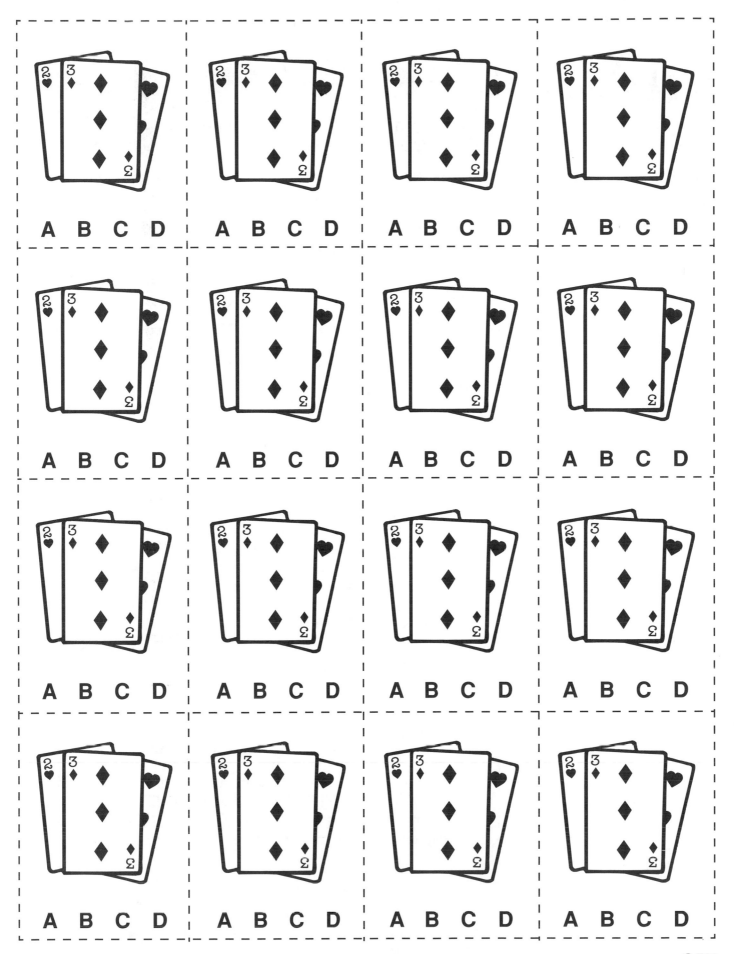

A B C D A B C D A B C D A B C D

A B C D A B C D A B C D A B C D

A B C D A B C D A B C D A B C D

A B C D A B C D A B C D A B C D

63

Balanced and Unbalanced

Grade A Experiment

Objective: Students will demonstrate that balanced forces produce no change in motion.

Question: What will happen to an egg when you squeeze it as hard as you can in one hand?

Science Background: A **force** is a push or a pull. A force can set an object in motion or change the speed or direction of a moving object. Objects can exert forces on each other. If the force exerted by one object is equal to the force exerted by the other, the forces will cancel each other out and neither object will move. Forces that produce no change in the motion of an object are said to be **balanced**. However, if the force exerted by one object is greater than the force exerted by the other, the objects will move in the direction of the stronger force. Forces that produce a change in the motion of an object are said to be **unbalanced**.

Consider an egg in the palm of your hand. You might think that squeezing the egg would cause it to break, but it doesn't. That's because when you squeeze an egg, the force you exert on it is equal to the force it exerts back on you—in other words, the two forces are balanced. How is that possible? An egg's shape gives its shell unusual strength. The oval shape transfers an applied force (such as a squeeze) evenly over the entire surface, enabling the egg to withstand the pressure of the squeeze.

Teaching Procedure:

1. Post the laminated graph chart at the front of the class. Label the top of the graph "Grade A Experiment."

2. Have each group cover its work area with newspaper. Distribute an investigation sheet and a super egg icon to each student.

3. Show students the eggs. Read aloud the question at the top of the investigation sheet. Refer students to the picture of the student holding the egg and briefly explain how the experiment will be set up. Answer any questions students might have about the procedure.

Materials:

- laminated graph chart
- page 260, reproduced for each student
- page 261, reproduced, one icon for each student
- uncooked eggs
- paper towels
- newspaper

4. Have students select an answer to the question posed on the investigation sheet about what they think will happen when they squeeze the egg in their hand. Tell them to record their answer both on the sheet and on the super egg icon. Collect the icons and use them to create a class graph as shown.

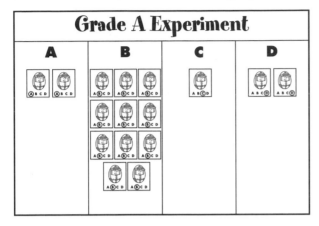

5. Distribute an egg and some paper towels (for accidents) to each group. Before they begin, remind students not to press with their fingertips—just their palms. Also tell them to remove any rings, as the rings may create pressure points that break the shell.

6. Now have students take turns holding the egg in their palm as shown in the picture on the investigation sheet. Tell them to squeeze as hard as they can. What happens? (The egg doesn't break.) Have students record their observations on the investigation sheet.

7. Discuss with students what they observed. Encourage them to offer an explanation for why the egg didn't break no matter how hard they squeezed. Once the class has had a chance to discuss their theories, introduce the idea that the egg exerted a force back on them equal to the force they applied to it with their hand. So the forces were balanced and the egg didn't break. Point out that the egg's special oval shape makes it able to withstand a lot of force.

8. Have students answer the conclusion question on the investigation sheet. Finally, have them draw a picture of the experiment on the back of the sheet. Encourage them to label their drawing and provide a caption that explains what happened in the experiment.

Try this for fun:

Students might think that they are simply not strong enough to break the egg. Squeeze an egg yourself as students watch. Even adult hands can't crush the egg!

Grade A Experiment

Question

What do you think will happen to an egg when you squeeze it as hard as you can in one hand?

The egg will _____.

    A explode

    B crack a little

    C squish like a rubber ball

    D do nothing

Procedure and Observations

Hold the egg in the palm of your hand. Squeeze as hard as you can. What happens?

_____

_____

_____

Conclusion

How can you explain what happened to the egg when you squeezed it?

_____

_____

_____

On the back of this sheet, draw a picture showing what happened in your experiment. Label your drawing and write a sentence that describes what it is showing.

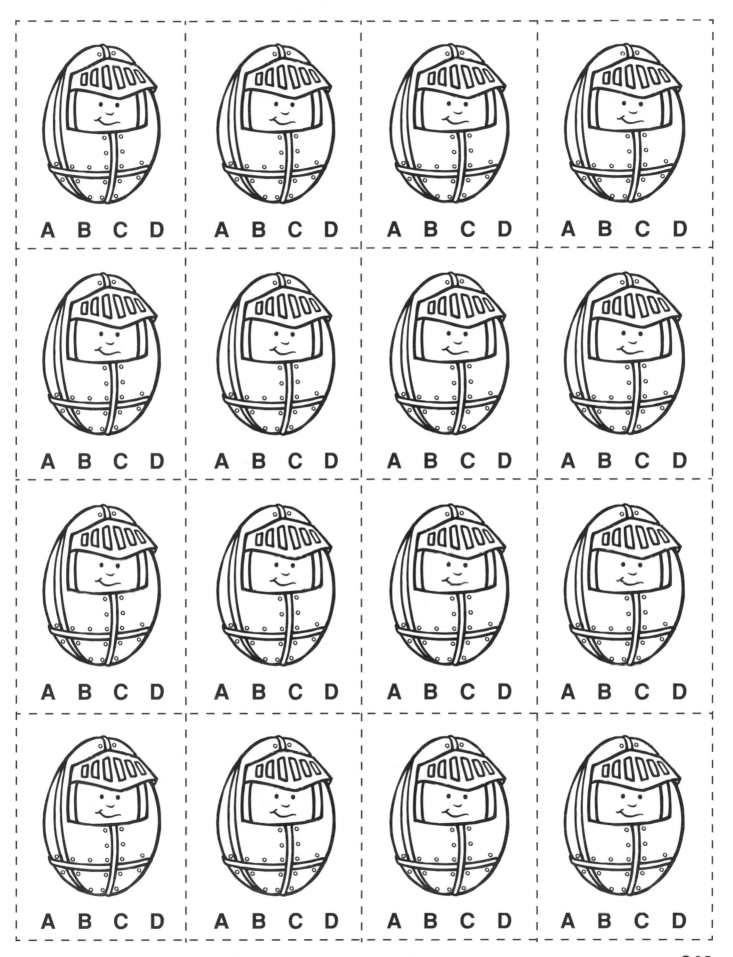

A B C D | A B C D | A B C D | A B C D

A B C D | A B C D | A B C D | A B C D

A B C D | A B C D | A B C D | A B C D

A B C D | A B C D | A B C D | A B C D

FORCES

64

Materials:

- laminated graph chart
- page 264, reproduced for each student
- page 265, reproduced, one icon for each student
- glass or plastic bottle
- cork
- vinegar
- water
- baking soda
- tissue
- pencils

All Gassed Up and Ready to Go

Objective: Students will observe that for every action, there is an equal but opposite reaction.

Question: What will happen when the pressure inside the bottle pops the cork off?

Science Background: Newton's third law of motion states that for every action, there is an equal but opposite reaction. Consider the chemical reaction that takes place when vinegar (CH_3COOH) and baking soda ($NaHCO_3$) are combined in a bottle and the bottle is sealed with a cork. Carbon dioxide gas (CO_2) building up in the bottle exerts a force on the cork, popping it out of the bottle (the "action"). At the same moment, the cork pushes against the bottle with an equal force in the opposite direction (the "reaction"). You probably wouldn't notice this if the bottle were sitting on a table, but you would feel the "back kick" if you held the bottle in your hands. By placing the bottle on rollers, students will able to see Newton's third law for themselves: The bottle actually travels backward as a result of the force exerted by the exiting cork.

Teaching Procedure:

1. Post the laminated graph chart at the front of the class. Label the top of the graph "All Gassed Up and Ready to Go."

2. Perform this experiment outdoors as a demonstration for the class. Make sure the cork you are using fits snugly in the top of the bottle.

3. Distribute an investigation sheet and a cork icon to each student.

4. Show students the materials to be used in the experiment. Read aloud the question at the top of the investigation sheet. Refer students to the picture of the experiment on the sheet and briefly explain how the experiment will be set up. Answer any questions students might have about the procedure.

5. Have students select an answer to the question posed on the investigation sheet about what they think will happen when the cork pops off the bottle. Tell them to record their answer both on the sheet and on the cork icon. Collect the icons and use them to create a class graph as shown.

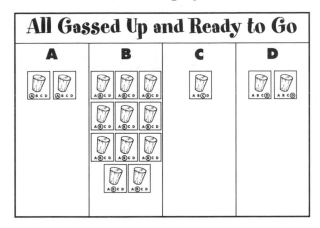

6. Bring all the materials outside. Gather students around.

7. Pour about ½ cup of vinegar and ½ cup of water into the bottle. Wrap 1 teaspoon of baking soda in a piece of tissue and drop it into the bottle. Quickly place the cork in the bottle and set the bottle down on its side on two or three pencils. Make sure the cork is facing away from students. (The vinegar and baking soda will fizz in the bottle. After a few seconds, the cork will pop off the bottle and the bottle will roll backward on the pencils.) Have students record their observations on the investigation sheet.

8. Discuss with students what they observed. Encourage them to offer an explanation for why the bottle moved backward when the cork popped off the bottle. Once the class has had a chance to discuss their theories, introduce the idea that a chemical reaction took place inside the bottle between the vinegar and the baking soda. This reaction produced a gas that filled up the bottle, putting pressure on the cork and causing it to pop off the bottle. As the cork was pushed forward, the bottle was pushed backward. Point out to students that Newton's third law of motion states that for every action, there is an equal but opposite reaction.

9. Have students answer the conclusion question on the investigation sheet. Finally, have them draw a picture of the experiment on the back of the sheet. Encourage them to label their drawing and provide a caption that explains what happened in the experiment.

Try this for fun:

Help students use what they learned in this experiment to construct and launch a bottle rocket. On what principle do rockets function? (the principle of action and reaction: as hot gases are thrust out the bottom of the rocket, the rocket is propelled upward)

Name _____

All Gassed Up and Ready to Go

Question

What do you think will happen when the pressure inside the bottle pops the cork off?

A The bottle will move backward.

B The bottle will move forward.

C The bottle will break.

D The bottle will fill with smoke.

Procedure and Observations

1. Watch as your teacher adds vinegar and baking soda to the bottle and plugs it with a cork. What happens to the cork after a few seconds?

_____

_____

2. What happens to the bottle when the cork flies off?

_____

_____

Conclusion

How can you explain what happened to the bottle in the experiment?

_____

_____

_____

On the back of this sheet, draw a picture showing what happened in your experiment. Label your drawing and write a sentence that describes what it is showing.

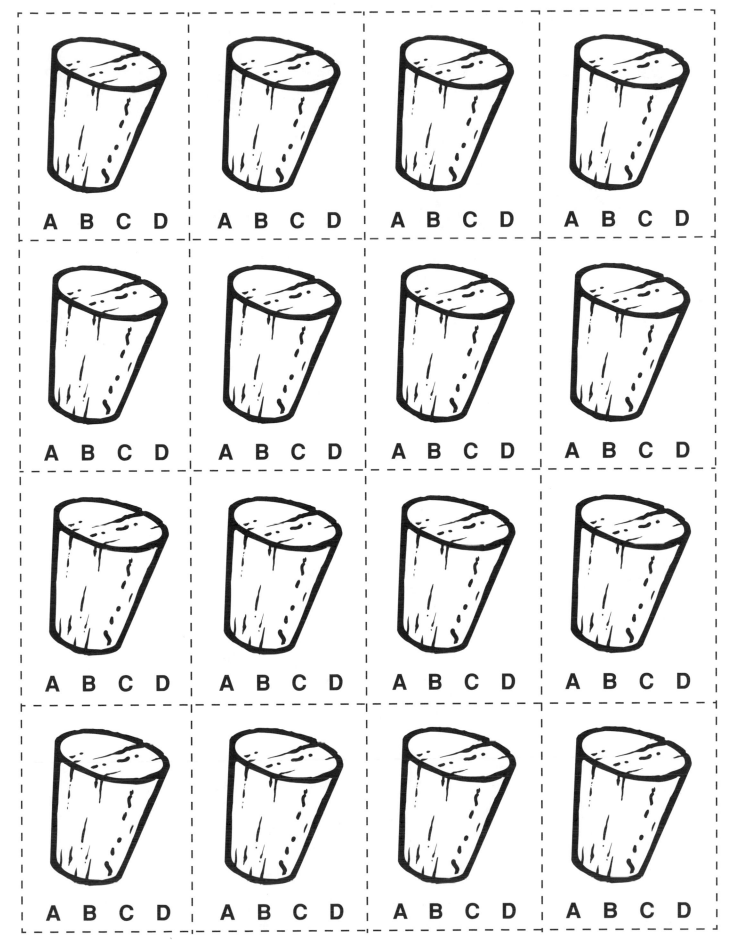

A B C D   A B C D   A B C D   A B C D

A B C D   A B C D   A B C D   A B C D

A B C D   A B C D   A B C D   A B C D

A B C D   A B C D   A B C D   A B C D

FORCES

65

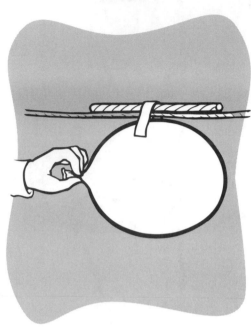

Materials:

- laminated graph chart
- page 268, reproduced for each student
- page 269, reproduced, one icon for each student
- balloons, identical
- straws
- string
- tape

Balloon Jets

Objective: Students will demonstrate that for every action, there is an equal but opposite reaction.

Question: Which balloon will travel farthest on the track: the small, medium-size, or large one?

Science Background: Newton's third law of motion states that for every action, there is an equal but opposite reaction. As air shoots out the back of the balloon jet, the balloon is thrust forward along the track. The three balloons are identical in every way except for the amount of air they contain, and therefore the level of air pressure inside them. The balloon that has been inflated the most will travel the farthest because it contains the most "fuel" (has the highest air pressure).

Teaching Procedure:

1. Post the laminated graph chart at the front of the class. Label the top of the graph "Balloon Jets."

2. Distribute an investigation sheet and a balloon icon to each student.

3. Show students the materials to be used in the experiment. Read aloud the question at the top of the investigation sheet. Refer students to the picture of the experiment on the sheet and briefly explain how the experiment will be set up. Answer any questions students might have about the procedure.

4. Have students select an answer to the question posed on the investigation sheet about which balloon they think will travel farthest. They should record their answer both on the sheet and on the balloon icon. Collect the icons and use them to create a class graph as shown.

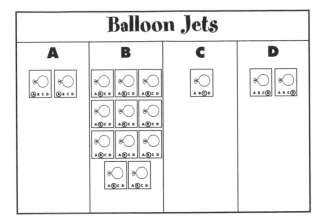

5. Distribute three 8-meter lengths of string, three straws, and three balloons to each group. Have each group thread one length of string through each straw, and then use the lengths of string to create three balloon jet tracks side by side. (Have the groups spread out around the room. Tell them to tie or tape the ends of their strings to a wall, desk, or chair. The tracks should be parallel and taut.)

6. Have students blow up each balloon to a different size—small, medium, and large—and pinch the neck of the balloons closed. Then tell them to tape each balloon to a straw, making sure the balloons are all pointing in the same direction.

7. Starting at one end of the string tracks, tell students to let go of all three balloons at the same time. Which balloon travels farthest? (the large one) Have students record their observations on the investigation sheet.

8. Discuss with students what they observed. Encourage them to offer an explanation for why the large balloon traveled the farthest. Once the class has had a chance to discuss their theories, introduce the idea that as air shot out the neck of each balloon, the balloons were thrust in the opposite direction. Point out that this behavior follows Newton's third law of motion, which states that for every action, there is an equal but opposite reaction. The large balloon traveled the farthest because it contained the most air and therefore had the greatest air pressure and the greatest thrust.

9. Have students answer the conclusion question on the investigation sheet. Finally, have them draw a picture of the experiment on the back of the sheet. Encourage them to label their drawing and provide a caption that explains what happened in the experiment.

Try this for fun:

Have students decorate their balloons to look like real jets. Or have them draw faces on the balloons that make them look like sprinting animals.

Name _____

Balloon Jets

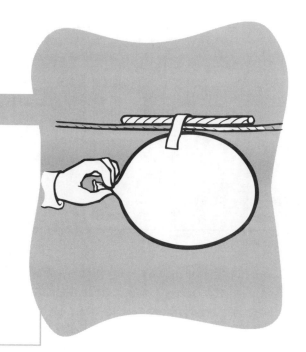

Question

Which balloon do you think will travel farthest on the track?

    A the large balloon

    B the medium-size balloon

    C the small balloon

    D All balloons will travel the same distance.

Procedure and Observations

1. Use string to set up three balloon jet tracks as instructed by your teacher.

2. Blow up the balloons to three different sizes: small, medium, and large. Hold the neck of each balloon closed.

3. Tape each balloon to a straw, line them up, and release all three at the same time. Which balloon travels the farthest?

_____

Conclusion

How can you explain what happened in the experiment?

_____

_____

_____

On the back of this sheet, draw a picture showing what happened in your experiment. Label your drawing and write a sentence that describes what it is showing.

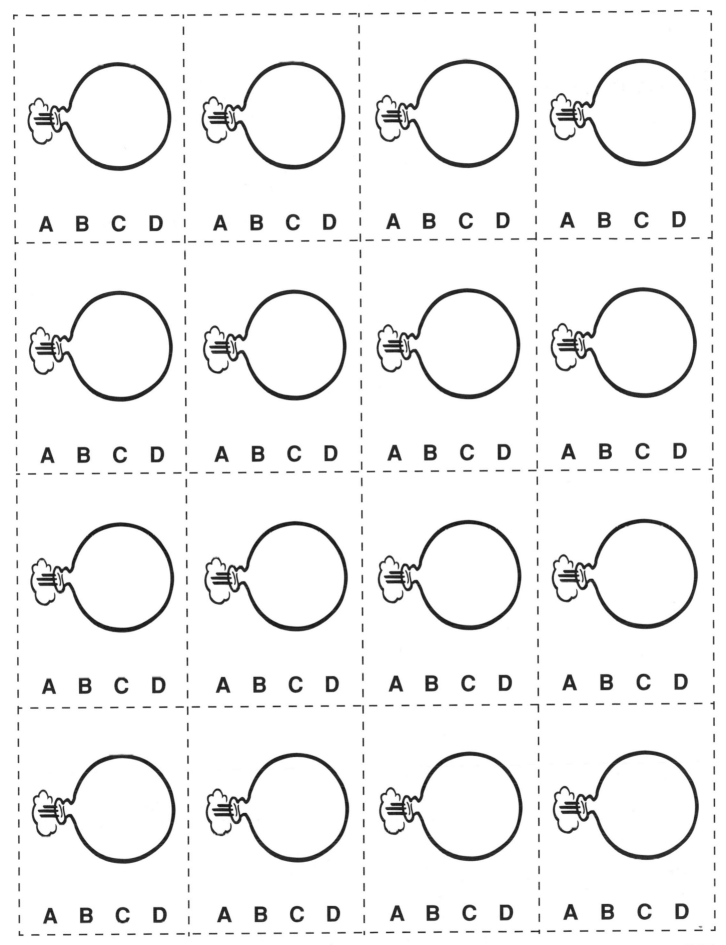

FORCES

66

Materials:

- laminated graph chart
- page 272, reproduced for each student
- page 273, reproduced, one icon for each student
- drinking glasses
- playing cards or index cards
- pennies

Card Sharks

Objective: Students will demonstrate that an object at rest will stay at rest unless acted on by an unbalanced force.

Question: What will happen to a penny resting on a card over a glass when the card is flicked off the glass?

Science Background: Newton's first law of motion states that an object at rest will remain at rest (and an object in motion will remain in motion) unless acted on by an unbalanced force. Newton's first law is also called the law of inertia. **Inertia** is the tendency of an object to resist a change in motion.

Consider a penny on a playing card that has been placed over the mouth of a glass. The penny is being acted on by two forces: Gravity is pulling down on the penny, and the card is pushing up on the penny. Because these two forces are equal and balance each other out, the penny stays put. When the card is flicked, the force exerted by your finger pushes the card off the glass. But because the force on the card acts quickly, the penny's inertia keeps it from moving sideways with the card. Once the card is gone, however, the only force acting on the penny is the force of gravity pulling it down. This unbalanced force causes the penny to fall into the glass.

Teaching Procedure:

1. Use drinking glasses rather than plastic cups in this experiment because lightweight plastic cups may not be able to stand up to the card flick administered by students. If you don't want to use glasses, place some pebbles or marbles in the plastic cups to give them some weight and keep them stable.

2. Post the laminated graph chart at the front of the class. Label the top of the graph "Card Sharks."

3. Distribute an investigation sheet and a playing card icon to each student.

4. Show students the materials to be used in the experiment. Read aloud the question at the top of the investigation sheet. Refer students to the picture of the experiment on the sheet and briefly explain how the experiment will be set up. Answer any questions students might have about the procedure.

5. Have students select an answer to the question posed on the investigation sheet about what they think will happen to the penny when they flick the card horizontally off the glass. Tell them to record their answer both on the sheet and on the playing card icon. Collect the icons and use them to create a class graph as shown.

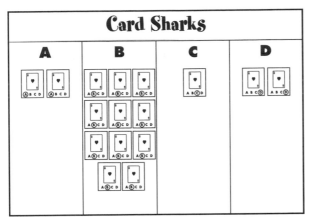

6. With a card and a glass (but no penny), demonstrate for students how to flick the card so that it flies sideways off the glass.

7. Distribute a glass, a playing card, and a penny to each group. Have students set the card over the glass and the penny on the card as shown in the picture on their investigation sheet. Then have students flick the card off the glass and see what happens to the penny. (The penny will fall straight down into the glass. Students may have to try a few times before succeeding.) Have students record their observations on the investigation sheet.

8. Discuss with students what they observed. Encourage them to offer an explanation for why the penny fell into the glass rather than flying off with the card. Once the class has had a chance to discuss their theories, introduce the idea that the penny and the card are separate objects (they are not attached to each other). The penny stays still unless acted on by an unbalanced force. This tendency to resist a change in motion is known as inertia. The moving card did not exert a force on the penny because it moved so fast. The penny was left sitting in the air for a split second before gravity pulled it down into the glass.

9. Have students answer the conclusion question on the investigation sheet. Finally, have them draw a picture of the experiment on the back of the sheet. Encourage them to label their drawing and provide a caption that explains what happened in the experiment.

Try this for fun:

Have students try the trick again using a marble instead of a penny.

Card Sharks

Question

What do you think will happen to a penny resting on a card over a glass when the card is flicked off the glass?

The penny will _____.

    A stick to the card

    B drop to the floor

    C drop in the glass

    D sit on the rim of the glass

Procedure and Observations

1. Set the card on top of the glass and the penny on top of the card as shown in the picture.

2. Flick the card hard from the side. What happens to the penny?

_____

_____

Conclusion

How can you explain what happened to the penny?

_____

_____

_____

On the back of this sheet, draw a picture showing what happened in your experiment. Label your drawing and write a sentence that describes what it is showing.

Inertia and Momentum

67

Quick Trick

Objective: Students will demonstrate that an object at rest will stay at rest unless acted on by an unbalanced force.

Question: What will happen to a plastic bottle sitting on waxed paper when the paper is pulled out quickly from the side?

Science Background: Newton's first law of motion states that an object at rest will remain at rest (and an object in motion will remain in motion) unless acted on by an unbalanced force. Newton's first law is also called the law of inertia. **Inertia** is the tendency of an object to resist a change in motion.

In this experiment, a bottle sits on a sheet of waxed paper that has been placed on a table. When the waxed paper is pulled quickly out from under the bottle, the bottle's inertia holds the bottle in place. The pulling force acted so quickly that it did not affect the bottle.

Materials:

- laminated graph chart
- page 276, reproduced for each student
- page 277, reproduced, one icon for each student
- plastic bottles, heavy-gauge
- waxed paper

Teaching Procedure:

1. Collect bottles that have some heft to them. If the bottles are too light, the trick may not work.

2. Post the laminated graph chart at the front of the class. Label the top of the graph "Quick Trick."

3. Distribute an investigation sheet and a bottle icon to each student.

4. Show students the materials to be used in the experiment. Read aloud the question at the top of the investigation sheet. Refer students to the picture of the experiment on the sheet and briefly explain how the experiment will be set up. Answer any questions students might have about the procedure.

5. Have students select an answer to the question posed on the investigation sheet about what they think will happen to the bottle when they pull the waxed paper out quickly from underneath it. Tell them to record their answer both on the sheet and on the bottle icon. Collect the icons and use them to create a class graph as shown.

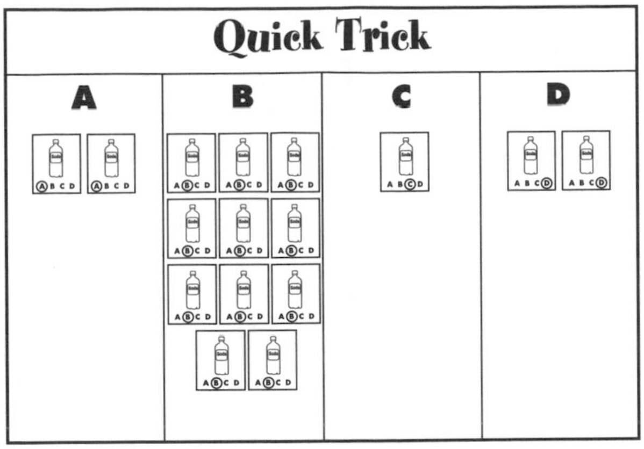

Quick Trick

A	B	C	D

6. Distribute a plastic bottle and a piece of waxed paper to each group. Have students set the bottle in the center of the sheet of waxed paper and then pull the paper out quickly from the side. What happens to the bottle? (The bottle should remain standing upright on the table. Students might have to try the procedure a few times before making it work.) Have students record their observations on the investigation sheet.

7. Discuss with students what they observed. Encourage them to offer an explanation for why the bottle was left standing on the table. Once the class has had a chance to discuss their theories, introduce the idea that the bottle and the waxed paper are separate objects (they are not attached to each other). The bottle stays still unless acted on by an unbalanced force. This tendency to resist a change in motion is known as inertia. The moving paper did not exert a force on the bottle because it moved so fast. As a result, the bottle was left standing upright on the table.

8. Have students answer the conclusion question on the investigation sheet. Finally, have them draw a picture of the experiment on the back of the sheet. Encourage them to label their drawing and provide a caption that explains what happened in the experiment.

Try this for fun:

Have students try the trick again, this time pulling slowly on the waxed paper. What happens? Why? (The bottle either moves with the waxed paper or falls over. Unless the pulling force acts quickly, friction between the bottle and the paper will cause the bottle to move with the paper.)

Name _____

Quick Trick

Question

What do you think will happen to a plastic bottle sitting on waxed paper when the paper is pulled out quickly from the side?

The bottle will _____.

    A ride along with the paper

    B tip over

    C remain standing in the same place

    D flip over and land on its top

Procedure and Observations

1. Set the bottle on top of the waxed paper as shown in the picture.

2. Pull the waxed paper quickly from the side. What happens to the bottle?

_____

_____

Conclusion

How can you explain what happened to the bottle?

_____

_____

_____

On the back of this sheet, draw a picture showing what happened in your experiment. Label your drawing and write a sentence that describes what it is showing.

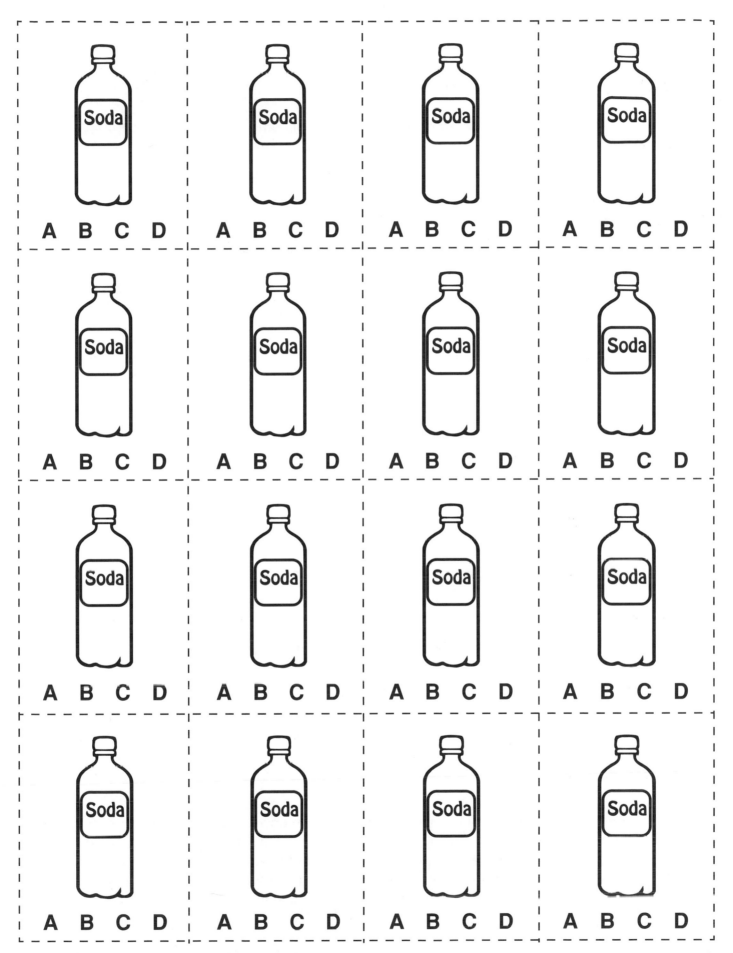

FORCES

68

Materials:

- laminated graph chart
- page 280, reproduced for each student
- page 281, reproduced, one icon for each student
- quarters
- dimes
- stiff rulers

Fast Cash

Objective: Students will demonstrate that momentum can be transferred from one object to another.

Question: What will happen to a dime placed at the end of a ruler when the opposite end of the ruler is hit by a sliding quarter?

Science Background: Momentum is a measure of the force a moving object exerts as it strikes another object. Momentum is determined by an object's mass and velocity ($M = m \times v$). The more massive an object is, and the faster it is moving, the greater its momentum.

Momentum is conserved in any one collision. Thus, a heavier object moving at a certain speed will cause a lighter object it runs into to move away at a greater speed. As an example, let's say that a 6-kg object moving at 2 km/hr strikes a 3-kg object that is sitting still. The 3-kg object will move away with a velocity of 4 km/hr ($m \times v = m \times v$; $6 \times 2 = 3 \times 4$).

When the quarter strikes the ruler, its momentum is transferred along the ruler to the other end, where it sets the dime into motion. The dime travels faster than the incoming quarter because it is lighter than the quarter.

Teaching Procedure:

1. Post the laminated graph chart at the front of the class. Label the top of the graph "Fast Cash."

2. Distribute an investigation sheet and a dime icon to each student.

3. Show students the materials to be used in the experiment. Read aloud the question at the top of the investigation sheet. Refer students to the picture of the experiment on the sheet and briefly explain how the experiment will be set up. Answer any questions students might have about the procedure.

4. Have students select an answer to the question posed on the investigation sheet about what they think will happen to the dime when the quarter hits the ruler. Tell them to record the answer both on the sheet and on the dime icon. Collect the icons and use them to create a class graph as shown.

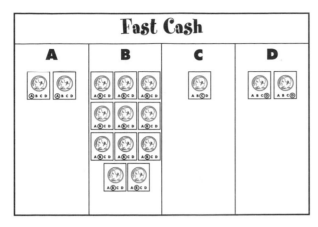

5. Distribute a quarter, a dime, and a stiff ruler to each group. Have students place the ruler on their desk and set the dime against the far end as shown on the investigation sheet.

6. Instruct students to slide the quarter across their desk, releasing it just before it strikes the near end of the ruler. (Students might have to practice this motion a few times before achieving the right combination of speed and accuracy.) What happens to the dime as the quarter strikes the ruler? (It slides away from the ruler.) Ask students what they noticed about the speed at which the dime moved. (It moved faster than the quarter.) Have students record their observations on the investigation sheet.

7. Discuss with students what they observed. Encourage them to offer an explanation for why the dime moved away from the ruler, and why it moved faster. Once the class has had a chance to discuss their theories, introduce the idea that the quarter struck the ruler with a force equal to the weight times the speed of the quarter. This moving force, called momentum, was transferred along the ruler to the other end, where it was transferred to the dime. Since the dime weighed less than the quarter, it was pushed away at a greater speed.

8. Have students answer the conclusion question on the investigation sheet. Finally, have them draw a picture of the experiment on the back of the sheet. Encourage them to label their drawing and provide a caption that explains what happened in the experiment.

Try this for fun:

Have students try the trick again, this time reversing the positions of the quarter and dime. What do they notice? (The quarter moves away from the ruler much more slowly than the dime struck the ruler.)

Name _____

Fast Cash

What do you think will happen to a dime placed at one end of a ruler when the other end is hit by a sliding quarter?

The dime will _____.

    A move under the ruler

    B jump into the air

    C slide away from the ruler

    D stay where it is

Procedure and Observations

1. Set the ruler on your desk. Place the dime at one end. Slide the quarter so that it hits the other end. What happens to the dime?

    _____

    _____

2. What do you notice about the speed of the dime compared to the speed of the quarter?

    _____

    _____

Conclusion

How can you explain what happened to the dime?

_____

_____

_____

On the back of this sheet, draw a picture showing what happened in your experiment. Label your drawing and write a sentence that describes what it is showing.

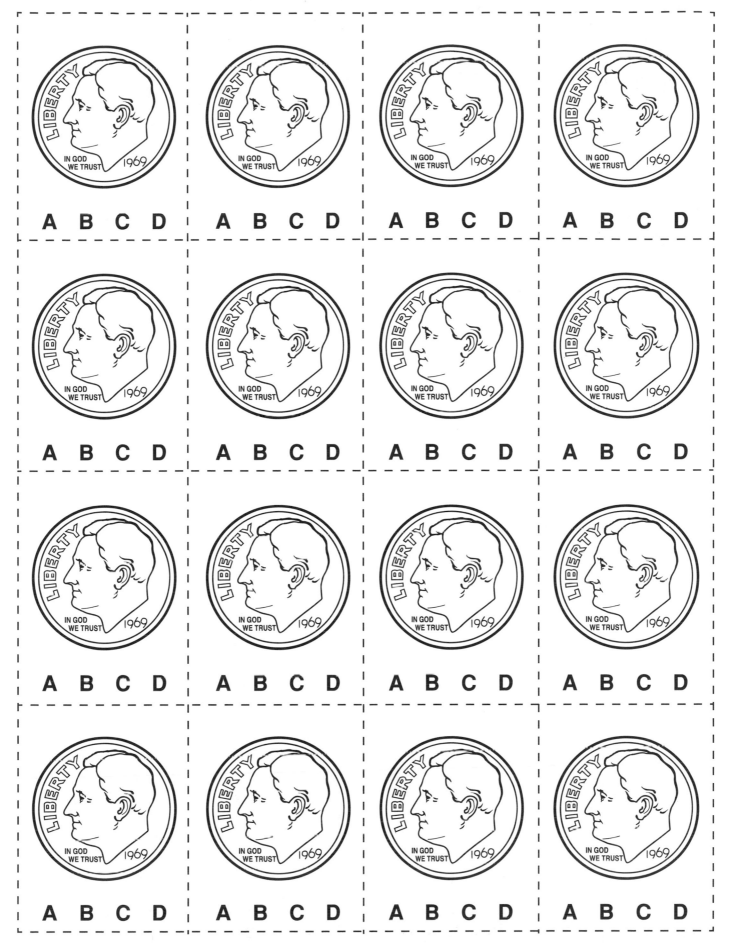

69

Look Out Below

Objective: Students will demonstrate that light objects fall at the same rate as heavy objects.

Question: What will happen when you drop a heavy object and a light object from the same height at the same time?

Science Background: Gravity is the attraction between objects that have mass. Earth has a lot of mass. Smaller objects have less mass. Thus, objects like paper clips and board erasers will fall toward Earth when dropped.

Newton's second law of motion states that the acceleration of an object by a force is inversely proportional to the mass of the object, and directly proportional to the force ($a = F/m$). Newton's second law explains why a heavy object and a light object dropped together from the same height will hit the ground at the same time: They both accelerate at the same rate.

Consider a paper clip and a board eraser dropped from the same height. Because the paper clip has less mass (m), the force of gravity (F) on it is smaller. The board eraser has more mass (m) and so has a greater force of gravity (F) acting on it. Because an object's "F" and "m" increase proportionally, "a" is always the same: 9.8 m/s^2. Because both objects accelerate at the same rate, they both hit the ground at the same time.

This explanation is too advanced for most students this age. In the discussion section of this investigation, simply explain that all objects fall at the same rate, regardless of their weight. This is a simplification, of course, but one that is appropriate for the grade level.

Materials:

- laminated graph chart
- page 284, reproduced for each student
- page 285, reproduced, one icon for each student
- large paper clips
- board erasers

Teaching Procedure:

1. Students will need two nonbreakable objects of different weights to drop. Large paper clips and board erasers are suggested here as examples, but use any objects you might have around that would work. Make sure none of the objects is light enough or shaped such that it will experience significant air resistance—for example, a tissue or flat sheet of paper. Air resistance works against gravity and can influence results.

2. Post the laminated graph chart at the front of the class. Label the top of the graph "Look Out Below."

3. Distribute an investigation sheet and a falling objects icon to each student.

4. Show students the materials to be used in the experiment. Read aloud the question at the top of the investigation sheet. Refer students to the picture of the experiment on the sheet and briefly explain how the experiment will be set up. Answer any questions students might have about the procedure.

5. Have students select an answer to the question posed on the investigation sheet about what they think will happen when they drop the two objects. Tell them to record their answer both on the sheet and on the falling objects icon. Collect the icons and use them to create a class graph as shown.

Look Out Below

6. Distribute a large paper clip and a board eraser to each group. (Any large object/small object combination will work.) Instruct students to hold the two objects at shoulder height and drop them at the same time. Which one hits the floor first? (Both objects should hit the floor at the same time. Students are often surprised by this result, because they think that the heavier object will fall faster.) Have students record their observations on the investigation sheet.

7. Discuss with students what they observed. Encourage them to offer an explanation for why the two objects hit the floor at the same time. Once the class has had a chance to discuss their theories, introduce the idea that gravity pulls on all objects and makes them fall to the ground. All objects fall at the same rate, regardless of whether they are large or small.

8. Have students answer the conclusion question on the investigation sheet. Finally, have them draw a picture of the experiment on the back of the sheet. Encourage them to label their drawing and provide a caption that explains what happened in the experiment.

Try this for fun:

Have students try the investigation again, using different objects.

Look Out Below

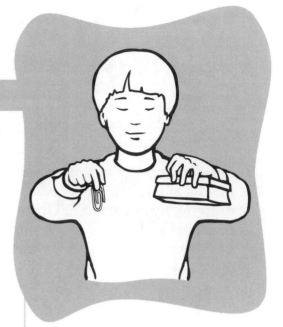

Question

What do you think will happen when you drop a heavy object and a light object from the same height at the same time?

     A The heavy object will hit the floor first.

     B The light object will hit the floor first.

     C Both objects will hit the floor at the same time.

     D Neither object will fall.

Procedure and Observations

1. Hold both objects at shoulder height. Release them both at the same time.

2. Which object hits the floor first?

_____

_____

Conclusion

How can you explain what happened in the experiment?

_____

_____

_____

On the back of this sheet, draw a picture showing what happened in your experiment. Label your drawing and write a sentence that describes what it is showing.

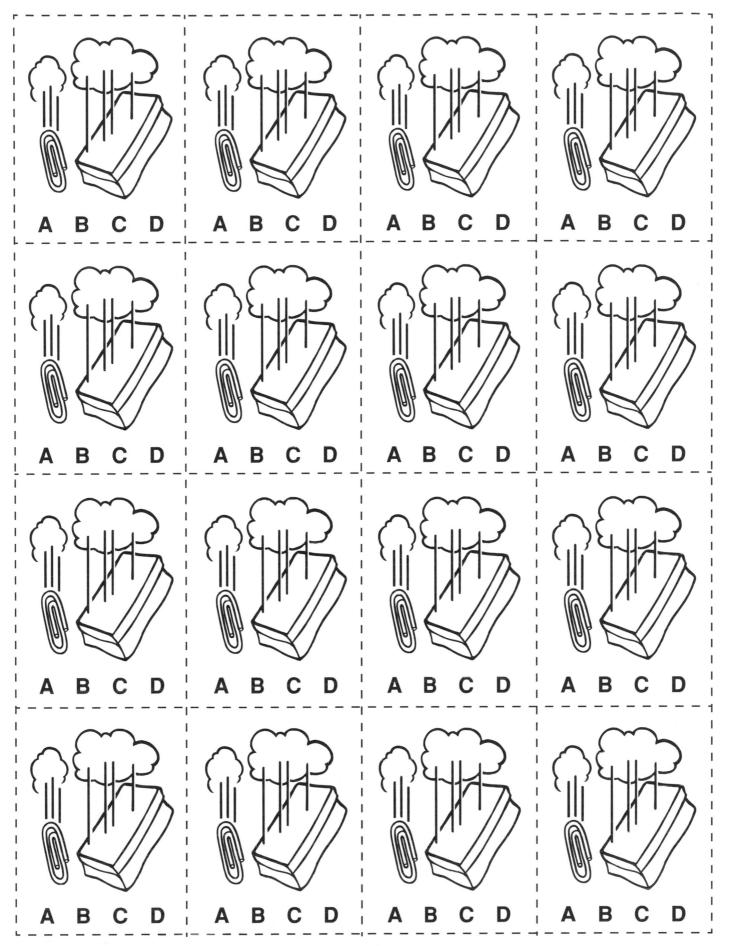

70

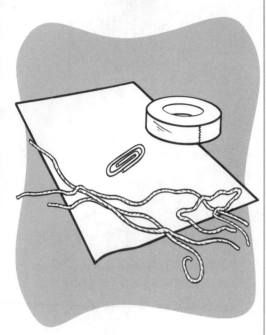

Materials:

- laminated graph chart
- page 288, reproduced for each student
- page 289, reproduced, one icon for each student
- large paper clips
- flat sheets of paper
- tape
- string

Drifting Down

Objective: Students will demonstrate that air resistance works against gravity.

Question: How will a parachute affect how a paper clip falls?

Science Background: Gravity is the attraction between objects that have mass. Earth has a lot of mass. A paper clip has very little mass. Thus, a paper clip will fall toward Earth when dropped.

As objects fall through the air, air particles push up on them. This is known as **air resistance**, as it acts against, or resists, the force of gravity. The greater the surface area of the falling object, the more air particles that push against it, and the greater the force of air resistance. An object's surface area can be increased by attaching a parachute to it. The parachute forms a kind of umbrella, which runs into lots of air particles and slows the descent rate of the object.

Teaching Procedure:

1. Post the laminated graph chart at the front of the class. Label the top of the graph "Drifting Down."

2. Distribute an investigation sheet and a parachute icon to each student.

3. Show students the materials to be used in the experiment. Read aloud the question on the investigation sheet. Refer students to the picture of the experiment on the sheet and briefly explain how the experiment will be set up. Answer any questions students might have about the procedure.

4. Distribute a large paper clip to each group. Have students drop the paper clip from shoulder level and note what happens to it. (It falls quickly to the floor.)

5. Have students select an answer to the question posed on the investigation sheet about what effect they think a parachute will have on the falling paper clip. Tell them to record their answer both on the sheet and on the parachute icon. Collect the icons and use them to create a class graph as shown.

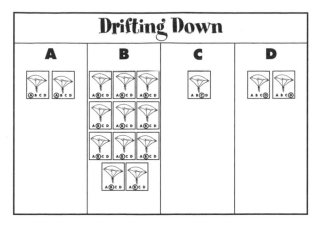

6. Distribute a sheet of paper, a roll of tape, and four 15-cm lengths of string to each group. Have them use the materials to create a parachute for the paper clip. (They can use tape to attach one string to each corner of the paper, and then tie the strings to the paper clip.)

7. Have students hold the clip (with attached parachute) at shoulder level again and drop the clip. What happens? (The clip drifts down to the floor this time, rather than falling quickly.) Have students record their observations on the investigation sheet.

8. Discuss with students what they observed. Encourage them to offer an explanation for why the paper clip drifted slowly to the floor when the parachute was attached to it. Once the class has had a chance to discuss their theories, introduce the idea that air pushes against an object as it falls. This pushing, called air resistance, acts against gravity and slows the object's fall. A parachute increases the amount of air resistance a falling object experiences by increasing its surface area. The greater the air resistance, the slower the object will fall.

9. Have students answer the conclusion question on the investigation sheet. Finally, have them draw a picture of the experiment on the back of the sheet. Encourage them to label their drawing and provide a caption that explains what happened in the experiment.

Try this for fun:

Have students improve their parachutes by using different materials (tissue paper, plastic, cloth) and different-sized parachutes. Which combination produces the best parachute (i.e., slows the paper clip's rate of descent the most)?

Name _____

Drifting Down

Question

How do you think a parachute will affect how the paper clip falls?

A The parachute will not affect how the paper clip falls.

B The parachute will make the paper clip fall more slowly.

C The parachute will make the paper clip fall faster.

D The parachute will prevent the paper clip from falling.

Procedure and Observations

1. Hold a paper clip at shoulder level. Drop the clip. What happens?

_____

2. Make a parachute out of the paper and strings your teacher gives you. Attach the parachute to the paper clip.

3. Hold up the paper clip again and drop it as before. What happens this time?

_____

Conclusion

How can you explain what happened once you added the parachute to the paper clip?

_____

_____

_____

On the back of this sheet, draw a picture showing what happened in your experiment. Label your drawing and write a sentence that describes what it is showing.

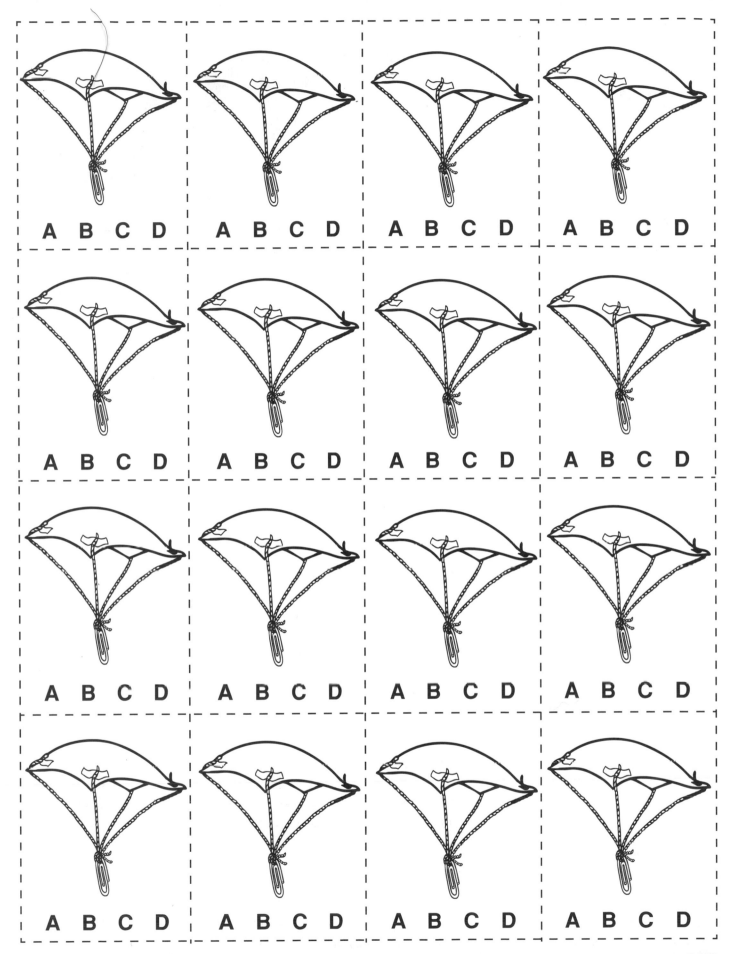

71

Materials:

- laminated graph chart
- page 292, reproduced for each student
- page 293, reproduced, one icon and one larger paper teacher for each student
- paper clips

Twirling Teacher

Objective: Students will demonstrate that air resistance works against gravity.

Question: How can you make the paper teacher twirl?

Science Background: Gravity is the attraction between objects that have mass. Earth has a lot of mass. A paper figure has very little mass. Thus, a paper figure will fall toward Earth when dropped.

As objects fall through the air, air particles push up on them. This is known as **air resistance**, as it acts against, or resists, the force of gravity. If a falling object has blades that are all tilted in the same direction, the air will push the blades in one direction and move the object in one direction. If the blades are placed opposite each other and secured to a center object, a circular motion is formed.

Teaching Procedure:

1. Students will need one copy of the teacher icon and one copy of the larger teacher to use in the experiment.

2. Post the laminated graph chart at the front of the class. Label the top of the graph "Twirling Teacher."

3. Distribute an investigation sheet and two teacher icons to each student.

4. Show students the materials to be used in the experiment. Read aloud the question at the top of the investigation sheet. Refer students to the picture of the experiment on the sheet and briefly explain how the experiment will be set up. Answer any questions students might have about the procedure.

5. Have students select an answer to the question posed on the investigation sheet about how they think they can get the paper teacher to twirl. Tell them to record the answer both on the sheet and on one of the teacher icons. Collect those icons and use them to create a class graph as shown.

Twirling Teacher

A	B	C	D

6. Distribute a paper clip to each group. Tell students to attach the paper clip to the feet of the figure as shown in the picture on the investigation sheet. Then have students try all the suggestions listed on the sheet. Which one worked? (when she was dropped with one arm bent forward and one arm bent backward) Have students record their observations on the investigation sheet.

7. Discuss with students what they observed. Encourage them to offer an explanation for why the teacher twirled when one arm was bent forward and one was bent backward. Once the class has had a chance to discuss their theories, introduce the idea that air pushes against objects as they fall through it. As the teacher figure fell, air pushed against her arms in a way that caused her to twirl.

8. Have students answer the conclusion question on the investigation sheet. Finally, have them draw a picture of the experiment on the back of the sheet. Encourage them to label their drawing and provide a caption that explains what happened in the experiment.

Try this for fun:

Have students repeat the experiment, this time without the paper clip attached to the feet. (The paper teacher will drift randomly to the floor.) Why was the paper clip added to the figure in this experiment? (The added weight steadies the figure as it falls.)

Twirling Teacher

Question

How can you make the paper teacher twirl?

The teacher will twirl when she is dropped _____.

    A with one arm bent forward

    B with both arms bent forward

    C with both arms straight over her head

    D with one arm bent forward and one
        arm bent backward

Procedure and Observations

1. Try all of the suggestions listed above. What did each suggestion make the teacher do?
Circle the suggestion that worked.

A: _____

B: _____

C: _____

D: _____

Conclusion

How can you explain what made the teacher twirl?

_____

_____

_____

On the back of this sheet, draw a picture showing what happened in your experiment. Label
your drawing and write a sentence that describes what it is showing.

72

Materials:

- laminated graph chart
- page 296, reproduced for each student
- page 297, reproduced, one icon for each student
- small, empty coffee cans
- clay
- books or wooden planks
- board erasers or other props

Gravity

Can You Rock and Roll?

Objective: Students will demonstrate that objects will come to rest so that their center of gravity is directly above their point of support.

Question: What will happen when a can with a lump of clay stuck to its inside wall is placed on an incline?

Science Background: Gravity is the attraction between objects that have mass. All objects are attracted to Earth and come to rest at a point where their **center of gravity** is directly on, above, or below their point of support. An object's center of gravity is the point where the object balances.

Consider a can with a lump of clay stuck to its inside wall. When the can is placed on its side on a flat surface, with the clay in the 10:00 or 11:00 position, the can will rock back and forth until it comes to rest with the clay closest to Earth (with the clay side of the can touching the ground).

If the can is placed the same way on an incline, however, two forces are competing. Gravity is working to roll the can so that the clay side is facing the earth (ground). But gravity is also working to roll the can down the incline. As long as the incline is not too steep, the force working to place the can over its center of gravity will win out over the force of gravity pulling the can down the incline, and the can will roll a few centimeters uphill to its centered position.

Teaching Procedure:

1. Post the laminated graph chart at the front of the class. Label the top of the graph "Can You Rock and Roll?"

2. Distribute an investigation sheet and a coffee can icon to each student.

3. Show students the materials to be used in the experiment. Read aloud the question on the investigation sheet. Refer students to the picture of the experiment on the sheet and briefly explain how the experiment will be set up. Answer any questions students might have about the procedure.

4. Distribute a coffee can and a lump of clay to each group. Have students place the lump of clay on the inside wall of the can. Now have them hold the can on its side so that the clay is in the 10:00 or 11:00 position, and place the can on

the floor. What happens? (The can rocks back and forth until the clay side of the can is touching the floor.)

5. Have students select an answer to the question posed on the investigation sheet about what they think will happen when they set the can down on an incline. Tell them to record their answer both on the sheet and on the coffee can icon. Collect the icons and use them to create a class graph as shown.

6. Distribute a book and a board eraser (or other prop) to each group. Have students use the objects to make a ramp with a slight incline. Now have students place the can in the middle of the incline with the clay once again in the 10:00 or 11:00 position. What happens when they release the can? (The can rolls up the incline a few centimeters, as the clay takes the shortest route to getting centered over Earth.) Have students record their observations on the investigation sheet.

7. Discuss with students what they observed. Encourage them to offer an explanation for why the can rolled uphill. Once the class has had a chance to discuss their theories, introduce the idea that objects come to rest over their heaviest point, their center of gravity. When placed on a flat surface, the can rocked back and forth until the clay side was resting on the ground. When the can was placed on a slight incline, the clay still took the shortest route to being centered over the ground. The force of the clay seeking its center of gravity was greater than the force of gravity pulling the can down the incline, so the can rolled uphill.

8. Have students answer the conclusion question on the investigation sheet. Finally, have them draw a picture of the experiment on the back of the sheet. Encourage them to label their drawing and provide a caption that explains what happened in the experiment.

Try this for fun:

Have students try the experiment again with the clay in the 2:00 position. What happens? (The can rolls down the incline, as "down" is now the shortest path to the can's center of gravity.)

Can You Rock and Roll?

Question

What do you think will happen to that same can when it is placed on an incline?

The can will _____.

    A roll down the incline

    B fall off the incline

    C roll up the incline

    D not move

Procedure and Observations

1. Stick the lump of clay on the inside wall of the coffee can. Turn the can on its side and set it on the ground with the clay in the 10:00 or 11:00 position. Release the can. What happens?

_____

_____

2. Set the can on its side in the middle of the incline with the clay in the same position as before. Release the can. What happens?

_____

_____

Conclusion

How can you explain what happened to the can on the incline?

_____

_____

_____

On the back of this sheet, draw a picture showing what happened in your experiment. Label your drawing and write a sentence that describes what it is showing.

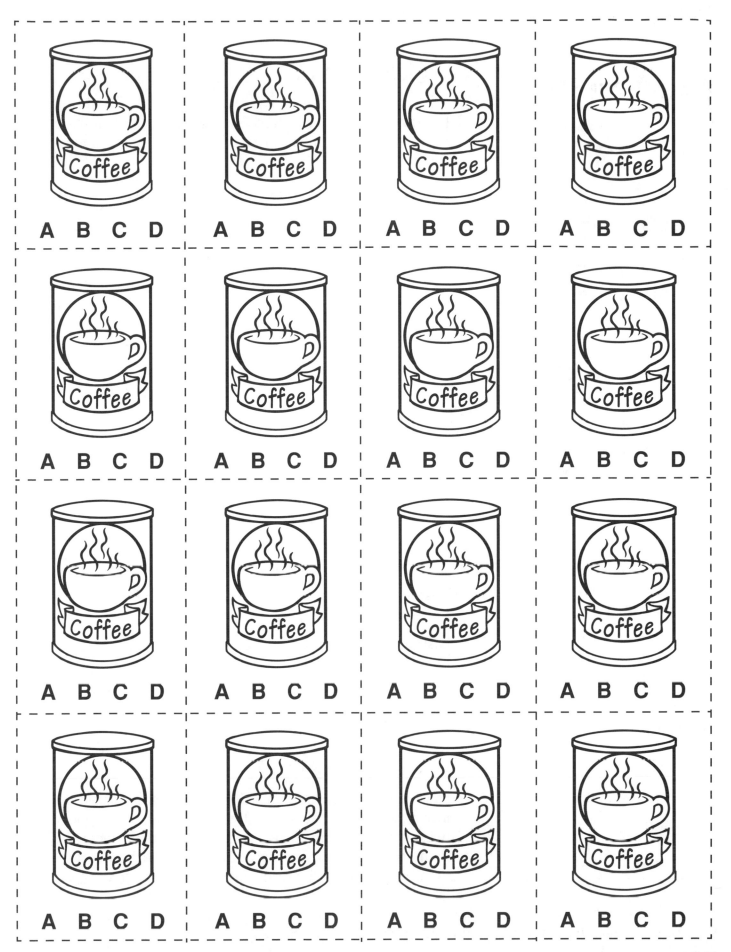

73

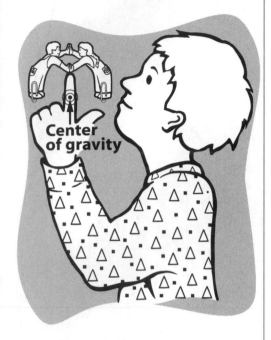

Center of gravity

Materials:

- laminated graph chart
- page 300, reproduced for each student
- page 301, reproduced, one icon and one larger copy of the twins for each student
- tagboard the same size as the large twins, one piece for each student
- paper clips
- glue stick
- scissors

To the Point

Objective: Students will demonstrate that objects can be balanced when their center of gravity is directly below their point of support.

Question: What will happen to the tagboard twins when they are placed on the end of your finger?

Science Background: Gravity is the attraction between objects that have mass. All objects are attracted to Earth and come to rest at a point where the center of their mass, or their **center of gravity,** is directly on, above, or below their point of support. Thus, even oddly shaped objects can be balanced as long as they are supported at a point directly above or below their center of gravity.

In this experiment, the tagboard figure's center of gravity is between the twins' feet. The paper clips add some extra weight that lowers the center of gravity to the point between the twins' feet. The added weight also helps hold the tagboard in place. If the cutouts keep falling off students' fingers, add more weight to the ends of the figure by taping pennies to them.

Teaching Procedure:

1. Students will need one copy of the twins icon and one larger copy of the twins, along with a piece of tagboard.

2. Post the laminated graph chart at the front of the class. Label the top of the graph "To the Point."

3. Distribute an investigation sheet and the paper and tagboard twins to each student.

4. Show students the materials to be used in the experiment. Read aloud the question at the top of the investigation sheet. Refer students to the picture on the sheet and briefly explain how the experiment will be set up. Answer any questions students might have about the procedure.

5. Have students select an answer to the question posed on the investigation sheet about what will happen to the tagboard twins when they are placed on the end of their finger. Tell them to record their answer both on the sheet and on the twins icon. Collect the icons and use them to create a class graph as shown.

To the Point

A	B	C	D

6. Distribute the large twins, a piece of tagboard, glue stick, and scissors to each student. Instruct students to glue the twins to the tagboard and cut on the cut lines.

7. Distribute two paper clips to each student. Have students attach a paper clip to the legs of each twin. Then have them place the tagboard twins at the end of their finger. What happens? (The twins balance on their fingertip.) Have students record their observations on the investigation sheet.

8. Discuss with students what they observed. Encourage them to offer an explanation for why the twins balanced on their finger. Once the class has had a chance to discuss their theories, introduce the idea that all objects have a center of gravity, and that objects can be balanced by supporting them directly over that point. The twins' center of gravity was between their feet, directly under the point where students placed their fingers.

9. Have students answer the conclusion question on the investigation sheet. Finally, have them draw a picture of the experiment on the back of the sheet. Encourage them to label their drawing and provide a caption that explains what happened in the experiment.

Try this for fun:

Have students remove one of the paper clips from the tagboard twins and place them on their finger like before. Will the twins still balance? Why or why not? (No, because the center of gravity is no longer between the twins. It is closer to the twin with the paper clip.)

To the Point

What do you think will happen to the cardboard twins when they are placed on the end of your finger?

The twins will _____.

    A tip to the left

    B tip to the right

    C spin around

    D remain upright

Procedure and Observations

Place the cardboard twins at the end of your finger, as shown in the picture above. What happens?

_____

_____

_____

Conclusion

How can you explain what happened to the cardboard twins?

_____

_____

_____

On the back of this sheet, draw a picture showing what happened in your experiment. Label your drawing and write a sentence that describes what it is showing.

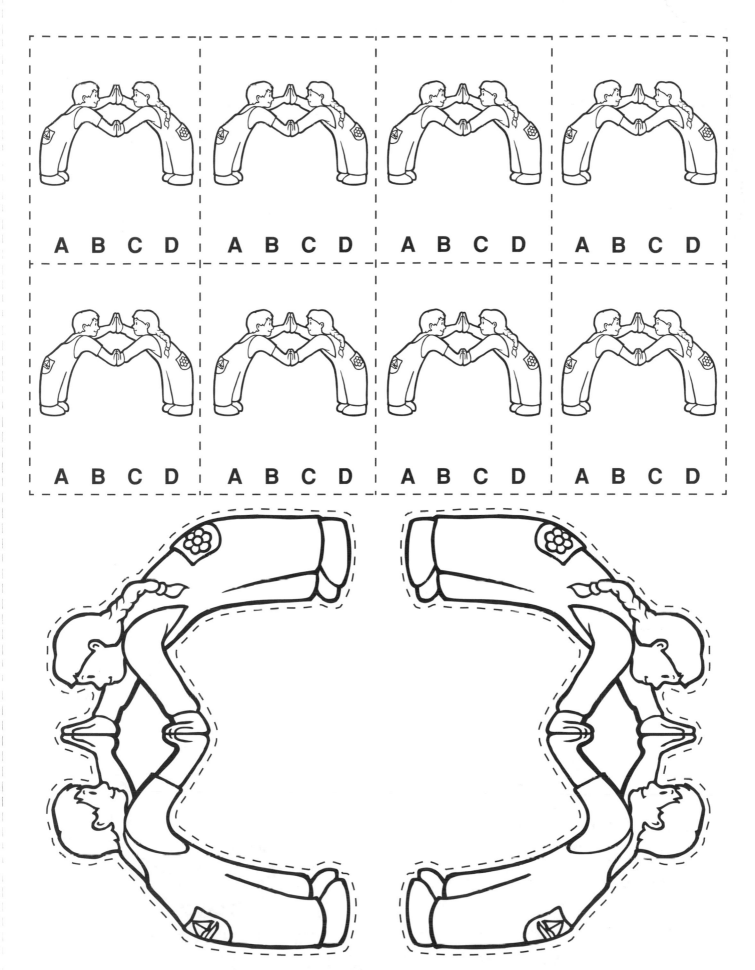

A B C D   A B C D   A B C D   A B C D

A B C D   A B C D   A B C D   A B C D

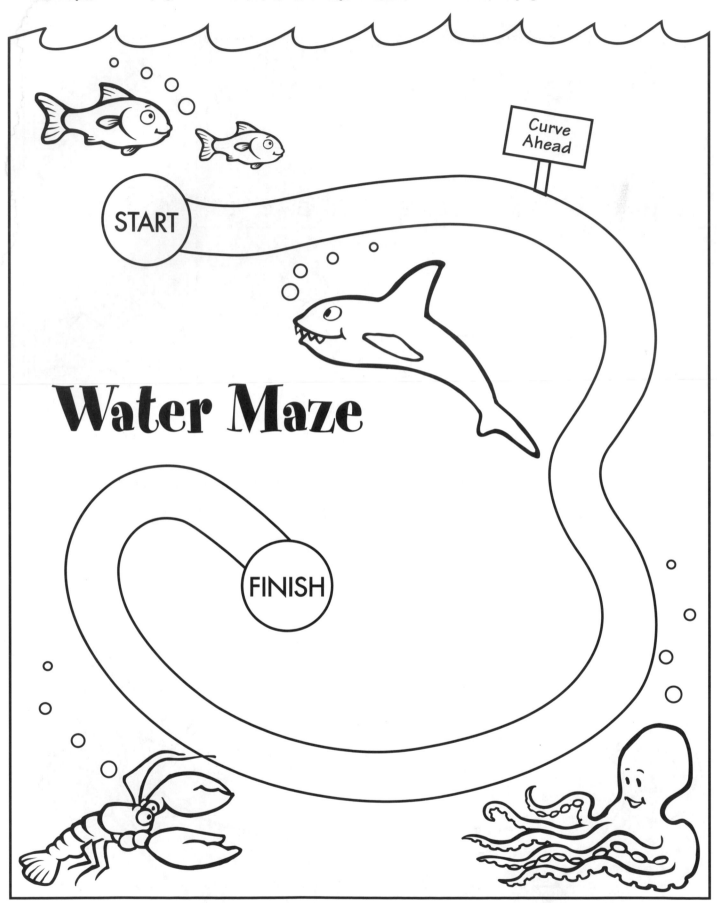

START

Curve
Ahead

Water Maze

FINISH

My Science Experiments

Name _____

My Science Experiments Log

Date	Experiment Name	What I Learned